Regina Barreca is a professor of English and Feminist Theory at the University of Connecticut and is the author of Perfect Husbands (& Other Fairy Tales); They Used to Call Me Snow White . . . But I Drifted; Untamed and Unabashed: Essays on Women and Comedy. *She is a regular contributor to the* Chicago Tribune, *and her work has appeared in the* New York Times, Ms., *and* Cosmopolitan.

Also by Regina Barreca

PERFECT HUSBANDS (& OTHER FAIRY TALES)

THEY USED TO CALL ME SNOW WHITE . . . BUT I DRIFTED:
WOMEN'S STRATEGIC USE OF HUMOR

UNTAMED AND UNABASHED: ESSAYS ON WOMEN AND COMEDY

LAST LAUGHS: PERSPECTIVES ON WOMEN AND COMEDY, *editor*

NEW PERSPECTIVES ON WOMEN AND COMEDY, *editor*

SEX AND DEATH IN VICTORIAN LITERATURE, *editor*

WOMEN OF THE CENTURY:
THIRTY MODERN SHORT STORIES, *editor*

FAY WELDON'S WICKED FICTIONS, *editor*

SWEET REVENGE

The Wicked Delights of Getting Even

REGINA BARRECA

BERKLEY BOOKS, NEW YORK

This Berkley Book contains the complete text of the original hardcover edition. It has been completely reset in a typeface designed for easy reading and was printed from new film.

SWEET REVENGE: THE WICKED DELIGHTS OF GETTING EVEN

A Berkley Book / published by arrangement with
Harmony Books, a division of Crown Publishers, Inc.

PRINTING HISTORY
Harmony Books edition published October 1995
Berkley edition / May 1997

The Putnam Berkley World Wide Web site address is
http://www.berkley.com

ISBN: 0-425-15766-0

BERKLEY®
Berkley Books are published by The Berkley Publishing Group,
200 Madison Avenue, New York, New York 10016.
BERKLEY and the "B" design are trademarks
belonging to Berkley Publishing Corporation.

PRINTED IN THE UNITED STATES OF AMERICA

10 9 8 7 6 5 4 3 2 1

This book is dedicated,

with love and gratitude,

to my father, Hugo Barreca

acknowledgments

There can be pleasure in paying back debts, especially those willingly incurred. Shaye Areheart, my editor at Harmony Books, leads the list of those owed: Shaye believed in this book from the beginning, and gave it her full support and her excellent advice. Her assistant Heather Julius was terrific, as was production editor Kim Hertlein. That I cannot show my thanks to this book's agent and protector, Diane Cleaver, is more than sad. Diane's death took from all of us the sweetest, toughest cookie New York City ever knew.

A number of people might want to get even with me, given how much work they've put into this project. Julie Nash, my good friend, research assistant, and co-conspirator, would have to be first among them. Julie's superbly supportive, efficient, and patient work on the manuscript made her my guardian angel; her writings on revenge in Charlotte Brontë gave me much to think about. Students in my revenge and literature classes at the University of Connecticut have me in their power because of all I owe them: Their funny stories, smart ideas, and hard work all fed this book along the way. I'd particularly like to thank those who worked with me on independent studies: Christine Cappazzi, Kara Copley, Josephine Feola, and Casey Leadingham.

At UConn, too, I'd like to thank Dean Tom Giolas and his staff at the Research Foundation for their support of this project, as well as my colleagues in the English Department, particularly Lee Jacobus, Margaret Higonnet, Barbara Rosen, Brenda Murphy, and, by proxy, George

Montiero. To Sue Donnelly and Helen Smith at the English Department, I am also under contract—for their generosity, their typing, their reading, and their suggestions. Other friends and colleagues have allowed me to profit from their experiences and wisdom: Bob Sullivan read the manuscript and made suggestions that improved it immeasurably, all while he was working toward his own book deadlines, and I owe him one (or more than one); Faith Middleton can own my soul (if she can find it) for all her joyfully wicked encouragement and for allowing me to appear on her radio program, *Open Air New England.* John Glavin helped me see, as always, where I was going, and helped me decide whether or not I wanted to proceed. Dr. Rose Quiello listened and laughed and added her own perspective. Bookstore mavens Roxanne Coady and Suzy Staubach provided sound advice and sounding boards when I needed them most. Denis Gosselin of the *Chicago Tribune Magazine* told me I was on the right track and then put the cover story of his magazine on the line to prove it. Fay Weldon's works and her conversations gave me food for thought without making me diet.

I would also like to thank the following friends and colleagues for their varied and valued support: Blanche Boyd; Dr. Natalie Becker; Richard Caccavale; Nancy Lager, Lynette Lager, and Tim Taylor; Pam Katz; Bonnie Januszewski; Deborah Morse; and Joe Cuomo. To Hugo my brother, his wife Wendy Schlemm, to my stepsons Matthew and Tim, to my father Hugo, my thanks for providing a world safe from life's worst wounds. Finally to my adored and restorative husband Michael Meyer, I want to say: You are the best compensation for the world's ills that I can imagine; if living and loving well are the best revenge, we've got them all beat.

contents

chapter one

HOW SWEET IT IS

The Secret and Shared Impulse Toward

Getting Even

Revenge: a. The act of doing hurt or harm to another in return for wrong or injury suffered; satisfaction obtained by repayment of injuries. b. A desire to repay injuries by inflicting hurt in return.
—Oxford English Dictionary

"I can't ask for money back that I loaned to a friend—the most I can do is, the next time I'm at their house, break something of approximate value."
—STAND-UP COMIC RITA RUDNER

IT IS A HOT, AIRLESS SUMMER AFTERNOON IN BROOKLYN and I am about five years old. There are countless aunts, grandmothers, and a handful of uncles scattered around the three-family house but none of them are nearby; everything is aridly silent, except for traffic kicking up gravel on the street outside the window. My brother, six years older than I, has damaged my infant pride by telling his friend, the one who plays basketball in the lot behind the house, that I still suck my thumb. They laugh and I am left holding a ballooning sense of outrage and help-lessness.

I hate myself for sucking my thumb, but I hate my brother more for revealing this secret merely to get a laugh out of the handsome boy I secretly plan to marry. I am determined to get back at my brother. I sneak into his room on the second floor with plans to turn his pet turtles over onto their backs. The blue curtains blow in a sudden breeze, and I hold my breath, terrified that some adult will catch me in my unholy mission. I am doing the worst thing I can think of doing to him; I am hurting those he truly adores as a way of extracting revenge.

I make it unseen into the supposedly inviolate sanctuary of his room and, one by one, very carefully overturn the small creatures. The turtles are uncomfortable and look ridiculous; they aren't actually in pain, but their tiny flailing limbs signal desperation and discomfort. It is precisely how I wish my brother to feel, but since he is older and therefore out of range for direct action, I have to settle for a sort of referred revenge directed onto those he loves and who are under his protection. I had once thought of myself as being in that category, but now I feel betrayed.

The betrayal is perhaps the worst of it. I thought we were allies; I thought it was him and me against the gang of adults who wandered through our house all day long. If it had just been some neighborhood kid who made fun of me, I wouldn't have even bothered taking my thumb out of my mouth to say anything. The hardest part was that my usually nice big brother should have treated me so lightly in front of one of his friends, handed me over for a laugh—that was the last straw, the straw that broke the camel's back and turned the turtles over on theirs.

After sneaking out of his room, I go downstairs and out into the alleyway to play with dolls, imitating the good little girl I once was but am no longer. I have been initiated. I suddenly feel older and wiser, the possessor of secret knowledge. I've done something to him without his consent just as he did to me; I have made things even. I have balanced the scales of justice, I think, in a way that makes it clear I'm not to be treated as if I don't count.

Having taken my revenge, I feel smug with satisfaction, as if what I've done is an accomplishment, as if I have learned a new song or memorized a new joke. My childhood, like any childhood, was filled with the impotent sense of always needing to look up to see what's really going on; revenge is an attractive, seductive, triumphant, and unusual feeling.

I got caught—it was probably pretty clear to everyone that the turtles didn't simultaneously pirouette into the air, and it wasn't likely that one of my aged aunts had taken it upon herself to have a little fun with the terrapins. But, frankly, I don't remember how I got caught. Being found out wasn't as important as committing the deed; punishment was nothing compared to how good I felt after doing it. The tension and satisfaction I derived from my miniature Medea fantasies were, at that moment, obviously worth the cost of whatever punishment I could anticipate.

I was, indisputably, the most likely suspect. They— meaning my parents, my brother, and a virtual chorus of assorted relatives—tried to embarrass me about my actions, but they couldn't; the embarrassment I felt about the thumb-sucking revelations was still smarting too intensely for me to feel bad about my response to it. Even though I couldn't really understand how they could get mad at me and not at my brother once I had explained the details of my gratuitous humiliation in front of the boy next door, I accepted my punishment with all the dignity a very small and grubby child could manage.

Punishment—in my case being denied dessert and Walt Disney for two weeks—was a price worth paying. Regardless of what they could do to me now, I wouldn't take back the look of powerless anger on my brother's face as he listened to my sentence being handed down. I got him back; that was all that mattered. Anything after that moment added up to nothing more than an epilogue.

So it goes with revenge. We are willing to run the risk of forfeiting those possessions usually held dear: self-esteem, pride, morality, ethics, love, and family. While revenge is purchased most often at the cost of our good impression of ourselves (and others' good impressions of us), somehow it feels worth it.

Selling Us on Revenge

Revenge sells everything from movies to magazines to hair coloring. "Don't Get Mad. Get Promoted," read the promotional blurb for the film *The Temp*. The April 1994 *Ladies' Home Journal* cover headlined "Diana Plots Her Revenge." For the last few years Clairol, a megacorporation, has used the slogan "Gorgeous Hair Is the Best Revenge" under its photographs of sultry women with sexy tresses. Upon whom exactly is one extracting this revenge? Your man? (One of the colors is called "Make Him Drop the Remote Control Red," so maybe he is the target; a lot of women I know would certainly buy the product if the color were called "Make Him Drop Dead Red," but more about that later.) Or is gorgeous hair revenge on women with dull hair who may have snubbed you or taken your man away? Who repays Mother Nature for gray hair? Or maybe it's revenge on other hair-product companies, ones that are less savvy about the power revenge holds over our collective imagination?

Clairol's new slogan is a far cry from thinking of dyeing your hair with "Nice and Easy." Revenge, obviously, is neither nice nor easy—and my best bet is that it's only within the space of a few years that "Gorgeous Hair Is the Best Revenge" could have come to promote a feminine beauty product. In a world where marketing managers have long considered the phrase "Only Your Hairdresser Knows for Sure" the perfect vehicle for women's attention, we're suddenly in a world where that phrase applies only if your hairdresser is Sonny Corleone.

Whereas it used to be, simply, "Blondes Have More Fun," we're now up to thinking that using color number 5, "Kick Down the Door and Bedazzle Him Blond," is the way to greater self-esteem and continued sexual attention. Clairol has kept the slogan for quite a while in a climate where slogans are dropped the minute they don't seem to be working, so obviously women are buying the product to get this promised revenge on this unnamed adversary.

A friend who works in advertising cynically suggested that Lorena Bobbitt could be the poster girl for Clairol's ad campaign, but I doubt this will happen. Then again, fifteen or twenty years ago, hair coloring was a personal secret; now it's a weapon. "I'm dying to get back at him," the Clairol models seem to whisper. "Vengeance is mine," the big-haired women seem to say.

Vengeance also applies as much to shopping as to hair, apparently. "Discounts with a Vengeance" is the slogan for paradoxically upscale discount vendor Loehmann's. When my old college roommate and I were going into the store, credit cards burning holes in our pockets, I asked her what she thought about the store's representation of itself. "It's appealing because everybody who spends thirty dollars for a designer T-shirt secretly wants to get back at the bastards who make them," she replied immediately. "With a vengeance" can mean merely with emphasis or extreme commitment, but the phrase also smacks of the same revenge potion we put on our roots.

We want the chance to feel as if we're not powerless in the face of inattention, exploitation, or the simple foolishness of many of our desires. Revenge can give us the illusion of having control over our lives. On occasion it works with satisfying alacrity.

Whether or not we act on them, fantasies of revenge play a large part in the lives of many otherwise nice, generous, calm, and caring individuals. This was brought home to me by a cheerful young woman at the local supermarket who, while she was ringing up my sale, told me, "I think about it constantly, probably twenty times a day. I think about how I'd like to do it and who I'd like to do it to. I think about doing it to people who got to me ten years ago and I think about doing it to the person standing in front of me if they act a certain way. I don't like to admit that I think about it, but I do."

It occurred to me that anybody listening would think she was talking about having sex. But the scenarios this woman was describing had to do with getting even, not getting into bed. It also occurred to me that, in the eyes of most of her customers, it would be far more acceptable for her to discuss her sexual fantasies than her revenge fantasies. We've learned to admit out loud (sometimes with quite a bit of gusto) that sexual fantasies make up part of most people's daily menu of passing thoughts, but what we haven't been so open about is that revenge fantasies can be just as rich, complex, and satisfying as any dreams of romance.

In *The Life and Loves of a She-Devil*, Fay Weldon's heroine Ruth, the abandoned wife, fantasizes as she prepares dinner about the revenge she would like to take on her husband's new mistress. "Mary Fisher, I hope such a wind arises tonight that the plate-glass windows of the tower crack and the storm surges in, and you die drowning and weeping and in terror. I take the thin curved strips of dough . . . and mold them into a shape much like the shape of Mary Fisher, and turn the oven high, high, and crisp the figure in it until such a stench fills the kitchen that even the fan cannot remove it. Good. I hope the tower burns and Mary Fisher with it, sending the smell of burning flesh out over the waves. I would go and fire the place myself, but I don't drive." Well, in the cases of most such fantasies—thank goodness—most of us don't drive. But that doesn't stop the idea of revenge from having a grip on our collective imaginations.

We can use our fantasies of revenge to get to the heart of what's bothering us. The desire for revenge is often uncontrollable, universal, irrational, and personal, but it can lead us to new levels of self-awareness and to an understanding of deeply buried emotions and needs. The insult you need to revenge is the one that attracts your most authentic fears and that inadvertently calls up your most hidden secrets.

What Qualifies as Revenge?

We can file a range of activities and emotions under the heading "getting even." These emotions might not be pretty or even ethically acceptable, but that does not mean they are not powerful or universal. Maybe you remember the shocked expression on your ex-boyfriend's face when you told him that you had thrown out his collection of 45s—after all, how were you to know that he would want those back? They reminded you of him and in a sentimental mood you had to put them in the incinerator, you're so very sorry. His new girlfriend is seven years younger and has nothing in her collection that's older than Blind Melon? Pity.

Or perhaps you still smile remembering the firm—for which you'd worked sixteen loyal years—losing more than half its clients when you were told to pack up your desk. These clients, who knew your value better than the bosses, chose to follow you with your expertise and personality instead of staying with that old bunch of yellow power-ties.

It could be that you and your older sister can now laugh about the time you substituted pure peroxide for her Sun-In hair coloring when you were ten, and angry that she had hidden the head of your Barbie in a fit of pique.

Revenge encompasses everything from passive-aggressive acts such as "forgetting" to call someone who waits by the phone or starching your partner's underwear "by mistake," to actively aggressive acts such as putting Tabasco in somebody's yogurt or reporting them to the toll-free IRS hot line.

But one thing is for certain: Though revenge may be wrong, selfish, or motivated by deep insecurities, it is rarely if ever boring. That is one of the reasons that books, movies, television programs, talk shows—and many people's lives—are filled with delicious and diabolical stories of revenge.

Putting the "Re" in Revenge

Revenge operates on the basis of a highly structured economy of emotion: Its basic methodology seems to draw from the marketplace, given its emphasis on "payment" for a past injury. The O[...] the word *revenge* as "a. the [...] another in return for wrong or in[...] obtained by repayment of injuries[...] injuries by inflicting hurt in return.[...] "repayment" of injuries is significant. Th[...] ing of revenge has already been drawn into [...] of feelings; he or she is acting in response to [...] committed by someone else.

"Re" is important because it underscores the reac[...] part of this activity, the sense that revenge is a return to the site of an earlier moment of pain. In the perpetual remembrance of pain, there can be very little freedom to accept the future. "A life of reaction is a life of slavery, intellectually and spiritually," writes novelist Rita Mae Brown. "One might fight for a life of action, not reaction." Her point is crucial, and highlights one of the reasons that revenge is destructive when it becomes a habit.

The Popularity of Revenge

Revenge has always been in vogue. It is impossible to calculate whether the initial audience witnessing *Medea* in 436 B.C. was any more or less receptive than the New York audience that saw Diana Rigg in the 1994 production. The New York show was an evident hit and received a great deal of critical attention. It was clear that the play still held significant sway over those watching it. After all, Medea gets to destroy her selfish ex-husband's life and, at the end of the play, gets carried off in the chariots of the gods, free from earthly punishment. This sounds good to many of us.

Revenge in popular culture bears a striking resemblance

ears a strik-
e everyday
t mate, may
if our con-
ely fitted to

s governing
nd what they
in ways that
ause revenge
wable for one
ns, for inner-

ford English Dictionary defines
act of doing hurt or harm to
ury suffered; satisfaction
b. A desire to repay
The emphasis on
e person dream-
he exchange
an action
ive

city dwellers, ...ned if used by another group. If, for example, a woman breaks the jaw of her spouse's lover after finding them in bed together, she will probably be judged differently from the man who broke *his* rival's jaw. The targets of the revenge in such a case would also receive different responses and sympathies: The woman would not have been expected to protect herself or to fight back, but the man would have been.

In a small town, it would probably be a grave act of revenge to boycott a store that had a history of biased hiring practices, but the same action would hardly count as revenge if directed by the same number of people toward a megachain store. In a city, their revenge would go unnoticed, implying that revenge on a grander scale would be called for if indeed they wanted to guarantee that someone in power would be affected. It is an accepted commonplace that whites in our culture are treated differently from people of color by the court and penal systems. If we look carefully at revenge, it is clear that the rules governing justice and appropriate behavior at perceived injustice are arbitrary or merely convenient rather than universal and unwavering.

The social script for revenge in the Western world has undergone fundamental and irrevocable change over the past several centuries. In most neighborhoods we no longer put the severed heads of our vanquished enemies on stakes for the community's edification and enjoyment. Nor is it common to set fire to a restaurant if the maître d' happens not to recognize your name. Yet the desire for revenge remains a fundamental human emotion even when it appears in less dramatic or obvious forms.

The first "interactive" movie, released in 1995, was titled *Mr. Payback. Mr. Payback* permitted viewers to use handheld devices to choose what punishments the evil villain would receive. Presumably the producers felt that the audience would be so involved in wanting to express their own revenge that they would pay for the privilege of believing that their input went into the process of revenge depicted on the screen. As if Charles Bronson or Clint Eastwood could hear their cries of encouragement behind their celluloid skins, the audiences of *Mr. Payback* were permitted to encourage retribution; it is my understanding that there was no button marked "forgiveness." Turning the other cheek was not an option.

Remind You of Anybody You Know?

You consider yourself a decent, responsible, considerate person. You're a good friend, a loving partner, a committed worker, and an asset to your community, at least as kind and comforting as most anyone around you. So why do you find yourself thinking about how good you're going to look at the office Christmas party, imagining how your competitive and smug coworker will be furious at all the attention you'll get? Why do you daydream about the look on the guy's face at the gas station—the one who has smugly told you for years that you're driving a piece of junk—when you drive in with a new Mercedes? Why are you secretly delighted when your daughter wins the spelling bee, triumphing over your neighbor's child, whose father always tells you his kids are going to be Yalies, just like their old man? Why do you think about taking all the files and just walking out when your boss tells you there'll be no bonus for you this year, even though you read in the paper this morning that the entire board—including the boss—will be given significant raises?

Why do you want to bump the back of the car that just cut you off, return everything you just bought when the salesclerk is deliberately slow in ringing up, or show up at your high-school reunion twenty pounds lighter and driving a Jaguar convertible just to smile and turn away from your old rival? Why did people applaud when Thelma and Louise blew up the truck whose driver had been harassing them for miles on the highway? And why did *Death Wish*, *Dirty Harry*, and *The Godfather* become hit films—such hits that they spawned other films in the same genre? Why? Because revenge is as human and as inevitable as hunger.

We might not call it revenge, or be conscious of the way we want to settle the score, but the fantasy of getting even with someone we believe has wronged us has captured the imagination of almost all of us at one time or another. The desire to get even creeps up on us when we least expect it, and sometimes involves people we love deeply and sincerely. Feelings of revenge aren't governed by logic or controlled by intellect, but instead emerge from the most buried parts of ourselves, the parts we are least comfortable acknowledging.

Revenge, Like Popcorn, Is Good at the Movies

In *The Godfather*, Michael Corleone understands that honor is played out in acts of retribution. Characters played by Charles Bronson and Clint Eastwood avenge on behalf of everybody. Sigourney Weaver faces off against a female Alien in a sort of sci-fi catfight. Glenn Close goes for broke in *Fatal Attraction*. Harrison Ford gets to expose and professionally discredit his foe in *The Fugitive*. And every day many of the nicest people surreptitiously plot to get even with bosses, companions, spouses, and total strangers.

From the first time I saw images on a screen, I liked movies laced with revenge. What I didn't like were the movies that my mother and my aunts dragged me to. These were tearjerkers designed for women who did not marry Omar Sharif, David Niven, or Laurence Olivier— women, in other words, whose lives of quiet desperation were inevitable. I squirmed in my seat to see genteel ladies on the big screen waste their time weeping prettily into hankies when nobody I had ever met actually behaved like that, much less let you blow your nose on the embroidered linen they all carried. I hated finely engraved black-and-white films about tight lives lived in small rooms.

Why didn't these frail movie blondes *do* something when they were abandoned or when they found out that they were married to brutes? I knew that my aunt Maggie had once shaved half my uncle Ronnie's head in his sleep because he'd been paying too much attention to a new neighbor upstairs, but starlets obviously lacked such imagination. When threatened with abandonment, all they could do was invite The Other Woman to dinner and try to Be Brave. These movies seemed to advocate putting up and shutting up. Suspecting that I couldn't do either, I knew I needed to find more satisfying stories. I watched old movies on television, and on Saturdays a friend and I were allowed to walk the three blocks to the theater as long as I paid for my ticket out of my own allowance.

As a kid, I usually liked my movies big and gaudy. I spent my own money to go see *The Ten Commandments* not because it reaffirmed anything I learned in catechism, but because I loved seeing the Egyptians get trashed by the tribes of Israel. I planned for something on a smaller scale to take place on the playground, as I cast myself as a miniature version of Charlton Heston. I would part the boys who ganged up on us girls at lunchtime the way Moses parted the Red Sea. Then I would transform Miss Morrow's erasers into snakes the next time she made me do math on the board because she knew that I couldn't add up my fingers and toes without a piece of paper and an uninterrupted afternoon. Even then, I adored *West Side Story* and preferred Rita Moreno's character to Natalie Wood's delicate heroine. I sang along with gusto to ''[I Like to Be in] America'' and practiced delivering smart, sassy answers while provocatively raising one eyebrow. However, the wonderfully exuberant action in *West Side Story* went downhill faster than in *The Ten Commandments*, because every cute boy had to kill or be killed. Of course, Tony had to kill Bernardo, who killed Tony's best friend. Viscerally grasping this long before anybody taught us about blood feuds via Romeo and Juliet, the girls in the audience held their breath and the boys (who came to see the gang scenes and not the mushy parts) practiced using invisible switchblades to defend their pre-pubescent honor. *West Side Story* taught that revenge was disastrous. What else could one glean from a film that left Rita and Natalie to become what we could only imagine to be old maids (a fate worse than death in a movie where the women make bridal gowns for a living)? But we also learned that revenge was bound up with loyalty and passion and honor. We learned, boys and girls alike, that it was wimpy to turn away when you needed to fight. Nobody wanted Tony to turn away from the brawl once his best friend was killed, even at the expense of his own life. Revenge was as inevitable as the final credits.

The one exception to my preference for big, gaudy movies was the classic comic film *The Lady Eve*. For some reason this played every other week on the local old-movie channel and I was hooked on it. In the film, a con woman masquerades as a society woman who plays cards for money, winning by cheating the all-too-eager rich in order to get into games of chance that are way over their heads but don't put a dent in their bank accounts. Eventually, the heroine marries a snobbish, uptight man with whom she was once in love just to get revenge on him, then she spends their wedding night making up stories about past lovers in order to torture him the way he had tortured her. Of course, all of this is resolved with the usual elegance of any Preston Sturges movie, but the idea that she could get revenge by *staying* with him instead of leaving him intrigued me before I understood its implications.

Knowing all the lines to *The Lady Eve* tempted me to act in a similar way when I was faced with my first real high-school love. It was the same old story: This guy was gorgeous and charming, and I was lost from the moment he laughed the deepest laugh I'd ever heard—I was, after all, only sixteen. For him, I broke up with a perfectly nice young man who brought me flowers every week, as if he'd read that this would magically guarantee happiness. I decided to take the big risk and opt for magic.

What a mistake.

For Mr. Charming, I took a minor role in a school musical even though I danced with all the grace and agility of a newborn giraffe and had to wear an outfit that made me look like one of the hippos from *Fantasia*—despite the fact that I wasn't overweight. For him I sang in the show with a voice that made street traffic sound good. For him I cut my hair, grew my nails, and tried not too laugh too loudly when I was amused. I gladly butchered and then bartered my personality as if it were so many pounds of lamb to be sacrificed at his altar—and I did it all myself, with very little encouragement from him.

To be fair, he liked me enough to indulge in notewriting and all the romantic stuff associated with school sweethearts, but he only did this until he fell for a girl who could sing, dance, and giggle with charm. Then he stood me up, going to a school dance with her instead of me. I finally showed up two hours late and alone, only to see them dancing together on the light-spangled floor with our friends—all of whom must have guessed precisely what happened.

There I was, with my deeply buried lessons learned from old movies, and a sudden need to apply them. Over the next several months, I did my best Claudette Colbert imitation; I made myself into the girl to rival the girl of his dreams. I didn't follow his prescription. Instead I just excelled at what I was already good at and began to shine in our high school's very tiny firmament. I directed a summer play. All our pals wanted to be in it, and they were suddenly all on my side. I aced the classes we were in together, and instead of not laughing, laughed with abandon. I let my hair grow and filed my nails and looked more like myself.

He started paying attention. He started calling. I flirted back. He asked me out. I agreed. We decided to meet at a local cafe. I sent four of my girlfriends. They sat at another table. They watched him wait for me; one took a snapshot of him alone, fiddling his thumbs. He caught on. He left. They came back to my house for pizza and we laughed so hard we couldn't eat. I had the photo made into a poster-size print and pinned it to his locker, and with that I could finally walk away without looking back. It wasn't how Preston Sturges would have written it in 1941, maybe, but for 1975 it felt just right.

A Child's Garden of Revenge

Revenge is a part of everyone's life—*everyone's*. No politician has ever ruled without it and no lover has lost without thoughts of it. Show me an employee who hasn't fantasized about it, a sibling who has not considered it, and a child who hasn't heard of it. We go to bed as cute, innocent, thumb-sucking little kids and drift off to fairy tales full of revenge.

Sitting down to read the Brothers Grimm or Hans Christian Andersen aloud to a child can be startling if you haven't held one of those books in your hands since your own childhood. When my brother and sister-in-law needed a baby-sitter ten years ago, I was only too happy to oblige—my brother, never one to hold a grudge, felt able to trust me with his children as well as his pets by this point. Delighted to see a familiar cover on one of the books, I eagerly began reading. Had these stories somehow changed since I was a kid? I checked the book carefully; it was the one my brother and I shared as kids—it was the very same book from which I had learned to read at five. But I didn't remember the stories being at all like this. I couldn't believe how many were, at their very hearts, tales of vindication and retribution.

Peter Rabbit spent his youth being warned by his mother about the evil farmer who had killed Peter's father (and eaten him in a pie). Needing to revenge the death of his father and secure his own position as a fully masculine bunny, Peter eventually triumphs over Mr. McGregor. Freud's *Totem and Taboo* converges on Potter, the Grimms, and Disney around every curve and corner. *Peter Rabbit* was written by an English lady and not a Viennese psychoanalyst, but almost all fairy tales use revenge as a primary or secondary theme.

Today's politically correct children's books are filled with stories of benevolent creatures all working together (dragons who seek therapy for their anger and monsters who are really only personality-challenged), but these can hardly be weighed against the visceral satisfactions provided by the uncut versions of childhood stories. Remember the climax of *Red Riding Hood*? The woodsman, rescuing Red and her grandmother, slices open the wolf with his hatchet. Nobody can tell me that this grand finale didn't help sustain an apparently inborn appetite for revenge as a suitable payoff.

Remember Hansel and Gretel? The witch ends up being kicked into the oven and baked like an apple. Snow White eats her stepmother's poisoned apple and falls into unconsciousness because of the wicked woman's envy of her youth and beauty (and it's surprising that kids don't like eating fruit? Can you imagine falling asleep to the story of a poisoned Klondike Bar?).

Forcing Snow White to eat is her stepmother's revenge; Snow White's revenge is a lifetime of happiness with a responsive man instead of a glaring mirror. The stories we hear in early childhood help shape the way we deal with revenge in our adult lives, even if the characters who taught us the ropes are more thoroughly buried than our old teddy bears and dolls.

"I'll Get You, You Wascally Wabbit!"

Cartoons, of course, use revenge as often as they use primary colors. Bugs Bunny and Road Runner are tricky and successful revengers because they are, to mix animal metaphors, the underdogs. They are relentlessly pursued by creatures who at first glance seem more powerful than themselves: Elmer Fudd is a card-carrying member of the NRA and always has his gun ready to misfire, and Wile E. Coyote has teeth and, more often than not, dynamite. Like their predecessor Goliath, Elmer and Wile are not prepared for any dispute about their superiority.

Of course, Elmer and Wile consistently and hilariously lose to those lower down the food chain. Not regarding their prey as equals, they are automatically what Bugs would label "maroons" for underestimating the opposition.

Understanding that the apparently helpless victim isn't without power is at the heart of many cartoons, mimicking on celluloid the dynamics found in traditional fairy tales. Tweetie Bird survives Sylvester the cat because Tweetie is a goodie-two-wings who happily reveals the evils of the rival sibling pet to the little-old-lady mother figure who then whacks lisping Sylvester with her huge umbrella. Tweetie's ultimate revenge on the hapless carnivore who shares the house is to remain the innocent favorite. They compete for attention in a small emotional space, as do coworkers, spouses, and siblings. No wonder revenge is usually an intimate phenomenon.

Revenge plots are hardly limited to fairy tales or the 'toon world; we don't give up on getting even once we hit adulthood. On the contrary: Revenge in mythology, literature, films, and popular culture is a recurring and symbolically important theme. Clytemnestra wants retribution for her daughter's death, Shylock wants his pound of flesh, Hamlet contemplates the task of avenging his father's death, Lizzie Borden wants to register her displeasure at her father's second marriage.

Civilized and Discontented

Revenge seeps into our dreams and secretly manifests itself in little, incidental ways in our waking lives. It's an inherited appetite, one passed on but nevertheless repressed in its journey up through the generations. The moment at which a group decides to adopt common rules and systems of punishment, and forfeit the right to personal vengeance, is often marked as a turning point. In *Civilization and Its Discontents*, Sigmund Freud argues that "this replacement of the power of the individual by the power of a community constitutes the decisive step of civilization. The essence of it lies in the fact that the members of the community restrict themselves in their possibilities of satisfaction, whereas the individual knew no such restrictions. The first requisite of civilization, therefore, is that of justice—that is, the assurance that a law once made will not be broken in favour of an individual." If Freud is right, then at one point in human history the threat of reprisal had an important function in the development of civilization, teaching one tribe to be wary of another. But revenge can hardly justify itself as a tool for survival—except metaphorically.

And yet the fantasy—and reality—of vindication still exist. The very nature of revenge is difficult to define in practice because it remains a taboo subject. Whatever revenge actually is, however, the idea of getting even can usefully serve as a catalyst for us, helping us to discover or uncover our deepest disappointments, angers, wishes, and desires. Revenge forces us to examine our conventional concepts of justice and prods us into questioning where we stand in terms of forgiveness, mercy, and the ability to get on with life after receiving an injury to our sense of self.

Many men and women have never consciously acted out their wishes for revenge, but that does not mean their lives have been free from the desire, need, and even effects of getting even. We often give ourselves away in the smallest details of our actions, the way we silently make a spouse feel guilty for wanting to go somewhere without us, or perhaps in just happening to fall ill on the day of a friend's or sibling's happiest occasion. "See?" revenge cries. "You can't expect me to just sit back and take this"—this happens even if the voice is muffled by apparently faultless behavior or even the best of intentions.

We want to get even when we're insulted, when we're deceived, when we're demeaned, when we're abandoned, when we're ignored for recognition, and when we're reminded of the vast inequities of daily life. More often than not, we bite our tongues and get past the need for revenge, but sometimes we find a way to get even—to achieve what can be called "reciprocity."

In her important and captivating essay "The Value of Vindictiveness," psychoanalyst Karen Horney confronts the fact that for many otherwise "perfectly normal" people, the impulse toward revenge is nevertheless familiar: "Are not impulses to get back for injuries done universal? Are they not even culturally sanctioned in many civilizations?" she asks.

Horney points out that societies universally attempt to redirect the desire for revenge into a more socially acceptable system of laws that attempts to channel the need for personal vindication. Yet she suggests, "While [social systems] implicitly acknowledge the general existence of needs to retaliate, they also take these needs psychologically out of the hand of an individual by rendering them a civic duty."

In other words, personal anger and the desire to get even are translated into the obligation to use existing laws and avenues of jurisprudence. A person is supposed to go to the local police station to seek justice, not to the home of his enemy in order to break the windows. But Horney's focus is on the various incarnations of revenge that are, psychologically speaking, very common. Even though they may not be identified as the desire to get even by those experiencing these emotions, Horney is perfectly aware that "conscious impulses, or action . . . are experienced as just punishment, as perfectly rational responses to injury done."

There are as many ways of thinking about getting even as there are menus for preparing dinner, but most recipes for revenge fall into one of the three sections Horney outlines in "The Value of Vindictiveness"—three ways that the desire for vindication can appear in various personal psychologies. They are worth looking at in detail because most of the behavior described in this book can be viewed through the lens she supplies.

Obvious Aggression

"Openly aggressive vindictiveness," Horney writes, "looks uninhibited in action. The person may aggressively strike out at others. He is openly exploiting. He is usually proud of this capacity, although, as mentioned, he does not experience the vindictive character of these actions. He may feel that he is simply more honest and straight than the others, that he merely is doling out justice, that his dignity refuses to be insulted with impunity." This is the sort of high-testosterone behavior we've seen in Charles Bronson and Clint Eastwood movies, exemplified by the swaggering lawman (more than willing to step outside the law at the least provocation) who is on a mission to clean up the streets and take justice into his own large, calloused hands.

As reported in the *Connecticut Law Journal*, the Richard L. Preston vs. Phelps Dodge Copper Products Company case appeared to involve "openly aggressive vindictiveness." "In August 1988, because of his frustration and anger with his employer, the plaintiff had entered the restroom used by the plant manager and the personnel manager and put poison ivy on the toilet seat and stall," according to the report. "The plaintiff then informed three of his friends as to what he had done, warning them not to use the toilet. The plaintiff felt this was his way of getting back at management. As a result, the plant manager, who is highly allergic to poison ivy, developed a severe reaction that took more than two months to cure." When the plaintiff sued the company for wrongful dismissal, his personal revenge story eclipsed—at least in the minds and imaginations of those not directly concerned with the trial—the events of his employment and firing. It was difficult for many of those following the case to see the plaintiff as a sympathetic and powerless victim of wrongdoing, when he had appeared to handle the situation with the panache of an expert avenger. His act of personal revenge might have jeopardized his position as a legitimate casualty of mismanagement.

In contrast, we can also recognize patterns of what Horney calls "self-effacing vindictiveness." If "openly aggressive vindictiveness" can be classified as traditionally "masculine," then "self-effacing vindictiveness" could be regarded as fitting into conventionally "feminine" behaviors. According to Horney, "Self-effacing vindictiveness operates subversively and indirectly. Suffering is used unconsciously to make others feel guilty. Emphasis on needs, suffering, appeal to pity and sacrifices, serve as unconscious bases on which to make demands." I am reminded of the old joke about "How many mothers-in-law does it take to change a lightbulb?" to which the answer is "None. I'll sit in the dark. It's good enough for an old woman like me who nobody wants to come visit. Go out, have a good time, I'll just sit here," et cetera ad nauseam. Delivered in the right tone of whining, the person telling the joke runs the risk of being throttled by someone having a flashback to the last time he was a victim of that sort of remark himself.

Horney says "self-effacing vindictiveness puts less stress on justice than the aggressive type [because the person] experiences himself as a particularly good person who is constantly abused by others. The vindictiveness in this instance is by no means less great or less effective but it evokes the puzzling impression of being done at the person's own expense." In many of these cases, men are taught to inspire fear, whereas women are taught to inspire guilt.

Evil Do-Gooders

A friend of mine came up with the term *Evil Do-Gooders* for those who practice self-effacing vindictiveness when we were preparing for an event following a poetry reading at the university. I suggested we ask one young woman to help plan the dinner after the reading, but Julie quickly pointed out that Rosalinda inevitably abused and soured whatever role she was allotted. "She agrees to telephone everyone who's coming to the dinner to find out their preferences," Julie observed, "and tells them just how difficult it's been to reach them, and how overworked she is, and how much is demanded of her. Everybody she speaks to believes she's both a martyr and a prime-mover, that she's given everything to The Cause and that nobody else has done a damn thing." Julie, an efficient, smart, and modest woman, is not usually given to such diatribes; I was curious about the source of what seemed at first like an overreaction. Is whining martyrdom really strong enough to merit the term *evil*, I asked.

Julie replied, "Absolutely. These folks sigh and moan through every task, wheedle and connive to be complimented on the most trivial matters even when everybody else is already doing twice as much. They control the power because they manipulate their position into one of extraordinary but unrewarded heroism. They volunteer on a regular basis just in order to be told that they're too good, too generous, and too nice. Meanwhile, they snipe in little ways at the others who are doing the same jobs and denigrate those who accomplish more with less effort. Their revenge on someone who is faster, smarter, or more accomplished than they are is to damn with faint praise.'' I asked for another example. ''When our committee formed, for the express reason of celebrating the successes of women in the profession, Rosalinda asked to be co-chair. She spent all her time saying 'If I could only be as high-powered and driven as these women, I might be recognized as special' or 'Too bad I'm still so wrapped up in providing love and care for my family that I can't get ahead the way these women do.' She wrote a letter inviting people to an end-of-the-year party which read like a litany for the Evil Do-Gooder society. It opened with the line 'I write to invite you to a celebration for women who have learned that getting ahead is the main thing in life, a lesson not all of us have learned.' '' When Rosalinda asked to help with the event, therefore, we suggested cheerfully that for once she should attend as one of the honored guests, come to enjoy herself, and leave the work to some new volunteers. Telling her to enjoy herself, Julie laughed, was her own little act of revenge.

Detached Vindictiveness

Finally, ''detached vindictiveness . . . the least dramatic of all,'' wherein ''sins are of omission rather than commission. Quietly but effectively the detached person may frustrate others by not listening, by disregarding their needs, by forgetting their wishes, by making them feel as disturbing intruders, by withholding praise or affection, by withdrawing psychically or physically.''

We have all dealt with ''detached vindictiveness'' every time we've waited on line at the Department of

Motor Vehicles, Immigration, Passport Control, or the pound where our cars are brought when they are towed off the street. More seriously, we can be victims of "detached vindictiveness" when we anger a teacher who then refuses to call on us or grade a paper on time, when a clerk whom we have slighted says she is all out of that garment in our size and they will not reorder that particular item, or when a child won't give us a hug because we didn't have time to help him do his homework the night before. Almost every individual fantasy or act of revenge can be easily slotted into one of these categories.

Why There Is No Instructor's Manual with This Book

This book lacks a pull-out "how-to" section. *Sweet Revenge* is not about how to understudy for Norman Bates (à la *Psycho*), how to leave a horse's head in your partner's bed (à la *The Godfather*), or how to wire explosives to your school (à la *Heathers*). Most people with wit, insight, intelligence, and subtlety—*and* a small measure of good sense on their side—find no need to resort to violence in order to reestablish a sense of equilibrium. They are clever enough to use their heads and hearts instead of their fists and firearms.

The impulse we have to restore our self-esteem when we feel someone has deliberately taken it from us is one of the most universal and reliable ones in human nature. Stealing candy from a baby, for example, will virtually insure that the baby then throws a toy at your head as soon as you turn around—not even infants are good-natured enough to be taken for granted. As soon as a sense of self emerges, so does the wish to get back at an adversary. Not that this is a good way of getting attention;

making friends and influencing people beats revenge hands down any day when it comes to getting the best out of life. But at one time or another we have all dreamed of revenge, and on occasion most of us have acted out greater or lesser versions of the dream. We smuggle our ideas and memories of revenge with us through life, showing the secret goods only to a very few close friends if we reveal them to anyone at all.

And yet in the same way that the memory of a particularly delicious success can make us sigh with remembered satisfaction, a remembered moment of illicitly secured triumph can sustain us when we're feeling powerless or damaged. Of course, we might also cringe at the remembrance of an occasion when our attempt at revenge boomeranged, leveling us with the impact we'd hoped to make on someone else. Or perhaps we realize, as did Erma Bombeck, that some familiar kinds of revenge just don't work: She once remarked, "I'm going to have to stop punishing my family by snapping 'All right then, I'll just do it myself' when they refuse to help around the house."

Isn't Living Well the Best Revenge?

That the desire for revenge is the outward manifestation of an inward lack of self-worth has been put forth by any number of theorists; if you feel good enough about yourself, they argue, you won't feel the need to "get back" or even "get even" with an old enemy. Singing the famous refrain "Living well is the best revenge," they make it sound easy to be free from anger, resentment, and the desire to settle the score.

I, for one, have never met anybody who feels so good

about herself or himself that a small but core part of the heart hasn't at one time or another hankered after immediate and personal justice. All human beings—whether priests, rabbis, ministers, homemakers, bakers, judges, social workers, lawyers, schoolchildren, doctors, truck drivers, or nurses—would like to see themselves and their positions vindicated. Revenge isn't something that *other* people do—most of us have participated in a revenge plot even if we haven't given it that name.

The temptation to get even was one a close friend of mine—one of the nicest women I know—couldn't pass up. When I was a graduate student—during a lean time for academics and working at two different posts in order to guarantee a future that would include regular paychecks—I hardly ever considered my peers as my rivals. We were all in it together, and it seemed imperative that we, at least, could offer one another support in a world that appeared determined to thwart our fairly modest dreams of teaching and writing. For three years I kept this vision of community without tinkering with it; everybody in the crowd was sincerely eager to celebrate success and mourn failure. Everybody, that is, except for Jim.

Byronically handsome and incisively bright, Jim was already smugly picturing himself as the success story of the class. An Ivy League graduate, he bragged about his performance on the comprehensive exams and clearly regarded himself as destined to become a tweed-jacketed, suede-patched professor well before thirty. This put him in stark contrast to most of the graduate students in the program, especially the women whose collective motto was "Tenure Before Menopause." Many women (and some of the other men) had only been able to begin their Ph.D. programs in their thirties or early forties, and Jim in his polished late adolescence was a rare creature in this city college. Still, no one actively resented his gleaming achievements, being too worried about their own situations to spend much time thinking about his apparently worry-free world. He had few friends but seemed not to mind the absence of any other company. He was obnoxious, but was regarded as harmless.

All of this changed when Sandy, a friend of mine, discovered that a local community college had called our department to offer her a part-time teaching position, one that could have led to a full-time job within the year. Sandy only learned about this call after Jim had already tried to set up an interview for himself for the job. Somehow he had seen her message and called first in order to try to take the appointment. Luckily an old college pal of hers had been in on the hiring plans and had explained what happened.

The message had been given to a secretary, who was asked to leave it in Sandy's mailbox. The graduate-student mailboxes were in an old-fashioned "pigeon hole" arrangement, so there was no privacy; all the mail was there for anyone unscrupulous enough to go through someone else's material. Sandy's friend told her that there was no mistake made: The college had not placed an open call for jobs—it was a replacement position for an ill faculty member and Sandy's name had been the only one promoted at a recent meeting. There was no way Jim could have known about the job except by reading Sandy's mail, an action that implied his reading everybody's mail since there was no reason to single out Sandy. It was creepy, and it was wrong.

What could be done? Sandy had hoped to avoid a one-on-one confrontation with Jim, but when all else failed, she confronted him with her information, only to have him hotly deny any shady practices. He claimed that he

had heard from an acquaintance that there was a job opening, and accused her of being jealous. He was vicious in
his counterattack on Sandy and left her wanting a more
hand-tailored satisfaction than she had desired initially.
Sandy wanted Jim to be forced to admit that he had been
rooting through other people's mail and that he had, in
fact, attempted to steal something from her. The chair of
the department, however, was unwilling to involve herself
in what she considered the petty domestic disputes of the
unruly masses, and the graduate-student board was busy
trying to keep tuition hikes from sending us all onto the
streets. There was no governing body to whom we could
complain and who might then be willing to act.

Sandy decided to leave a message for herself written
on department letterhead (the secretary was a friend) asking that she, Sandy, be prepared to discuss the details of
her accusation in a closed session with various administrators. The letter said that this matter was of the utmost
importance and that it would be dealt with immediately.
It was folded and left in Sandy's box, looking for all the
world like the real thing; anybody reading it would think
that Sandy was bringing a very serious matter before the
governing body of the graduate school.

If somebody feeling guilty were somehow to read this
letter, he would be pretty upset. But then, of course, nobody should have been reading mail addressed to her. It
was better than a mousetrap set with sharp cheddar; the
rat couldn't resist it.

That night Sandy received what she considered the inevitable call from Jim (who had somehow managed to get
his hands on her phone number as well as her job offers),
accusing her of attacking him and setting the administration against him. He said that he had heard from one of
the dean's secretaries that this meeting was being held the

next day, and he was deeply resentful of the secrecy and of being denied a chance to defend himself. None of this was true, of course, since there was no actual meeting planned. Jim was tangled in the skein of his own lies and narcissism.

Sandy's revenge was to hang up the phone in the middle of his harangue and take it off the hook so that he could not reach her. Knowing that he would twist himself into a pretzel trying to figure out how to handle the nonexistent meeting and might even get himself into trouble with the administration by trying to clear himself of her accusations—perhaps by running into the chair's office and demanding that the meeting be canceled—Sandy was able to feel a sense of satisfaction based on her belief that Jim was now going to inflict his own punishment on himself for his unethical behavior.

She told only a few of us in the program about her scheme, and we watched with a certain amount of glee as Jim tried to cajole information out of random colleagues, none of whom had the least idea what was going on. Having spent his time prying into other people's lives and attempting to take what was theirs, he now believed that everyone was doing the same to him. "What goes around comes around," Sandy laughed, and even though English teachers are supposed to avoid clichés, it was too appropriate a summary to pass up.

I examined my response to this incident and still couldn't figure out how I was feeling about it. Sandy was a close friend and the process had taken up quite a bit of emotional time for everybody. So what overriding sense of things was I left with? Disappointment in Sandy? Disappointment in myself for supporting her in "stooping" to retaliation? Anger at being backed into a corner by Jim?

I dragged the sensation into the light, faced it, and examined it. What were my feelings about the revenge tale I'd seen acted out—with me in a front-row seat? Pure delight. It was a pleasure similar to the one I get from reading a beautifully balanced poem or a well-planned mystery novel; it was like listening to a perfectly orchestrated opera. It appeased my love for symmetry and my fondness for closure.

I had hoped for something more noble from my inner sense of ethics, but what I felt primarily was that now we had all finished with recriminations and nastiness and could get back to our ordinarily decent lives. In some corner of my mind, I'd attempted to tell myself that ignoring my own responses was healthy, but it was never satisfying. Offering Jim a healthy taste of his own medicine offered a chance to obtain closure on the situation.

Beyond (Behind, Underneath, and Sidestepping) the Rules

Even folks usually adept at turning the other cheek can be tempted to indulge in small-scale revenge. A priest I once knew always cooked with garlic because he knew it bothered his bishop. It was a venial sin, surely, a minor infraction, but the larger canvas still shows a landscape of the desire to exact revenge on a powerful figure who often dominated his life. "I've been kicked to the curb too many times by that man," confessed the father, smiling. "I had to find a way to kick back, even just a little."

"Revenge is everywhere," echoes one of my twenty-year-old students, a smart and sweet young woman whom you wouldn't expect to have thought deeply about the subject. But she had decided that at certain points revenge was as inevitable and uncontrollable as gravity. When I asked a student in a class on "Revenge in Literature" to define the term, she wrote that "revenge is part of almost everyone's daily existence. It could be ignoring your boyfriend because he played Genesis instead of visiting you or badmouthing your roommate because she didn't wait to go with you to dinner. The 'I'll show you' or 'You'll be sorry' mentality comes as a natural reaction to daily emotional injuries. It's only when revenge becomes more conscious and deliberate that it's considered dangerous or even negative."

But while the desire for revenge is all too human, the right to revenge remains divine. In Romans 12:19 we are told, "Vengeance is mine: I will repay, saith the Lord." Yet as Mark Twain once put it, "Revenge is wicked and unchristian and in every way unbecoming. . . . (But it is powerful sweet, anyway.)"

The desire to get even can be regarded in a fairly simple way as the need to employ an unofficial and personal form of justice. It usually emerges in cases where an individual believes the ordinary paths to justice are blocked or lead in the wrong direction. The way we feel about revenge— whether we punish it or celebrate it or both—is a vitally important index of the relationship of public laws and public rules to personal power, personal space, personal property, and personal morality. Its implications range from the literary to the historical, from the realm of the individual to the world of the institution, from the social to the cultural. A desire for revenge is what prompts George from *Seinfeld* to declare, "If I were a dictator, I would institute the death penalty for double-parking."

Certain moments, however, remain memorable in our personal histories not because the emotions involved are unconventional but because our response to them is innovative. A person is rarely more creative than when he or she is planning a way to rectify a wrong, especially if the task must be accomplished without the perpetrator being discovered. And, often, people are surprised to find that they respond with less tolerance than they are expected to have at their disposal.

"Okay, Everybody Off!"

Even small acts of revenge can move us from private outrage to public action (even if we remain anonymous). The same incident that today prompts your feelings of revenge might have occurred in the past without your making so much as a comment, but now you are completely fed up. Instead of merely seething inwardly, all hell breaks loose.

There's an old story about a woman sunbathing naked in a field. A butterfly passes directly over her nose and tickles her but she only smiles. An ant walks across her stomach and she looks at it, turns over, but doesn't flinch. Finally a bee comes over and stings her right on the rump. "Okay," she yells, "everybody off!" There comes a time when we know that enough's enough.

Deciding *when* enough is enough can be a pivotal moment for most of us and, at its very best, can mark the decision not to accept helplessness as a natural state. Maybe you vanquished the seemingly unstoppable schoolyard bully after you discovered his deep fear of spiders and pulled a jar full of them out of your jacket pocket when he grabbed you by the collar. Not only didn't he ever grab you again, he started leaving other kids alone, too (especially if they seemed to be carrying anything in their pockets).

Dreaming of Revenge

Revenge, like illicit sex, rich foods, ornate decorations, extravagant cars, and hundred-dollar haircuts, often appears desirable because it is taboo. It's shameful. It's wasteful. It's extreme. It's unnecessary. But when have these reasons ever stopped anyone from wanting to fulfill such desires?

Once you feel a sense of entitlement to revenging an action or comment, you want the revenge as quickly and as effortlessly as possible. You write anonymous letters in your head, catalogs of dastardly deeds. You want someone else to sanction your appetite, but you'll go ahead and satisfy it even without a benediction. You are beyond living by the rules; rules no longer apply in your case. You need this, you tell yourself, because you deserve it. You'll never be able to get along without it. Revenge becomes the first item on your private agenda, and even as you go through your daily routines, you find yourself thinking of what it would be like to get even.

Getting even may well become the object of your daydreams, especially since we often secretly hope that getting even will, in fact, allow us to get ahead. You want to win. The desire for revenge increasingly resembles the desire for love as it occupies your imagination.

Like a lover, you imagine what surprise encounters would bring; you fantasize about conversations in which you are witty and smart; you dream up elaborate scenes from which you emerge triumphant. You find yourself smiling smugly as you think of how you'll get the last laugh, utter the last word, leave a lasting impression. Some sigh for revenge for the most trivial things, of course, like the comedian who described struggling into a size-twelve dress at a posh boutique, when a reedlike youngster came in and asked for the same dress in a size four. "She then calls out from the dressing room, 'This is too big. Do you have a two?' and I'm thinking that this girlie really needs a near-death experience, preferably while I watch." These may be fleeting thoughts, hardly worth the name of "revenge," but they are there, nevertheless, and unavoidable even for the best as well as the worst of us. There are better and worse ways, too, of handling this emotion. Zsa Zsa Gabor, a woman of considerable experience when it comes to outrage (as evidenced by the fact that she once slapped a member of the LAPD), pointed out that even she "never hated a man so much that I gave him his diamonds back." Revenge is a banquet table full of luscious possibilities and you are the delighted and eager guest.

chapter two

JUST LIKE A WOMAN

Distinctly Feminine Revenge

"When a judge let a rapist go because the woman had been wearing a miniskirt and so was 'asking for it,' I thought, Ladies, what we all should do is this: Next time we see an ugly guy on the street, shoot him. After all, he knew he was ugly when he left the house. He was asking for it."
—STAND-UP COMIC ELLEN CLEGHORN

"Heaven has no rage like love to hatred turned,
Nor hell a fury like a woman scorned."
—WILLIAM CONGREVE, *The Mourning Bride*

DO WOMEN TRADE RECIPES FOR REVENGE OVER THE backyard fence the way they once traded recipes for pot roast? Has a generation of women grown up believing that Glenn Close is in fact the *heroine* of *Fatal Attraction*? Should you take out extra insurance every time you make a copy of your house key for a new girlfriend?

Certainly women and revenge is a topic explored and exploited by every media, including, of all things, comic strips. Cathy Guisewite's ''Cathy'' is one of the most widely syndicated and merchandised characters in the Western world, and the heroine's romantic, domestic, workplace, and familial trials and tribulations have made her the darling of many eighteen- to forty-five-year-old female readers. The usual competition for boyfriends and doughnuts, however, was once replaced by an interesting discussion among Cathy and her pals at work concerning the elaborate revenge fantasies they all harbored.

"Alex and I had a fight," reveals Cathy, "and suddenly all I could think of was how much I wanted to sneak over to his house and let all the air out of his tires. . . ." A sheepishly grinning coworker admits, "Hee, hee . . . Out of nowhere one day, I started dreaming about pouring superglue in my husband's remote control and mailing his golf bag to a phony address in Europe!" Another woman gleefully chimes in, "Sometimes I lie awake planning how I'll pop out of bed in the morning, bake Walter's favorite pie, and hurl it right through the sports section into his face!"

As all three women leave the coffee machine smiling, the male boss who has overheard the conversation realizes, horrified, that "after a lifetime of hoping, a man is finally privy to the secret fantasies of women." And those secret fantasies aren't the ones promised by 900 numbers.

Why Men Fear Women's Revenge

One male friend, a journalist in his mid-forties who writes frequently about relationship issues with great insight and sensitivity, looked nervous when I asked him about revenge and gender. "I'm terrified of women when they're mad," he said, to my surprise. "I know that if I anger a woman or disrespect her—even without doing it intentionally—that she's going to make me pay. At least a guy will tell you to drop dead or hit you in the gut or something—but a woman will kill you so slowly you won't even know she's doing it.''

When I asked for examples, he rattled them off as if in alphabetical order, starting with stories of the way his two older sisters used to put his underwear on the dog when they were mad at him and then let the dog run around outside while they called his name; to a high-school girlfriend who got her pals on the yearbook to print the worst possible version of his senior picture—the one with his eyes half-closed and his mouth half-open—and claim it was a clerical error; to the bitter ex-wife who kept sending him magazine subscriptions at work with titles like *Big Penis Quarterly* and *Bottoms Up*, which the mailroom and his secretary saw first; to a coworker who unplugged his office fridge while he was on vacation, thereby ''making it into its own little biosphere, where entire ecosystems were formed.''

And this was a funny, attractive, seemingly nice man, but as I listened to his stories, I suddenly found myself wondering whether he really *was* such a nice guy after all. Surely he must be a Bluebeard in disguise to have brought this all down on himself? So I decided to ask him. If he was as decent as I thought, why would these things be done by so many women? ''Because the women in my life just didn't fight fairly. Because they didn't want to be overtly aggressive and simply toss a brick at my head, they devised far more perverse plans. Believe me, I'd have taken the brick any day.''

Feminine Aggressions

A woman's revenge doesn't usually involve anything as direct as tossing a brick through a window, let alone at a head. Taught from infancy onward to be nice, forgiving, and gentle, a woman is more apt to find her natural expression of anger turned inward toward repression or self-inflicted pain, experiences about as pleasant as an in-grown toenail. Because women aren't encouraged to accept anger or rage as legitimate responses to certain situations—even dire ones—they resort to "feminine" methods of expressing their aggression.

Revenge is high up on this list. As French novelist Colette commented in her 1920 work *Chéri* about a girlish woman, "Life as a child and then as a girl had taught her patience, hope, silence; and given her a prisoner's proficiency in handling these virtues as weapons." If patience, hope, and silence are the tools given to women, it should not be surprising that even these can be fashioned into ammunition when a woman is up against the wall of her own sense of pain and injustice.

"If women aren't permitted to assume genuine autonomy over their lives, which would allow them to prevent something bad from happening, then we cannot be surprised that, in their resentment, they feel as if they can only act after the fact," New York–based psychoanalyist Dr. Natalie Becker explains. "For example, a woman who might not be able to prevent a boss from treating her badly because she's too worried about losing her job can still inflict hidden punishment on him in response. Everyone loses when the power base is uneven; it would be far preferable if women—if everyone—could prevent an injury instead of merely responding to an injury." Revenge, she argues, comes easily to women because many mainstream forms of expression and action are denied them. "If we lived in a world where everyone actually had equal access to justice, the incidence of revenge would go way down," Dr. Becker argues.

In other words, revenge is a compensatory mechanism for a number of women, especially those who believe themselves to be barred from "legitimate" avenues of recompense and restitution. For those women who are fed up with being voiceless and overlooked, or those who feel gagged and bound by a society that they believe attaches the labels "bitchy" or "unfeminine" to women who refuse to take an insult lying down, revenge can serve as an outlet—whether the planned revenge is carried out or remains a fantasy.

A Few Choice Words

"I found out about my husband's affair with a neighbor's twenty-year-old daughter after the kid left to go back to college." Jennifer runs a catering business and I watch her pound and knead a mass of dough as she speaks. Before she began this tale, she described it as a "cute revenge story," but, though she smiles as she talks, the vigor behind the punches into the dough would certainly make me nervous if I were married to her. "The neighbor's daughter was home for the summer, my husband was briefly out of work and spending too much time around the house, and things happened. I was gone most days and some evenings because of my job, but I never thought he would cheat on me. One quiet week I was home cleaning out the basement and I came across a pile of letters she'd written to him. He had them stuffed in his toolbox, which even at the time struck me as too appropriate for words. I left them there, but I attached a note that said, 'I guess I know which tool you've been using on her.' I put the box back in its place and waited for him to find it. I pretended like I knew nothing. The next weekend he went downstairs to fix something and I suddenly heard him say 'Oh shit' and I knew that he had found my note. I immediately got in the car and left for the whole day. No explanation, no nothing. Let him wonder.

''When I came home around midnight, he was in tears and had obviously been miserable the whole time. He begged me to take him back. He pleaded and cried and I told him that I would come back under one condition— that he have tattooed across his butt the following sentence: 'I adore my wife Jennifer.' I thought about having it say 'If you can read this, you're too close,' but decided against it. He got the tattoo and I never asked him another question about his affair. He'd done something permanent to my idea of myself and I wanted to do the same thing to him. If he hadn't been willing to get the tattoo, I don't think we would have stayed together.'' Jennifer looks up from punching the bread and I can see that she means what she says.

When dealing with the idea of women and revenge, the concept of the woman-as-witch emerges with significant cultural power. It's not unusual for men to think of women as having a connection to unnatural powers. ''My wife can read my mind'' is not an uncommon assertion, and while there are times when a wife's mindreading seems ideal to her spouse (when he's busy planning dinner), there are also times when it can be unnerving (when observing a beautiful woman at a party). ''The threadbare vocabulary of the serial novels describing woman as a sorceress, an enchantress, fascinating and casting a spell over man, reflects the most ancient and universal of myths. Woman is dedicated to magic,'' explains Simone de Beauvoir in *The Second Sex*. No wonder men are scared.

A Taste of His Own Medicine—or Wine

One evening, a group of us were told an astonishing revenge story by a wealthy woman. She explained how she had been ridiculed in front of guests by her pretentious husband for not pronouncing a foreign term with what he felt was the necessary "panache." We quietly gasped in recognition of her feelings of betrayal and muted anger. What could she say? She was made to feel ignorant, even ludicrous, by a husband who was himself deeply insecure and defensive about his own lack of sophistication. Not wanting to cause a scene and make their friends feel more uncomfortable than they already did, she vowed silently to exact her revenge at a later time.

Her husband had arranged an important dinner for the next weekend, to entertain a couple he hoped would sponsor them for admission to an exclusive country club. That night, he brought the guests downstairs to his wine cellar to show off his valuable collection and to retrieve a bottle of champagne, only to discover that his wife had painstakingly removed every one of the labels on every one of the bottles. He had no idea which were the expensive vintages and which were the inexpensive table wines received as holiday gifts. Of course, he could no more get furious in front of the people he was so desperate to impress than his wife could have gotten angry at the earlier dinner. When he drew out blank bottles, looking as if they contained homemade brew, he was busy stuttering out some implausible explanation to his guests. His wife, who told the story with a smile, said that she simply asked him if everything was all right and "it was wonderful to hear him try to sound normal as he spoke through gritted teeth."

Wanting him to understand her actions and her anger, his wife wrote him a long note calmly explaining why she was uncomfortable with his attitude and his actions, and explaining why she did what she did. She pinned it to his pillow and spent the night in the guest room. "When he came down for breakfast the next morning, he actually offered me his hand to shake, and we called it a truce. After a while, we could even laugh about it. We subsequently hosted a 'mystery wine' meal and invited close, old friends and had a terrific evening."

Women Only?

Medea, queen of revenge, declared that "a woman's weak and timid in most matters; the noise of war, the look of steel make her a coward. But touch her right in marriage, and there's no bloodier spirit." And Medea hadn't even heard of Lorena Bobbitt. Juvenal, the Rush Limbaugh of antiquity who was clearly not touched by issues of political correctness, made the provocative observation that "indeed, it's always a paltry, feeble, tiny mind that takes pleasure in revenge. You can deduce it without further evidence than this, that no one delights more in vengeance than a woman."

Is this true? Are women prone to the paring knife and bemused by the burning bed? Do many women believe, as cartoonist Libby Reid suggested, that the quickest way to a cheating man's heart is a knife in his back? The assistant prosecutor in Lorena Bobbitt's trial, Mary Grace O'Brien, declared in a summation that "we don't live in a society governed by revenge." As we all know, her side lost.

Talking It Over

My own most recent experience with plotting to get even took place a few months ago. A best pal from high school had been wronged, sort of in the way that Frankie was wronged in *Frankie and Johnny*. "I told him he could take me or leave me," she wailed, "but instead he did both—and in that order." Five of us had been sitting around a table for hours, drinking endless cups of coffee that by midnight had started to look like runoff from the Exxon Valdez oil slick.

Five women, a grievance, and a sense of defiance makes for a heady, potent atmosphere, believe me. "Lipstick on his collar," sang Rose with a touch of venom, "should at least equal sugar in his gas tank, don't you think?"

"I heard a story about a Detroit woman who was dumped by her sales-rep boyfriend," offered Clara. "To get back at him, she called the recorded weather number in Cairo and left the phone off the hook for the ten days he was on the road. It cost him a fortune."

Many of us giggled in an unseemly fashion for women our age. "You could always call the IRS and anonymously suggest that they look into his last three tax returns," offered a CPA who had recently emerged from a messy divorce and was only too happy to join in the fray.

I was originally invited to join this clan because I'd once explained to Cindy that I personally translated the word *vendetta* as Italian for "What do you mean, you want to see other women?" She liked my translation.

Our coven of plotting women posed no actual danger to the men under discussion and it certainly posed no problem for men at large. We are all nice women who are not supposed to crave revenge, even when we experience pain, betrayal, humiliation, or ingratitude, so it was fun, for those few hours, to be not so nice. The evening's rampages remained reined in by reality and eventually we laughed one last time at our imagined mercilessness and went home. But it is also true that we left with a sense of exhilaration at having been able to give breath to these most secret wishes for quick, unrepentant personal justice. Dishing about dishing it out was enormously gratifying. Exciting, uncomfortable, delicious, and distasteful, revenge fantasies cannot be exorcised completely—that is, if they can be exorcised at all.

Since the desiring or powerful woman remains threatening to traditional definitions of femininity, there is a need in our society to regard her as deviant: freakish, obsessed with anger, and incapable of living rationally. A woman's revenge is initially dismissed with a slight contempt of the ''Isn't she cute when she's mad?'' variety—unless the severity of her intentions is evidenced by violence or the threat of ''real'' (read: traditionally masculine) power. Women's revenge is characterized by the need for subterfuge and delay. If revenge is a dish best served cold, you have a lot of women learning to use the deep freeze.

Or they might be learning to use other kinds of equipment. When comedienne Roseanne and her ex-husband Tom Arnold split up, stories hit the media about the fact that Roseanne was determined that Tom not get his hands on their dream house, the place where they were supposed to live happily ever after and which was still under construction at the time that divorce papers were being served. The house, she decided, would be razed to the ground. ''I'll drive the bulldozer myself,'' Roseanne was quoted as saying. While Roseanne is obviously not a contender for the Solomon school of wise behavior, certainly her feelings are understandable.

Veni, Vidi, Vindicate

Often excluded from the usual machinery of power, the female revenger must invent a method particular to her situation. It is perhaps the inverse of situational ethics; what we have is situational retribution. The woman in such a case will not be looking for restitution, since in all probability she will not want to be "restored" to any original position. "I don't want him back," said my betrayed friend from high school. "I just want him heartbroken." The women in these cases are looking for vindication and affirmation of an elusive sense of entitlement. They want acknowledgment for the fact that they were exploited, hurt, or taken for granted. They want to re-create in their lovers the same sense of loss they have felt themselves.

In her widely acclaimed novel, *The First Wives Club*, Olivia Goldsmith taps into a river of resentment flowing beneath the highly polished floors of the lonely ladies populating Manhattan's upper-middle-class neighborhoods. A group of women whose husbands have left them have the following manifesto: "It's time for what goes around comes around. Let's talk about the total destruction of these men. Emotional, financial, social. We make sure their marriages fail, their businesses go sour, their friends desert them. They did it to us. We can do it to them." Unnervingly unapologetic about its particularly feminine take on the issues, the book was nevertheless applauded by the mainstream press: *The New York Times Book Review* called it "a credible and deeply satisfying tale." Men tended to ask the double-standard question: If such a book were written by a man about destroying a group of successful women, would it have received the same sort of critical approval? Probably not. But that's how tales of revenge work to a great extent: We most enjoy those where the apparently powerless get even with the powerful who have hurt them. And since, at this point in our culture men remain more powerful than women, stories of revenge against ex-husbands sell books.

The BMW vs. the DMV

Some tales of revenge are particularly satisfying in the short term, when anger is new and outrage is impossible to ignore, and many of the revenge tales told to me involved a newly divorced woman wanting to settle the score with her former spouse. "My ex-husband was a control freak," began one forty-five-year-old divorced mother of two, "and he hated being asked to do things he considered trivial—such as housework, child care, or social activities. I was designated to take care of all of these because I 'didn't work'—as he never ceased reminding me. I told him repeatedly that I worked at least as hard as he did, but since I didn't have an outside income he never took me seriously. I did everything for him, from his laundry to his taxes. When he left me for another woman, I was horrified and furious. He had enough money to buy me off, he didn't really care whether anybody invited him to dinner again, and so there were few avenues to get back at him.

"I decided that the worst thing I could do to him was inconvenience him. Every two weeks for six months I went to the parking lot behind his office and removed the license plates from his BMW. I carefully unscrewed them, never damaging the car, and took them home." I was puzzled about this particular revenge—what was so satisfying about the act? "It meant he had to go down to the Department of Motor Vehicles and apply for new plates all the time. He had to wait on line like everyone else and be just a regular guy caught up in a bureaucracy. He spent more time at the DMV than he did in his BMW and that gave me enormous joy."

In situations involving ex-spouses and ex-lovers, we usually want to get even to the same degree that we once loved. In this way, revenge becomes paradoxical since it insures that we maintain a continuing intimacy with the other person. Our heads are full of imaginary encounters and rehearsed conversations when we're in the heat of a wish for vindication.

For example, let's say you imagine the crestfallen expression on your old flame's face after he catches a glimpse of you holding hands with an exotic and glamorous new lover. Let's say you also imagine, for good measure, that your ex stumbles across your name as a keynote speaker at a professional meeting and understands that this high-voltage new job is only a partial measure of your success without him. As fantasies go, these are fairly representative.

The flaw lies with the fact that you're still filling your fantasy life with meetings, conversations, and emotions starring someone from your past. You're still hooked. You become as caught up with the idea of revenge as you were once caught up with the idea of romance—in part because they uncannily resemble each other.

"Arsenic and No Lace"

A lengthy anthropological/sociological study whimsically titled "Arsenic and No Lace" offers a hint of its unwhimsical and disturbing subject. Researcher Ferenc Gyorgyey discusses a rather unusual practice that occupied women in a small Hungarian town for a number of years, that of killing their menfolk. Now, some people might think, Well, this is what happens when guys just won't give women the right to hold public office, and to a certain extent they wouldn't be wrong. Gyorgyey writes, "There was some suspicion that the Hungarian government, reluctant to reveal that this custom of radically eliminating menfolk had gone back not twenty years but indeed for a century or more, had placed a twenty-year limit on exhumation. Whether this suspicion had any validity or not, the records of both the trial and investigation show that the twenty-year time limit was scrupulously honored."

The number of suspicious deaths exceeded 200, according to published reports. The number of confirmed arsenic victims can be estimated at around 165, according to Gyorgyey, who flatly declares, "The murders were committed solely by women." Prosecuting attorney Janos Kronberg stated in his summation of the second trial: "It is in the basic nature of women to enjoy the suffering of others. That is why most poisoners are women. Women are cowards, therefore they murder insidiously." That's one reason. Looking at typical behavior patterns in the village might lead to other explanations. Women killed men who beat them, who beat their daughters, who half-starved their children. Having no recourse in the eyes of the law—or believing they had none—they chose to take fate into their own hands. The acts were not so much ritualized as they were simply acts of revenge, but this was revenge on a *remarkable* scale. This was, in effect, war.

As if they were soldiers, ruthless in avenging past wrongs on their vanquished enemies, these women took out their anger on the men who had hurt them. "One of the most enigmatic aspects of this phenomenon is its conspiratorial nature," Gyorgyey notes. "It is common knowledge that gossip, rumors, leaks and squealing have always accompanied illicit group activity everywhere. But here, the whole village, at least the whole female population of the village, knew—had known, not for a year or two but for at least two decades—why and how all these men had died. Yet, the secret was so ancient, so overpowering, that with the exception of a couple of anonymous letters at the end, no one broke the silence. One cannot help wondering why the men never caught on and became suspicious. It is equally remarkable that a group of people came to accept a gruesome, unnatural practice as the norm and followed it without hesitation or guilt."

Here, of course, lies the rub. In part, these women were responding to the violent, gruesome, and unnatural practices that had been used against them for years. The horrors that befell this community can in no way be justified—but the horrors that preceded the poisonings cannot be sanctioned any more than the ones offered by the women in response.

"A Lot of Patience to Lose"

Affection, respect, and desire are not zero-sum games; if someone else feels good, it doesn't mean they've taken our happiness. If we lose a sense of self-respect, it isn't usually because somebody else stole it. It's usually because we gave it away. The person who we think has our fate in his hands is probably oblivious to the fact that he has walked off with all our invisible emotional baggage. "We have been taught to forgive our enemies, but where is it written that we have to forgive the people we love?" asks my pal Rose. It is a good question.

"I've got a lot of patience, baby," Laura Nyro sang on my favorite record during junior high, "and that's a lot of patience to lose." As we've already seen, we learn to damp down our wishes to get even as we get older, but they can remain a smoky, smoldering part of ourselves if we don't deal with what got us all fired up in the first place.

Basic Instincts

Revenge fascinates everyone, but let's face it—we have a particular appetite for stories about feminine young women getting mad and then getting even. Lorena Bobbitt, Amy Fisher, and Tonya Harding may have looked like sorority girls, but they acted like the three witches from Macbeth. Lizzie Borden remains an icon in American culture in part because she is the poster child for the "good girl gets mad" school of thought—and because she got away with it. These women, for better or worse, have captured our collective imagination.

We seem to look to these tales for both confirmation and denial of our basic instincts: We see that they confirm the maxim that the female of the species is deadlier than the male, and that, as Nietzsche suggested, "in revenge and love, the woman is more barbarous than man." But we also comb revenge tales for a challenge to the other assumption about women: that women are passive and powerless. We look to these mythologies not to excuse the villain but to explain and explore our own fears, rages, and sense of injustice. It seems that we care less for the real story than for the mythological one; discovering that the actual, flesh-and-blood women and men are tragic and tortured doesn't detract from our preoccupation with their actions. In other words, what actually happens is less significant than what we imagine it to be.

We become fixated particularly on the women who choose to act out their revenge far more often than we focus on their male counterparts. In October 1992 *The National Law Journal* reported that in the first nine months of that year alone, seven disgruntled men killed a total of three ex-wives, two lawyers, and two relatives in court while wounding more than a dozen others. The statistic did not make headline news. (Some men not too high up the evolutionary chart might look at those 1992 statistics and cynically comment, as did one of my more bitter male acquaintances, "Too bad about the relatives.") For the most part we tune out male violence. "Homicide is justifiable when committed by the husband upon one taken in the act of adultery with the wife, provided the killing takes place before the parties to the act have separated," reads a 1961 Texas law. Apparently things haven't changed as much as we'd like to think, except that clearly you no longer have to wait until you catch "them" in bed together. In 1994 one judge awarded a sentence of one and one-half years to a man who, having discovered his wife in flagrante delicto, murdered her. The judge went on to explain in court that, if it were completely up to him, he would have let the murderer go without any prison time whatsoever. It's just guys being guys: mad about unfair laws and alimony. Just guys with guns, and guys with weapons. They don't make news, not unless they were once seemingly gentle, highly photogenic football heroes and traveled in the super-rich circles of Los Angeles.

Portraits of the Avenging Woman

In contrast, stories of women's anger and violence have a "dog-bites-man" quality of reversal that gives them media appeal, simply as novelty. Give a woman a knife, and then watch the cameras roll and the copy scroll off the computer screen. After all, it's a standard plot for a drive-in movie, sort of like the forty-foot woman scaled down to apartment size. A woman who gets mad is still monstrous enough to make the front page and to guarantee a box office hit.

And don't think that it's only women who are watching or reading about women and revenge; this is not a Mary Tyler Moore rerun. Many guys are completely enthralled. Saloons that once showed only world-class wrestling suddenly started showing clips of figure skating after Nancy Kerrigan was put out of commission by Tonya Harding. The skate-off between the two women was one of the most-watched Olympic events in television history.

A woman who gets even with her man is the stuff of male fantasies about women. The odds of violent revenge actually occurring in their lives probably ranks right up there with other unlikely events that populate the male imagination, like finding out the Doublemint Twins are nymphomaniacs looking for a date. Yet when Tom Hanks's character in *Sleepless in Seattle* yells at his pre-adolescent son that "*Fatal Attraction* . . . scared the shit out of every man in America,'' the audience burst into applause.

It's not just the movies that are offering these portraits. In *Presumed Innocent*, Scott Turow's 1987 best-seller, we hear about a woman who believes that any revenge that leaves the lover living is ineffective. ''She has a wish,'' Turow writes of the hero's quiet, mathematician wife, ''a wild secret hope that the woman he was sleeping with could end up dead. When the wife's rage is at a peak, she's ready to abandon her husband and head for open spaces. But there would be no satisfaction in that if the other woman is alive, because the husband, helpless slob that he is, will just go crawling back to her and end up with what his wife thinks he wants. The wife can get even only if the other woman is gone.'' The enraged woman with the knife or the gun is a dangerous extension of an icon we all recognize: the femme fatale.

Maybe if the women at the center of these revenge spectacles looked like prison matrons in grade-B movies, we would not be as hooked on their stories as we are. If they were members of the underclass, we might not grant them the same number of pay-per-session exclusive interviews or television movies. If they were very unattractive, or very fat, or very old, we would probably push them as far off the stage as possible. We don't like seeing the pain and anger of those who are genuinely and irrevocably outsiders. What we like seeing is Michelle Pfeiffer as Cat Woman. We like a nice figure of a woman in our Medeas.

Attractive and deadly women are terrifying—and fascinating. What we can't understand—and what therefore holds our attention—is that such figures often appear to be ''real girls'' of the lip-gloss-wearing, hair-spray-using, high-heel-wearing sort. They look as if they'd cry if you insulted them, not cut off your penis, shoot your wife, or try to break your knees. They don't look tough, but obviously those around them learn to sit with their backs to the walls of restaurants and to sleep very, very lightly. Maybe with a nightlight.

"She Has Thought Much Worse Things About You..."

What about the kinds of revenge—crafty, subtle, emotional rather than mechanical—that women are far more likely to perpetrate? Women are far less likely to want a shoot-'em-out showdown at noon than men are, but that doesn't mean the aftermath of their anger is any less deadly. "Never feel remorse for what you have thought about your wife," wrote French author Jean Rostand. "She has thought much worse things about you."

She, the ex-wife, certainly thought worse things about you, the ex-husband, if you've left her for another woman. For one thing, she's likely to get some revenge by telling people all she knows about the woman you left her for. She might, for example, blame your fear of her success on your abandonment. According to Cynthia Heimel whose collections of essays include one with a revenge-driven title, *If You Can't Live Without Me, Why Aren't You Dead Yet?*, the contemporary woman is informed: "Get a job, your husband hates you. Get a good job, your husband leaves you. Get a stupendous job, your husband leaves you for a teenager."

The popular women's magazine *Marie Claire* includes as one of its regular features the inspiring "Role Models" section, presumably to raise our hopes and spirits by showing us how well other women are managing to get through life. One imagines stories about Mother Teresa, Oprah Winfrey, or at least Hillary Rodham Clinton. Even

I was surprised, therefore, to see an article entitled "Revenge of the Dumped" by Lisa Simmons in this section. Simmons clearly enjoys her less-than-ordinary discussion of how "personal scandal and public humiliation didn't keep these four women down. We are happy to report they are back on track and better than ever. Let their stories be an inspiration to you." Bringing to our attention a group of famous women who have gotten back at their rotten spouses or rotten circumstances, we find ourselves consorting with a bevy of unlikely heroines, including Ivana Trump, Vanessa Williams, Tonya Harding, and Mia Farrow. The thrust of Simmons's argument is that living richly and famously is the best revenge, which is really a slight letdown for those of us who were hoping for stories about how Ivana threw all of Donald's cuff links into the sewers outside the Plaza Hotel.

Nice Girls Don't Get Mad, They Get Even

The desire for revenge is a fundamental human emotion (and I'm not just saying that because my last name ends in a vowel). The Bible declares that man was created by God in His image, and we know that the God of both the Old and New Testaments has a taste for revenge. Indeed, He has such an appetite for revenge that men want exclusive rights. Are women (and men) coming too close to playing God when the idea of justice and revenge is removed from institutionalized and ritualized forms and interpreted by us? What informs the difference between the revenge fantasies of men and women?

Clearly John Wayne Bobbitt (and did you ever think you'd hear somebody's middle name being used this often after they let William Kennedy Smith go?) thought his wife was a good girl, one who might shrink a favorite shirt on purpose but not shrink his anatomy. Guys just don't think about revenge the same way women do. For example, guys often think of destroying somebody's property when it comes to getting revenge, but it's my impression that they don't usually think in terms of a woman keying her husband's car to get revenge. Guys sense, with itching-collar intuition, that many women don't buy the idea that living well is the best revenge. Women, especially the sweetie-pie, soft-spoken, real-girl sorts, often believe that *revenge* is the best revenge.

Lorena Bobbitt wanted to be called *Mrs.* Bobbitt, remember. None of this ''Ms.'' stuff for Lorena, who apparently bought the white-wedding fantasy wholesale. This was not a woman who was campaigning for NOW but a woman whose wedding picture showed her being lifted high in the air as if she were a flag for her husband to carry into battle. She apparently liked being the little woman, at least initially. Resembling a character from *The Stepford Wives,* Lorena Bobbitt seemed to play the good little wife to the hilt. Her revenge was evidence of powerlessness, not strength. Her act of vengeance was made not in order to control but because her marriage was out of control.

This was not cool Al Pacino in *The Godfather*. This was hysterical Kathy Bates in *Misery*.

"Who Am I, That I Should Be Kind?"

Part of the issue, of course, is that traditionally girls have been brought up to be nice instead of victorious, triumphant, or powerful. Only after being pushed to extremes of disappointment or outrage can women abandon the idea that they have to forgive everyone who has hurt them, no matter how bad the damage. Like Miss Havisham, the central female character from Charles Dickens's *Great Expectations*, women who seek revenge have long since refused to be placated by the dictum that they should forgive and forget injustices because they are bound by codes of nurturance and gentility. Such women may well echo Miss Havisham's words. "Who am I," she cries, striking her stick upon the floor and flashing into wrath to the surprise of those around her. "Who am I, for God's sake, that I should be kind?" Only after serious wounds have been carved into their souls do most women believe they can or even should reek vengence on a world that denies the validity of feminine experience.

Miss Havisham is not kind, but we cherish and remember her for her malicious cruelty, her obsessive desire for revenge, and her manipulation of those around her. Miss Havisham and her apprentice revenger Estella are at the heart of Dickens' 1861 novel, although they are not technically the main characters. Miss Havisham is the bad mother (Estella once calls Miss Havisham "mother by adoption"), the dark guardian who mistakenly or manipulatively defends her ward not against evil but rather against a natural development, or the development of any possible good: as adopted-daughter Estella says, telling her male friend Pip why she can be so angry at the world: "You have not your little wits sharpened by [the world] intriguing against you, suppressed and defenseless . . . I did." Brought up by her mother-figure Miss Havisham to emotionally seduce and betray the love of men (as Miss Havisham was herself emotionally seduced and betrayed), Estella is doomed to spend her life in a joyless life based on refusal and revenge.

Joyful Revenge

But revenge does not have to be joyless. Some of the best revenge depends almost completely on a celebration of feminine anarchy—on a woman's breaking away from and out of society's traditional roles. As Simone de Beauvoir put it, nearly fifty years ago, in *The Second Sex*, "She [woman in general] is servant and companion, but [her male mate] expects her also to be his audience and critic and to confirm him in his sense of being; but she opposes him with her indifference, even with her mockery and laughter." Women's revenge and women's humor often act as a record of rebellion.

While it is true that traditional forms of masculine behavior have recorded men's revolt against certain inequities in a given social system, there remains a difference between how men and women approach the subject of their irreverence. And the difference between men's and women's revenge is often the difference between revolt and revolution. When a woman's revenge is directed toward authority, it can bring down the house. Virginia Woolf wrote in one of her political essays, "Three Guineas," "The fear of ridicule which great psychologists, like Sophocles, detect in the dominator . . . is also peculiarly susceptible according to the same authority either to ridicule or defiance on the part of the female sex. . . . Laughter as an antidote to dominance is perhaps indicated."

Laughing at the oppressor is not limited to women—certainly Mark Twain and Will Rogers, Garrison Keillor and Dave Barry have shown us that—but women will use humor as revenge in a particularly inflammatory way. Audiences all over the country whooped and hollered at the scene in *Fried Green Tomatoes* when our now familiar revenge heroine, Kathy Bates, drove her vehicle into the parked car of two snotty teenagers who not only stole her parking space but made fun of her, laughing that they were younger and prettier and could do what they wanted. Bates, having reached her tolerance limit, replied, "Yes, but I'm older and I have more insurance," as she repeatedly rams their cute little car. While this was the climactic revenge scene in the film, the novel paints an even richer portrait of revenge fantasies entertained by Evelyn, the character played by Kathy Bates. In her daydreams, Evelyn thinks of herself as "Towanda the Avenger." *Fried Green Tomatoes at the Whistle Stop Cafe* author Fannie Flagg explains that "few people who saw this plump, pleasant-looking, middle-aged, middle-class housewife out shopping or doing other menial, everyday chores could guess that, in her imagination, she was machine-gunning the genitals of rapers and stomping abusive husbands to death in her specially designated wife-beater boots.

"And while Evelyn went about her business with a smile," Flagg continues, "Towanda was busy poking child molesters with electric cattle prods until their hair stood on end [and she] forced that doctor, who had told her mother she had cancer, to walk down the street naked while the entire medical profession, including dentists and oral hygienists, jeered and threw rocks. . . . She allowed rats to chew all the slumlords to death. . . . Graffiti offenders were to be dipped in a vat of indelible ink. No more children of famous parents could write books."

And many of Evelyn's revenge fantasies are fairly gender-specific: "She went to Hollywood and ordered all the leading men to act opposite women of their own age, not twenty-year-old girls with perfect bodies. . . . Tonight, while Evelyn was cooking dinner, Towanda had just put a roomful of porno and child-exploitation film producers to death. . . . She placed tiny bombs inside *Playboy* and *Penthouse* magazine that would explode when they were opened. . . .''

Along similar lines was John Waters's 1994 film *Serial Mom,* starring Kathleen Turner as a Donna Reed clone with a very, very bad temper. Waters, director of the infamous film *Pink Flamingos,* creates a female revenger who isn't caught up in romance but is instead a vigilante on behalf of family values. Like Flagg's Evelyn, Mom goes after all sorts of no-goodniks, even those who haven't done anything worse than aggravate her or a member of her family. Repeatedly running over her son's creepy math teacher, for example, brings her great satisfaction undiluted by pangs of conscience or second thought. Directly after the ''accident'' (which might be more appropriately termed an ''intentional'' in this case), she comes out of the kitchen with a plate of homemade cookies, smiling and cheerily announcing, ''I don't know what it is about today, but I feel great.'' Mom kills the boy who stood up her daughter for a date, and she is adamant about her right to get rid of annoying folks the same way she insists on getting rid of chewing gum. Like Evelyn, she tortures a woman who once stole a parking space from her, but unlike Evelyn, she plots out her revenge carefully and proceeds with caution. This is the domestic-comedy counterpart of *Fatal Attraction*—this is what the Glenn Close character would have turned into once she moved to suburbia and joined the PTA. Her target is no longer the lover who betrayed her but the untidy and unkind world at large.

Vituperation as Victory

Nineteenth-century feminist Elizabeth Cady Stanton declared, "If women would indulge more freely in vituperation, they would enjoy ten times the health they do. It seems to me they are suffering from repression." Her words mirror the repression that women continue to feel today because we have not come such a very long way after all. We often tell ourselves that we seek revenge for higher reasons: to right some grievous wrong, to create balance where there had been dislocation and inequality. Wouldn't you like to exact some form of revenge on, let's say, the president of the prestigious college who declared in the late sixties, "It is ridiculous and naive to suggest that a B.A. can be made as attractive to girls as an M.R.S."? I was told the story of a woman with a B.A. who got herself elected to the board of trustees and successfully encouraged the departure of this president.

Sweet revenge indeed, because often these selfless actions are at least initiated by a moment of personal desire to "get even" rather than to "make right," with justice as a by-product of the momentum of revenge. Women, it seems, have a genuine appetite for both hearing and telling their stories; revenge virtually cries out for the attention it has so long deserved. This is not about true confessions. It is about the way that people cut off from power learn to practice a kind of emotional terrorism in order to regain their self-esteem in a world that often seems bent on robbing them of even that.

The administrative assistant who supports her family cannot afford to put her job in jeopardy no matter how much ritual humiliation is inflicted by her boss. She doesn't dare go over his head to a supervisor for fear of reprisal, so she broadcasts his conversation with his mistress over the speakerphone "by accident." She swears up and down that the coffee she's been giving her boss all day is decaf, knowing full well that he'll now be awake for the next six weeks on all the caffeine flooding his system. She takes justice into her own hands, and resorts to being a pink-collar terrorist.

And if women get vengeful on their own behalf, they double their efforts when it comes to their children. Women can become ferocious even when they simply think their families *might* be in some danger. In Maxine Hong Kingston's *The Woman Warrior*, the heroine's mother is virtually obsessed by revenge, because she is very certain that the inhabitants of her new American culture are trying to take advantage of what they regard as her ignorance. When a pharmacy sends a prescribed drug to their house by mistake, the mother takes this random action as a personal insult: "Revenge. We've got to avenge this wrong to our future, our health, and on our lives. Nobody's going to sicken my children and get away with it."

Her daughter understands that the pharmacy has merely made an honest mistake, but her mother insists that there is a plot against them that must be avenged. She believes as she does because revenge is woven into her family's particular history and culture, and also because this is her own legacy of coming of age in a world where women are not permitted to act for themselves. Now the formidable matriarch of the family is intent on destroying the enemy, even if the enemy isn't real.

"Being Ladylike Is Not Everything It Is Supposed to Be"

But sometimes the lessons learned from appropriate revenge scenarios have long-reaching and ultimately positive results. "I was so upset that it felt as if somebody was pouring an electrical current through my body," a soft-spoken woman in her sixties revealed, blushing slightly and lowering her eyes. She betrayed her Southern background in a dozen charming ways, hinting at an earlier version of feminine behavior that was not overridden by either her decades in Boston or the fact that she has lived alone for the last fifteen years.

"I went to the library and studied all sorts of consumer ratings so that I could finally buy myself the large television I've always wanted, so that when I retire next year everything will all be in place. With my husband gone I'd not really investigated these sorts of purchases before, but I felt it was time that I treat myself. Although I was nervous about maneuvering my way through one of those big electronics stores, I found a good sale, armed myself like a warrior with all these documents, and walked into the store. Salespeople descended on me like ants at a picnic, but I chose to go with one lady, not too much younger than myself, because she seemed very, very knowledgeable.

"She was persuasive, and I spent more money in that one place than I ever had in my lifetime. I bought a television that cost more than my wedding ring, a VCR, and one of those extra-warranties. The saleswoman swore that it would all be delivered by the next week, so on the scheduled delivery date I took off from work to wait for it. I was very excited and, I'm embarrassed to say, felt like a little girl waiting for Santa Claus. Imagine my disappointment when, by late afternoon, no one had come or even had the courtesy to call. When I telephoned I was told that it would arrive the next day, without question. It didn't. They then swore on their mothers that one more day and it would be there, that the truck had broken down, whatever. The trouble is, I believed them. They all sounded so sincere and so overworked that I thought, Well, they don't need me to add to their troubles. But by then I'd missed three days of work. These were counted as vacation days, so while I wasn't losing pay, I was still eating up my own time sitting in my little apartment. The next day came and went and no television.

"By this time I was fit to be tied. I called Customer Service, and some manager told me that he would get to my order as soon as possible, but that he couldn't make promises. I told him that I'd already been promised a great deal. He told me that everybody had problems; I told him that he was being rude. He told me to stop being a selfish old biddy. Honest to goodness, I thought I was going to faint. How could someone who was a manager in Customer Service treat a paying customer this way? He wouldn't have said it to a man, I know that much.

"Well, I decided that if he was going to call me a selfish old biddy, then I was going to act like one. I called a local television station and reached some young woman who was an assistant producer or whatever and explained, sweetly and in my most little-old-lady voice, that I'd been treated very badly by this one store and I thought that it was because of my age and the fact that I was female. She understood and loved my story, and they had a car come and take me to the station. They interviewed me on the air, and I told my story as if I were Sarah Bernhardt's baby sister. Then they took the cameras to the store and tried to interview the saleswoman, who wouldn't speak, and the manager, who wouldn't speak, either. It made them look real bad. Before the program even aired, I got a call from the man who'd been so rude to me. He told me that they were sorry and that they would not only guarantee delivery of everything by the next day but that *he* would pick up the tab for the warranty and maybe the VCR, too. I canceled the order on the spot and hung up on him feeling like a queen.

"The next night a group of my friends and I watched the segment on a television at a local restaurant, and everybody cheered me when I came on to tell my story. It was wonderful. I bought an entertainment system at a competitor's store and they took a photograph of me as a satisfied customer to put in their window, figuring that everybody had seen what happened to me with the other store."

She concludes, with a lovely, warm smile, "I had never been so unladylike before, but it was worth it. And, after all these years, I suddenly realized that being ladylike is not everything it is supposed to be."

What's wonderful about this story is that this normally sweet woman understood and admitted that she wanted satisfaction for herself. Often women deny with astonishing vigor the fact that they might want to rectify a situation out of a sense of personal anger. "I'm not out to get anything for myself," says the voice denying revenge while playing it out. "I just don't want it to happen to someone else." But the voice of the woman seeking revenge is also the voice of a woman who has decided that, if the world will not defend her, she will defend and vindicate herself.

"Let no one think of me as humble or weak or passive; let them understand I am of a different kind: dangerous to my enemies, loyal to my friends. To such a life glory belongs.'' This is a line from *Medea*, but it could be the motto for a contemporary woman who decides that enough is enough.

Fat Chance

Occasionally one hears about a woman who delights in the fact that she has redressed a balance. ''I guess my husband married me in sickness and in health, for richer or poorer—but I should have put in the ceremony the line 'in thinness and in weight.' '' Georgia, a big, beautiful woman of thirty-one, explained that after she put on twenty pounds, her husband felt it was perfectly justifiable not only to make remarks about her shape but also to comment on the preferable shapes of all the women with whom he came into contact. From Georgia's description, this was no movie star we were dealing with; he, too, was twenty pounds overweight, but was convinced that it made him look good.

''I decided to diet. But if I was going to diet, then he was going to diet. I made the worst food in the world, which is tough to do if you're as good a cook as I am, and served it night after night. I made beans constantly, so that he would have gas at work the next day—his buddies down at the shop loved that—and I made him special vitamin-filled milk shakes that made him spend half the day in the can. I threw away candy he hid in his dresser. I threw away his beer. I felt better and he felt worse. I started to cut pictures of Fabio out of magazines and leave them with little notes in his lunch box saying 'You want to be as cute as him, dontcha, honey?' until he came back from work one day begging me to go back to how we used to live.

"I told him that if we did, I never wanted to hear my body compared to another woman's under any circumstances. He promised and I made macaroni and cheese. We do eat better now, and I've kept off some of the weight, but the main point was I rectified the situation. I felt that a sense of balance had been restored in our relationship." Georgia tried asking for sympathy, she tried to make her husband see the unfairness of the situation, she appealed to his affection for her, but when none of those worked, she chose revenge. The creativity of her plot was the offspring of her hurt feelings, but it was no less clever because of that. Sometimes revenge is the mother of invention.

Sometimes the Wrong Answer Is the Right One

One of the most satisfying types of a particularly feminine form of revenge depends on a shameless refusal to be embarrassed by a bully who believes that you can be whipped into submission by authority. My favorite illustration of this dynamic comes from a well-known and much-loved author who was slated to appear on a rather pretentious talk show, where she would be asked to discuss her favorite works of art, literature, and music. A few minutes before the program went on the air—where she and the host would appear in front of an audience and be broadcast live around much of the known universe— she was told by the host that he thought her to be one of the shoddiest, poorest writers in publishing today. As they walked onto the stage he told her that he argued against allowing her on the show but that the producers overrode his good judgment.

At first speechless, with humiliation and rage, she bit her tongue as he introduced her. Composing herself, however, she prepared for his first question. "If you were permitted to take only one piece of music with you to a deserted island, what recording would you choose?" Now, most cultural figures asked this question came up with the likes of Mahler or Mozart, the host beamed, and then they would discuss the lyrical nature of the symphony or opera mentioned. When she was asked this question, without hesitation she responded, "I would take the soundtrack of *The Wiz* with me." It was the host's turn to blush and stammer, "*The Wiz?* W-w-why?" "Because I really like the song 'Ease on Down the Road,' of course," she responded cheerfully. The audience laughed and applauded, clearly delighted by her irreverence and lack of pretensions. They were delighted, too, by the pole-axed expression on the face of the usually unflappable interviewer. He hated her smart-alecky ways, but he wouldn't budge; he remained serious and sinister even as she became increasingly flippant at his expense. She answered all the questions in the same vein: She would take a copy of *Smart Women, Foolish Choices* to the island as a great work of literature, and she would bring a *Magic Eye* poster to represent great art. She said she really liked when you could finally see the picture of the bunny emerge from the background.

Delivering all her answers with a beatifically calm expression and great earnestness, she could not be regarded as either openly sarcastic or silly. She could only be regarded as in control. Sometimes the only way to win the game is to change the rules of play. Her wrong answers, paradoxically, were her revenge. Speaking up and speaking out when silence is expected can be an enormously triumphant moment, especially for a woman who is no longer willing to put out, shut up, or simply get by. Her voice can be a song of vindication.

chapter three

THE FIRING LINE BETWEEN LOVE AND HATE

Revenge in Sexual Relationships

"Though the husband's interest in another woman may be a matter of the past, though it may merely consist in insignificant attentions, a wife may torment him and keep tormenting him in such a blind fury— sometimes against her own better judgment—that she may seriously jeopardize the whole marriage."
—PSYCHOANALYST KAREN HORNEY, "THE VALUE OF VINDICTIVENESS"

He who can lick, can bite.
—FRENCH PROVERB

STAND-UP COMIC SUSIE ESSMAN WALKS ONSTAGE AND explains, in a sad voice and with downcast eyes, "My boyfriend just broke up with me to go out with a younger woman." Everyone in the audience makes sympathetic "Aww" sounds. Essman then looks up and reassures the audience cheerfully, "Don't feel bad. He's dead now."

Her opening routine, as the routine of every successful comic must, plays on the assumption that her audience will get the punch line instantly, understanding that a guy who dumps her for a teenager must be made to pay for it. Men laugh as much as women at Essman's line because the instinct to hurt the lover who leaves is perhaps the least gender-specific of any instinct apart from breathing or wanting the last piece of chocolate. Like watching somebody else take the last piece of chocolate after you've bravely said, "No, you go ahead," watching a lover walk out of your life is infuriating even when you've told yourself it's perfectly okay and you didn't want any more to do with him, anyhow.

Sexual revenge stories were the ones most people wanted to tell, whispering and laughing in libraries, bars, cabs, and classrooms, speaking in a low voice as if somehow this made their actions more acceptable. In this manner I discovered a virtual orgy of revenge tales, many revealed to me by very unlikely sources. It became clear to me that anyone who has discovered a partner's affair, who has been left waiting by a telephone for a promised call that didn't come, or who has been on the receiving end of unfair humiliations in an otherwise reasonable relationship has entertained thoughts of revenge, however fleetingly.

A Confession...

Perhaps I heard so many of these stories because I had one of my own to trade, like an emotional baseball card. While working as a tutor in the writing center when I was a college sophomore, helping other students with their papers and tutoring ones whose skills needed sharpening, I became deeply infatuated with another student. He was definitely not my usual type. Big, burly, and bearded, he came into the center because his English professor had given him an ultimatum: Learn to write a sentence or you're off the rugby team. Wearing T-shirts bearing witticisms such as "Rugby Players Eat Their Dead," this guy looked more like a refrigerator with a head than a card-carrying member of the human race. For whatever reason, at that point in my life he looked very good to me.

It's hard to admit, but I was thrilled whenever he walked into the room and flattered that he always asked to see me for help. I found myself forgoing the usual jeans and T-shirts for pink sweaters and green corduroy skirts (which I had to borrow from a surprised sorority-girl co-worker). I tried to help him grasp ideas of such magnitude as punctuation and paragraphing, but there really wasn't much hope; he looked at me the way a beached whale looks at a life raft. This wasn't going to work. What I did—and this is where the embarrassing part comes in—was to practically write the damn things for him. He'd come in with an essay assignment and I'd tell myself that I was just outlining it for him, or writing a detailed pattern for him to follow when he went back to the frat house. I even went to the library to track down sources for him, and when I wrote up the bibliography, I told myself that I was just being extra nice because he'd been trying so very hard and had been so sweet to me.

I suckered myself into believing that my dishonest actions were not really dishonest and that my intentions were selfless. What I really wanted, of course, was a real date with him, maybe to one of those fraternity parties I'd spent years avoiding and disdaining. Like the pink sweaters, the parties suddenly had some appeal—because of the idea of his hand in them.

This went on for some weeks. He would walk into the room, filling the rectangular frame of the doorway with his bulk, and crush himself into one of the small chairs that lined the edges of the wood-paneled study. Then he would smile his sheepish smile and I would melt and begin working on his assignment. He would look over my shoulder, compliment, make noises representing some form of understanding, and gaze soulfully into my eyes as I explained the difference between *then* and *than*. It didn't matter that he didn't hear a word; what mattered to me was that I had, at the very least, done my job by saying them.

What I wouldn't do was type his papers. His hands, big and inflexible as paws, flopped over the keys, but I wouldn't give in. I repeated, as much for my own benefit as his, that I wasn't doing his work for him—I was only helping him along. I told him to double-check the sources I provided and rework the outlines I created in order to arrive at his own conclusions. No matter that the odds were better that an insect-eyed alien from Mars would enter the library before he did. I insisted on mouthing the words of the virtuous even as I committed the deeds of the unscrupulous. I figured that he'd be asking me out pretty soon, probably right after we saw him through the big term paper. Working harder for him than I worked for myself, I spent hours in the stacks finding obscure critics who wrote long books on the nineteenth-century American author he'd chosen for his topic, writing up synopses of their major points, and supplying all the information he'd need to footnote appropriately.

It was one afternoon while I was in the basement stacks, dust in my curly hair and mold from the pages making my fingers slick, that I overheard two women giggling a few aisles away. I caught my breath as I realized that they were talking and laughing about my rugby player.

I stopped breathing altogether when I realized they were also laughing about me.

At such moments you think you'll never forget the exact phrases as they cut themselves into your consciousness, carving out word by word the pain they cause, but the great thing about life is that you do forget—at least you forget the details. What I remember is the gist of the conversation: that this guy they both knew—and clearly knew well—had conned some moon-eyed moron in the writing center to do all his work for him, that he was stringing her along until his midterm paper was finished, but that he couldn't even handle thinking about going back every week until finals. He figured that if he aced the paper next week, he could afford to slack off for the rest of the term. At least he wouldn't get thrown off the team. They kept giggling as they walked back upstairs into the light.

I waited for myself to cry, but I couldn't. I was numb, then enraged, and finally more clear-headed than I'd been in weeks. For his next assignment, I went to the main library and retrieved the most famous essay about the author written by the most famous critic. I copied it out word for word. The next day, I kept my anger out of sight, like a sword in its sheath—sharp but hidden. I handed the paper to Mr. Rugby, all smiles, and warned him merrily that he should understand that these were just some of my own ideas and to make sure he did the research and wrote the paper on his own. Anything less wouldn't be right. He gave me a big grin, rolled the paper in his paw, and took off for fraternity row.

I think it might have even made the student newspaper when he was suspended for plagiarizing. Word got out that his professor wasn't really surprised that he'd cheated, but what shocked even this veteran teacher was that the student had cheated so stupidly—copying out word for word the most famous essay on the subject without a single reference.

Satisfied by the outcome, I was nevertheless humiliated by my initial foolishness and my own self-deluded dishonesty. While I followed the letter of the law, I'd certainly compromised the spirit behind it. I felt guilty for having been so eager to give up my principles for a handsome face. Never would I do such a thing again, but I didn't feel guilty for handing him that paper. He obviously felt stupid and embarrassed enough not to take any revenge on me for having set him up. We were even. When he was reinstated the next term, I heard from friends of friends that he had hired a private tutor.

Real Life Matches Fiction

So perhaps it's not surprising that women *and* men felt happy enough to share their own revenge stories after I'd started us off by telling my own. Some revenge stories even involve relatively happy couples. Sometimes, it seems, there are just moments when the relationship needs a wake-up call or one of the partners feels the other needs to be made aware of an imbalance. While retaliation ranges from the heartbreaking to the humorous, it is inevitably fascinating. Innumerable made-for-television movies have lovingly devoted themselves to the topic, but I've found few to equal the real-life scenes directed by those who have been burnt in a relationship.

It's Curtains for You...

One of my favorite revenge stories involves a thirty-five-year-old woman, living in suburban London, who was horrified to discover that her husband of fourteen years had been having a long-term affair with a woman they both knew well. The wife had suspected that he'd been unfaithful, although she could never prove anything, and had decided to try to work even harder at keeping their marriage together. When he accused her of not looking as young as she might, she signed up for aerobics. When he accused her of not being suitably domestic (she was a graphic artist), she signed up for cooking and sewing classes. Apparently the moment when she decided that enough was enough was when she discovered that the other woman she was trying to win him back from was one of her close friends.

"That's when it became war," as my correspondent, a friend of hers, wrote. "She had lived with the idea of her *husband's* betrayal, but that her good *friend* betrayed her was truly a blow."

Their divorce took a long time to arrange because the settlement matters were difficult. The husband fought long and hard for the right to keep the house and finally won that right in court—despite the fact that the wife had always paid half the mortgage. "He should have known that she wouldn't just leave quietly," my friend explained. "Those of us who knew her knew that she'd get her own back."

She did pack up and get ready to leave without much of a fuss. She didn't spray-paint the walls with red graffiti and she didn't set fire to the kitchen. But she did leave a little piece of her anger behind.

Before leaving for good, the now ex-wife decided to make use of those sewing skills she'd worked so diligently to acquire. She sewed miniature shrimp into every hem of every curtain in the house, and left. In this manner she found a way to leave the new couple with a reminder of their fishy and deceptive ways.

Before long, old friends were telling her that her ex-husband and his new wife no longer entertained at home because they had discovered that there were problems with the house. This came as a surprise, of course, because the man had lived there for many years without anything being amiss. The couple had extensive—and expensive—work done to remove the pervasive and unpleasant odor, but nothing seemed to work. Windows were left open day and night. Finally they had no choice but to move.

The ex-wife was delighted for now she could walk around the village without having to worry about bumping into reminders of her past life. As satisfying as it was for her to find out that her ex-husband was moving away, it was even more satisfying to hear that they took most of the furnishings with them to their new home—including all the curtains.

Just Get Over It?

There are a number of ways of looking at this woman's actions. She could be seen as merely spiteful, a petty thief of someone else's happiness. After all, what good did her shellfish game accomplish? Shouldn't she have simply gone her own way without looking back? Isn't the best way to get over the pain of a relationship to "let it all go," as we're inevitably counseled by those unaffected by the breakup?

Yes and no. Getting over a miserable time of life—especially one involving a sexually intimate relationship—is difficult to do without going through a stage of wanting to take revenge on the lover who's gone. Similarly, when a man anonymously mails nude photographs of his ex-wife to her new boyfriend, he desires to humiliate her to the extent that he feels she has humiliated him by leaving or by fooling around behind his back.

Mary from Maine was hurt and angry that her boyfriend was not willing to introduce her to his mother, who was coming from out of town to visit, despite the fact that Mary and this man had been together in a steady relationship for nearly a year.

"I'd always wanted to get to know her because they were fairly close for a mother and son, but when he said wimpishly, 'I don't think this is the right time for you to meet her,' I was stunned. He wouldn't consider it. So the next day I ordered the largest bouquet of pompons I could find and had them delivered to his house, when I knew they would just be sitting down to dinner. The day after she left, I stopped by. He lived in a rather sparse apartment, all clean lines and simple shapes. And as soon as I walked in I saw this mass of color. On his dining room table, in a vase that was obviously too small, were these flowers. He hadn't even cut the mums off to the right size, so they were sort of hanging all out of this vase, looking like monsters out of a bad dream. And I said to him, 'Well, how did it go?' He said, 'Those flowers. All they did was stare at us the whole night. All she did was ask about who sent them, and all we did was talk about you. It would have been easier if you'd just been here.' Which is, of course, what I'd wanted him to say all along."

Imagining His Response

Spending the night with a married man who brought her back to his apartment only to rip the straps off her dress in his eagerness to make love to her, Gloria Wandrous steals his wife's expensive mink coat and wears it over her underwear as she returns downtown. Gloria, protagonist of John O'Hara's *Butterfield 8*, had awakened alone in this man's apartment and was overcome by a sense of despair. The only thing that made her feel better was the idea of stealing the coat and imagining how the husband would explain the loss to his wife when she returned from out of town. "The despair was going away. Now that she knew what the bad thing was that she was going to do, she faced it and felt all right about it. She could hardly wait to do it." It is not financial gain that prompts Gloria's actions—it is the fierce desire to get even with the man who unceremoniously seduced and abandoned her. Left with a dress and her sense of self in tatters, Gloria sees no reason for him not to be inconvenienced.

Of course, there are tragic revenge stories about acts of desperation and despair that irrevocably damage the lives of even the most innocent bystanders. Perhaps getting even with an ex-lover is the most problematic of all the revenge fantasies because revenge traffics in the same materials as the first stages of love: passion, focused attention, and aroused imaginations. As D. H. Lawrence, author of *Lady Chatterley's Lover*, wrote: "The lust of hate is the inordinate desire to consume and unspeakably possess the soul of the hated one, just as the lust of love is the desire to possess or be possessed by the beloved, utterly. But in either case the result is the dissolution of both souls, each losing itself in transgressing its own bounds." The opposite of revenge can be said to be not forgiveness but indifference—which is also the opposite of love.

Selective Editing

"I felt like a fairy-tale character in a state of suspended animation who suddenly realizes that the clocks in the kingdom are working again," Allison, a fact-checker for a national magazine, announced. "My boyfriend from college and I had discussed marriage from our second date onward, and even though we weren't officially engaged, I still took it as a given that we were in an exclusive relationship. He stayed on at the university for a graduate degree in creative writing when I came here to New York to work, but as far as I knew, everything was going fine. I spent tons of money on phone calls and would shop for the perfect cute cards to send him. I even baked him his favorite cookies and Express Mailed them to him weekly.

"Then I get a letter which tells me that for the last three months he's been seeing this woman in his class on a regular basis, and that he felt he should write and tell me how deeply he felt for her. It was a really painful letter for me, not only because he made me realize that I'd been a sucker for three months but because he went into detail about why he was making the right decision in choosing *her*—how wonderful she was, how she eschewed (his word) all commercialism and would tease him about the cards I sent, saying how adolescent our relationship was. He told me he had come to agree with her. The letter was incredibly smug and self-indulgent even as he was trying to make himself sound hip and adult.

"He ended it by telling me that I must find a new life for myself, that I must broaden my circle of acquaintances (since many of our old college friends were more his buddies than mine, he said), and how I shouldn't weep too long after reading what he called 'this missive of misery.'

"I read it over *too* many times, and even though it's been a couple of years now, I hate to admit that I still remember his words by heart. It was a miserable experience."

Allison, who had been fairly subdued as she told her story, suddenly brightened. "But I decided that I was going to take his good advice and not weep. Instead I made photocopies of his letter and sent the pages around to my pals in the office, friends at home, and our old friends from college, asking them to comment on its style and critique the prose generally. Most of them were wonderfully scathing, calling his writing 'turgid' and 'sentimental.' I sent him copies of their responses. I knew that the most important thing to him was his overinflated sense of himself as a great writer and that these letters would land a punch. He thought I would be ashamed to admit to people that we'd broken up. Instead I celebrated it, and invited the people who knew us to join in the celebration. I have never regretted convening that impromptu editorial group, because I no longer felt like a sacrificial victim in someone else's script." Allison's story is an interesting one for several reasons, not the least of which is its emphasis on her need to renew her own sense of worth by making his pompous, hurtful letter available to a bevy of critics.

Allison got to add her own finishing touches to the story, and not remain alone with an inappropriate sense of rejection. She focused on what would make her feel better—and, significantly, make her feel the support and loyalty of her friends—and she did not allow an undue amount of time to pass before acting. She dealt a swift blow to her desire to withdraw from everybody and, by doing so, she ensured that the process of grieving over this loss would not be something she would have to endure alone. Achieving closure in these cases is paramount. The drive toward both symmetry and closure are at the heart of most revenge tales. There is, after all, a love of precision that informs the need for revenge.

Allison could well have patterned herself after a long line of accomplished women, living at various times, who managed to break the stranglehold of socially enforced feminine passivity long enough to make themselves heard when the occasion demanded it. Her story reminds me of one about the early twentieth-century writer and actress Ilka Chase. Chase had been married to Louis Calhern, who divorced her in order to marry Julia Hoyt. Sorting through her possessions shortly after the unhappy episode she found some visiting cards she had had printed for herself with the name Mrs. Louis Calhern. Generously, and bearing in mind her own experience, she sent them on to the new Mrs. Louis Calhern with a short note: "Dear Julia, I hope these reach you in time." Only an intimate would be able to strike so precisely into the heart of her direct rival's vulnerability.

Help Yourself

In an astute parody of the usual self-help books, *How to Avoid Love and Marriage*, Dan Greenburg and Suzanne O'Malley counsel couples on how to get even with their mates no matter what the situation. They propose that one of the most effective ways of punishing your mate is to make yourself sick. "Only serious diseases are effective punishments. To imply that your mate has given you a headache or dandruff or stomach gas is small potatoes. To make your punishment effective, go for the biggies. . . .

If you succeed in contracting one of these, you will probably be letting yourself in for a great deal of pain and, ultimately, death. But just think of what revenge it will be on your mate!'' In their factitious suggestion, they touch on a method of revenge that has a long history in the annals of relationship lore.

"Well, if I cannot keep Heathcliff for my friend—if Edgar will be mean and jealous, I'll try to break their hearts by breaking my own," declares Cathy in Emily Brontë's *Wuthering Heights* when her husband's jealousy of her first love threatens to ruin Cathy's life. "That will be a prompt way of finishing all, when I am pushed to extremity!" Cathy is wise enough to realize that making herself ill is "a deed to be reserved for a forlorn hope," but one she nevertheless embraces fully when her husband, Edgar, refuses to relent and allow Heathcliff into their lives. Cathy in effect starves herself to death, dying in childbirth, in order to punish the two men she loves. The irony is that they both passionately love her in return, and neither wishes for her to die. Cathy's rage can only be directed against her own body since she does not have access to other, gentlemanly forms of aggression such as a duel at dawn or a knife across the throat at dusk. Like the anorexic who refuses to eat in order to punish her mother for being overpossessive or the patient who refuses to get well in order to punish the doctor for not taking an illness seriously, the lover who destroys the self tragically relies on the power of her ability to remove herself from rescue.

Cathy's husband, Edgar, mourns her death and gives her a Christian burial, but Heathcliff vows revenge on Cathy even upon her death. "With frightful vehemence, stamping his foot, and groaning in a sudden paroxysm of ungovernable passion [Heathcliff cries] 'Why, she's a liar

to the end! Where is she? Not there—not in heaven—not perished—where? Oh! you said you cared nothing for my sufferings! And I pray one prayer—I repeat it till my tongue stiffens—Catherine Earnshaw, may you not rest, as long as I am living! You said I killed you—haunt me then! The murdered do haunt their murderers. I believe—I know that ghosts have wandered on earth. Be with me always—take any form—drive me mad! Only do not leave me in this abyss, where I cannot find you!' "
Women have cried over this scene in the book for nearly a hundred and fifty years—and have cried over the movie, miniseries, and even cartoon versions, for slightly less time.

Wuthering Heights has long been regarded as the paradigm for the gothic novel, but it is also a classic tale of self-destruction as sexual revenge. There ought to have been a way for Cathy and Heathcliff to have loved without this loss; there should have been a way for Cathy to get even with Heathcliff and Edgar that did not involve the destruction of her body. In all revenge tales, but especially those concerning sexual revenge, one is struck by the fact that *ought* to have been ways to avoid pain, to offer compassion, to reach understanding—but when these things do not come to pass, the desire for revenge rushes in to fill the void.

Bang, Bang, I Love You

That we want to settle scores with those we love most dearly is paradoxical, even if it is familiar. I remember watching a Western as a child that ended with a shoot-out between the female town marshal and her boyfriend, the town horse thief. Having killed off most of the town's inhabitants inadvertently during a number of gun battles, they hid behind trees and shot at each other while declaring the veracity and scope of their true love. I was maybe six years old, and more than glad to suspend my disbelief (if I could clap until Tinkerbell revived in *Peter Pan*, I could believe anything), but I remember that I had trouble making sense of this movie. I knew that my parents fought constantly and still seemed to love each other, but this shooting it out while saying "I love you" worried me. It still does.

The most dangerous forms of revenge are those that involve the need to punish while still depending on the need to be loved. To get back at someone you once loved makes the same sort of sense that getting back at a boss you once respected might have—you were hurt, it's over, you want closure. But to torture someone you still love, all the while saying "Please love me back," is troubling because there is no possible positive ending to this sort of repetitive pattern. If you keep returning to the need to get even, then a problem exists that cannot be solved by one quick and clever retributive measure.

But there can be a lighter side as well, one that involves getting even as a way of getting over it. It uses revenge to achieve closure, to bring down the curtain on a final act of a play best forgotten.

Being able to achieve a sense of release from the old relationship is what the best kind of revenge accomplishes in such situations. This can be done without the breaking of crockery or the smashing of car windows, but it is rarely done without someone getting bothered. "There's nothing either good or bad, but thinking makes it so," declared Shakespeare's Hamlet, and quite a number of revenge stories concern actions that, out of context, do not appear destructive in and of themselves.

Doing Unto Others What You Feel Has Been Done Unto You

When Freddy took Genny's dog to the vet to be neutered, he might well have been doing her a favor. Taking her dog to be neutered was, however, an act of revenge. Genny's schedule was certainly a busy one, and she had often chided Freddy in the past for neglecting to initiate household tasks. When Freddy found out that Genny had initiated a few out-of-household tasks herself with a handsome new neighbor, he decided to make up for his neglect.

Genny had paid an enormous sum of money for the pooch's pedigree, with an eye toward breeding the dog as soon as he matured. What Freddy had done to the dog was what he felt Genny had done to him by sleeping with their neighbor. Perhaps without even making it a conscious choice, Freddy got back at Genny by acting out his revenge in a way that infuriated her but harmed no one directly. Thousands of animals are neutered daily and there is nothing in the procedure itself that is inherently mean or nasty. What made Freddy's gesture one of revenge was his intention, not the action itself.

The road to hell in tales of sexual revenge is rarely paved with anything except the very worst of intentions. Pushed to the breaking point by disappointment in love, a person who is otherwise gentle and considerate could find himself or herself thinking cold, dark thoughts. Or warm dark thoughts—especially when it comes to playing with fire.

Too Hot to Handle

Fire figures largely in tales of sexual revenge, perhaps in part because of the ways in which we have always talked of "burning with love" or of being "consumed by passion." From classic songs such as Peggy Lee's sultry "Fire" or even Elvis's "Hunk of Burning Love," to Mary Chapin Carpenter's "Walking Through Fire" or Bob Seger's "The Fire Down Below," fire is the element connected to eroticism, energy—and going up in smoke. Fire, like passion, consumes that which it embraces. No wonder it is at the hot core of any number of revenge fantasies.

It seems that women, in particular, see fire as a friendly element, one that can get even for you. It is enjoyed by any number of disgruntled women and made popular by ex-wives and lovers. As far back as Charlotte Brontë's nineteenth-century novel *Jane Eyre,* readers have been introduced to the wife as fire-wielding avenging angel. Brontë first gave us abused wife Bertha Rochester, and a hundred years later Jean Rhys took up her story and wrote *The Wide Sargasso Sea*, which would be made into a popular independent film in 1992. Part of Bertha's appeal as a revenger is derived from the level of intolerable behavior to which she has been subjected. Regarded as merely a madwoman in the attic by her husband, Rochester, Bertha is locked away and treated like an animal.

Animals have no access to fire; human beings do. Bertha's humanity is ironically underscored by her last desperate, mad act of revenge—Bertha burns down her husband's house, as she had once witnessed her own home burn as a child. Her ultimate consummation by fire seems to indicate an outward movement of the anger and rage she has internalized for so long; it is as if, confronting her own power, she is consumed by it. The fire is only its most outward and obvious manifestation. She dies in flames set by her own hand; Rochester, however, lives. Crippled and partially blinded, he nevertheless goes on to marry Jane Eyre and to father a son. Bertha's revenge is finally incomplete and ineffective, tragic only insofar as it affected the woman herself.

Later versions of Bertha, however, were permitted by their authors to be more successful. In Fay Weldon's *The Life and Loves of a She-Devil*, Ruth also sets fire to the marital home after her husband leaves her for another woman. But, unlike Bertha, Ruth knows that it is not the loss of the symbol of their lives together that will get to her husband—it is the loss of property and money. Ruth sends her kids to McDonald's, gets the dog and cat out of the house, and, after lining up the beanbag chairs full of polystyrene foam and turning old electrical appliances on "high," throws a lit cigarette into a wastepaper basket full of bills underneath a long set of curtains. The kitchen explodes, and the rest of the house is burned to the ground.

But this is not sufficient for Ruth's purposes of revenge. Her most deft blow is dealt when the insurance man comes to call. He offers Ruth a cigarette, which she accepts with alacrity. "Thank you, I've smoked a lot since my husband left. You know how it is. Nerves," she explains, with full knowledge of the effect of her words. "Perhaps that's how it started? A cigarette in a wastepaper basket?" offers the insurance adjuster, disingenuously. "It might have been. Now I come to think of it," Ruth tells him in response to his questions about how the fire originated, "I was sorting papers in Bobbo's room, and started crying—oh!'' She clapped her hand over her mouth. ''What have I said?'' Knowing full well that by admitting guilt in starting the fire, albeit by accident, Bobbo will not be able to collect the insurance money. Ruth gets her revenge.

In Terry McMillan's 1992 novel, *Waiting to Exhale*, we find Ruth's American counterpart committing almost precisely the same act when put in the same position by her philandering husband, who leaves her for a younger woman. Bernadine, another wife relegated to the margins by a husband setting out on a new life of his own, is at home alone taking Xanax and getting depressed until an idea takes hold of her. ''There was too much order in this damn house,'' Bernie decides, and begins the process of creating chaos. She gets into her husband's ridiculously neat closet—the suits are in alphabetical order by designer, starting with Adolfo—and begins throwing his expensive tailored garments over her arms and taking them down to his BMW, now parked at the end of the driveway. She makes repeated trips to collect his fancy shoes, colognes, ties, boxer shorts (kept neatly separated from his jockey shorts)—and a can of lighter fluid.

''She struck the match, tossed it inside the front window, and stepped away from the car. . . .'' When one of the firemen informs her that the insurance money won't cover this, she replies, ''I'm aware of that.'' When he asks her to burn something smaller and less expensive next time, she assures him, ''It won't happen again.'' After an act of premeditated chaos and destruction, Bernie is beginning to gain a sense of perspective. Her next act of revenge is to have a garage sale where every expensive ''toy'' owned by her husband—from his skis and golf clubs to his antique car, vintage wine, and gold jewelry—is sold for exactly one dollar. She lets her kids keep the money. After all, as Bernie tells her absent husband, "Since you want to start a new life, motherfucker, see what starting from scratch feels like."

And fire doesn't have to be all-consuming to be a form of getting even. In Marge Piercy's poem "What's That Smell in the Kitchen?" we hear the wife's true, if unconscious, motives for her "mistake" in burning dinner: "If she wants to serve him anything it's a dead rat with a bomb in its belly ticking like the heart of an insomniac. . . . Burning dinner is not incompetence but war."

There are myriad other revenge stories involving what goes on behind closed doors—when the closed doors in question lead to the kitchen, that is.

Cooking Up a Surprise

Helen, a hairdresser, still smiles when she remembers the time she took revenge against her philandering ex-husband. "I met him when I was sixteen, married him at seventeen, and had our first child at eighteen. He was in the service, and I understood that we would be separated, but I absolutely believed that he would honor our marriage vows because I knew—or thought I knew—how deeply committed he was to our family and to traditional beliefs. One weekend he brought the wife of one of his buddies to dinner because their marriage was in trouble and she needed company. I tried to do my best to make a nice meal, and I even put the kids to bed early, before dinner, so we could all sit down and have a good heart-to-heart talk and talk about grown-up things. I was making an effort to be welcoming to this woman because I felt terribly sorry for all her troubles.

"When I came in after checking on the babies in the

nursery, I heard them laugh together as they'd been laughing together all evening—she was very happy for somebody who was supposedly having a bad time in her marriage—and I realized that they were having an affair. They broke apart a little too quickly when I entered the room; they were looking at each other a little too much and holding each other's eyes a little too long. I just knew. Everything was set to go for dinner except the rice, and I went into the kitchen. I banged pots and pans around but I was listening. I heard the whispers: 'Do you think she knows' and 'We have to be more careful.' My mind went blank. I just stood there over the sink, looking out into the ugly little yard, thinking about what a fool they were making of me.

"Then I took my underpants off and strained their rice through them. I went into the dining room carrying this nice shrimp dinner and I was much better company because I was pleased with myself. What was so humiliating about realizing they were having a relationship was that they shared this big secret and left me out of it. So I turned the tables—or at least the plates on the tables—on them. I was the one who now had a secret, if you want to think of it that way. And I knew everything they thought I didn't know. I got through the evening without making a scene. I'm horrified when I look back on what I did, but I don't actually regret it. The next day I called our chaplain for counseling, a moving company for practical matters, and a lawyer to handle the rest."

The Quest for Quid Pro Quo

Wanting the ex-lover to feel what one has felt—alone, hurt, unworthy—is a typical part of the bad—or post—

relationship blues. It is a stage to be accepted and dealt with, and it can offer its own insights and possibilities for healing the wounds.

That might sound contradictory, since thinking about revenge is usually considered a blockade to emotional progress. After all, in his classic essay on revenge, Sir Francis Bacon declared in no uncertain terms that "a man that studieth revenge keeps his own wounds green," and few have disputed his claim. Yet I would argue that the inevitability of feeling as if you have earned the right to settle a score after your lover leaves should help defuse rather than aggravate the emotions; saints as well as sinners have considered revenge when feeling abandoned. It is important, once again, to stress the fact that you need not act out these impulses for them to be cathartic.

Nice Guys Also Get Even

Women are not the only ones who are capable of the kind of crafty revenge associated with post-relationship trauma. Several men I interviewed had stories of their own about revenge no-less-carefully plotted than their female counterparts had.

"When my girlfriend decided that her ex-husband was much better for her than me, I thought I could just go on with my life," said a forty-one-year-old high-school teacher. "I was upset, of course. I'd spent years trying to help her get her life back together after her divorce from this man whom she described as cold and ungiving, and there she was running back to him. But I figured that, hey, I'm a nice guy. What can I do? But after a week or so I found myself feeling more and more like a chump. I fantasized about ways to make her feel rotten, but I didn't

want to make her feel guilty about the breakup or anything. After all, I agreed that we should still be friends,
something I suspect she wanted in order to have somebody to come running back to if her new old relationship
didn't work. I didn't want to hurt her, but I wanted her
to feel as bad as I did for a while.

"Knowing that she found cute, folksy decorations to
be definitely annoying, I figured out a way to get at her
with kindness. She had a new secretary, and I called to
say that, as an old friend, I believed that what she would
love more than anything else would be for everyone in
the office to send her a cute, sweet, arts-and-crafts item
on her birthday next week. I knew she'd love to decorate
her office with them. Maybe, I suggested, this secretary
could pass the word around?

"I also knew that my girlfriend had a tough time keeping staff and that she couldn't afford to alienate anybody—I figured I wasn't putting the secretary in any
jeopardy. And sure enough, when her birthday came and
I went to her office with a box of chocolates, the place
looked like a toy shop. There were all the things she hated
absolutely everywhere. Handmade gingham bunnies. Pot-
tery planters with pictures of ducks painted in pastel colors. Indian corn. Music boxes in the shape of kittens.
Somebody even brought her a little copper pan to put on
the wall saying that it was great to work for a woman
who liked to make her office feel like home. They gave
these gifts to her at a luncheon party, so she had to open
them one by one, as everybody oohed and aahed, and she
had no choice but to put at least some of them up.

"Telling everybody to take their damn trinkets and put
them where the sun doesn't shine is clearly what she
wanted to do, but she couldn't without seeming mean-
spirited. And she couldn't afford to seem mean-spirited to

this office full of sweet people who looked long and hard to find just the right hand-stenciled computer cover. So she sat there miserable in her Armani suit with a miniature butter-churn-pencil-holder at her elbow. She suspected I had a hand in the arrangement, but neither of us said anything. It was the last time I saw her, and I've not had any revenge fantasies since.''

"Sometimes emotional pain is simply too much to bear alone. You need to cause somebody else emotional pain if only to know that you're not the only one feeling it," explained one recently divorced woman of twenty-three. "If I called my ex-husband in the middle of the night, even if I only let the phone ring twice, at least I knew I wasn't the only one pissed off and awake at three A.M. I'd think to myself, Good. Now he'll look like hell at work tomorrow morning, too.''

Common to everyone's experience at one point or another is the wish to make your former lover as unhappy when the relationship is over as you once wanted to make him happy when the relationship was beginning. Perhaps, as one friend of mine believes, this desire to wound the one who wounded you lessens with age, diminishes when we fully appreciate that, with so little time in our lives, we can't afford to look back. But for many people, especially after the dismantling of a long-term relationship, the wish for retaliation is well within the bounds of normalcy.

The Blurring of the Boundary Between Love and Hate

Retaliation is, in fact, the sort of revenge we've been reading about since we got our hands on dog-eared paperbacks in high school. Nathaniel Hawthorne's classic novel of illicit love, *The Scarlet Letter,* is built on the theme of revenge. "It is a curious subject of observation and inquiry, whether hatred and love be not the same thing at bottom," wrote Hawthorne. "Each, in its utmost development, supposes a high degree of intimacy and heart-knowledge; each renders one individual dependent for the food of his affections and spiritual life upon another; each leaves the passionate lover, or the no-less-passionate hater, forlorn and desolate by the withdrawal of his object." Revenge and obsession are bedmates, and that is one reason that we so often and immediately associate revenge with personal betrayals of the heart.

It isn't only the dog-eared books from junior year that include revenge as a theme. Heading the school of thought that writing is the best revenge, traditional and popular authors alike target those who have hurt them in an earlier part of their lives. The ex-wife of novelist Jay McInerney of *Bright Lights, Big City* fame wrote a first novel titled, not surprisingly, *Burning Down the House.* When asked why she wrote a story chronicling the marriage and divorce of a Manhattan literati couple, Merry McInerncy replied, "Oh, it was revenge," according to the article "Knifelike Fiction" in *New York Newsday.* Worried that her ex-husband would satirize their marriage in his own new work, she began writing to "drive out the demons." In the process, she discovered the joys of telling her own story.

"I think, at first, it was like purging myself, like a bulemic would," McInerney admitted. "My marriage was pretty much my whole life, and then I lost it pretty suddenly. . . . I resent how he's written fiction about my depression. And I feel he exploited me. . . . I resent that [his new novel] is about out relationship. . . ." In putting her pain on paper, however, she saw her writing become "funnier and funnier, more and more fictional." She was clearly able to transform her desire for revenge into an act that allowed her to go through—and get over—her long-standing resentments.

Another revenge novel, *Torch Song*, is also mentioned in McInerney's article, which quotes author Anne Roiphe as explaining that "revenge is part of every writer's motivation, male or female. . . . I would not feel at all insulted if someone said that *Torch Song* was a novel written out of revenge. . . . There's also anger and an attempt to take back power that has been lost. That all seems perfectly legitimate."

Usually it's the person who's been left who desires vindication, but occasionally even the lover who chose to walk might want to get revenge for perceived injustices earlier in the relationship. If, for example, someone decides to leave what has been an emotionally abusive relationship, it might take several months to achieve a sense of psychological well-being so that this person can allow himself or herself to be angry. For some, it might take even longer to get to a point where he or she can admit to the desire to get back at the person who caused them pain. It is to be hoped, especially in such a scenario, that one can derive some satisfaction and closure from the *wish* itself without having to act on the desire for retribution.

With This Ring

"She had a genius for making me miserable," Lewis, a twenty-six-year-old banker from San Diego, admitted. "She was gorgeous, funny, and rich. There was nothing to stop every man on earth from being attracted to her, and most were. She knew this, and for the three years we lived together she made sure I knew it, too. She made a high art of deflating me, of cutting me down, with one quick, innocent-sounding phrase. I would buy a new sports coat and she would say, 'You shouldn't shop alone.' On our way to a dinner party, she would tell me that I should 'try for once to talk about *something* besides banking and stocks,' so that I felt like a jerk if anybody asked me what I did for a living. She could make me feel so unintelligent that I would be silent all evening. She could flatten me in five seconds.

"I put up with it until I discovered that she was sleeping with a loud-mouthed creep from her office who, I'm sure, told everybody that they were getting it on. I was humiliated, in addition to being shocked and hurt. She moved out but we still saw each other, and I thought it would be okay, but as time passed, I had a delayed reaction. I started therapy and realized how much she was like my mother. I guess every man must say that in therapy, but in this case it was very true. I understood that I'd subjected myself to this sort of abusive affection my whole life, and that I was responsible for it. I also saw that I'd never be able to get over this relationship until we made a clean break.

"I had stored up an incredible amount of resentment, and it came flooding out once I admitted that the relationship had no future. By this time, however, we were back to an exclusive dating situation and I couldn't figure out what to do. I wanted to retaliate not for how she was acting now but for how she betrayed me when we were living together. I bought her a handsome engagement ring. Only this engagement ring was a very realistic cubic zirconia and not a diamond. I spent a thousand dollars on it and, trust me, you couldn't tell the difference unless you had it appraised. I went to her office one morning, got down on my knees in front of the whole place, and asked her to marry me. She accepted. She told everybody.

A week later I broke it off. I cavalierly told her to keep the ring. A few days later she left a furious message on my answering machine screaming at me for giving her a fake diamond. It was interesting that she didn't scream at me for giving her a fake marriage proposal. The whole episode proved to me that I'd made the right choice in getting away from her. I felt that I had vindicated the poor slob, the earlier version of myself, who had once loved this woman blindly.''

Had he followed through and married his girlfriend, he would still have not exceeded the boundaries of revenge. Tales of revenge that include marriage can be found in some of the culture's most popular stories. After a particularly devastating rejection, some people run out and marry the next available and willing soul they encounter. "And if I married him right away, it would show Ashley that I didn't care a rap—that I was only flirting with him" Scarlett says in *Gone With the Wind*. Faced with Ashley's refusal to take her declaration of love seriously, Scarlett vows to revenge herself by marrying one of her many suitors simply out of spite. "Coolness was beginning to come back to her and her mind was collecting itself. A frost lay over all her emotions and she thought that she would never feel anything warmly again. Why not take this pretty, flushed boy? He was as good as anyone and she didn't care. No, she could never care for anything again, not if she lived to be ninety." Luckily for Scarlett (and for Charles Hamilton, the young man in question), he dies in the war, leaving her a pretty widow. Scarlett's ploy is ineffective, as all her machinations will be when applied to Ashley; he appears quite pleased at the announcement of her engagement.

In John Osborne's classic play, *Look Back in Anger*, a confused and depressed young wife explains to her aristocratic father that she realizes her working-class husband only wanted to win her and marry her out of a sense of spite. He wanted to revenge himself on the gentry by stealing away a product of their good breeding. Jimmy marries Allison in order to revenge himself on the world he believes has excluded him, to get back at everything she embodies: money, class, elitism, and self-righteousness. The tragedy, of course, is that Allison is merely a young woman trying to muddle through her own life and not an elected representative of her childhood environment. When she realizes that Jimmy has married her for *what* she is rather than *who* she is, she sees with despair that her marriage was built on hatred rather than love.

An older, Victorian novel, *Great Expectations* by Charles Dickens, also contains the prototype of love-as-an-act-of-revenge. We saw earlier that one of the main characters, Miss Havisham, felt she owed the world nothing. Left standing in her wedding gown at the altar, abandoned by her fiancé, Miss Havisham decides, like Jimmy, that she will be revenged on a whole category of people. Whereas Jimmy wanted to get even with the rich, Miss Havisham wants to get even with men. She adopts poor and beautiful Estella and raises her "to wreak revenge on all the male sex." Estella is brought up to attract men and then to spurn them the way Miss Havisham had once been spurned: "Sending her out to attract and torment and do mischief, Miss Havisham sent her with the malicious assurance that she was beyond the reach of all admirers, and that all who staked upon that cast were secured to lose."

Having no sense that her sacrificial victims—Estella included—are the great losers in her plan, Miss Havisham can only see that she will cause suffering in the hearts of men and have her revenge.

"I adopted her to be loved. I bred her and educated her, to be loved. I developed her into what she is, that she might be loved," hisses Miss Havisham at the young hero who worships Estella. "Love her!" The definition of love is what is at stake here. The narrator tells us that "if the often repeated word had been hate instead of love—despair—revenge—dire death—it could not have sounded from her lips more like a curse."

When you're part of a triangle, no matter what the configuration, you should consider getting out of your own corner. According to one man who told me his story, there is such a thing as a "preemptive strike."

"My revenge?" this man said. "When I had strong suspicions that my partner and my wife were on the verge of starting an affair, I 'innocently' got out photographs taken of her in high school and showed him what she looked like with her old nose. He had been attracted to her because she had such 'natural' beauty." The thirty-six-year-old contractor telling this story believes that his wife and partner have never acted out on their attraction. While he doesn't think his gesture had anything to do with preventing the affair directly, "it did help, because it reminded her of how far we had come together. And it showed him that I meant business about keeping her. It was all unspoken, but it was clear, even though we laughed about it. Maybe it was more preventative than revengeful, but I did it in anger and I was glad that it worked."

Empty Promises, Sweet Talk, and Hand Kissing

The next revenge story, told by an actor in his early thirties who had been unceremoniously dumped by his live-in girlfriend when she met a richer, older man, depends on a similar sense of mischief. Though unable to compete with his rival's financial and social success, he knew that his old girlfriend was still attracted to him. On her wedding day, he dressed in a perfectly tailored—albeit rented—suit and, making his way into the party, kissed her hand in the receiving line. "There she was, hooked for life to this guy old enough to be her father, and there I was, letting my warm lips linger on the back of her hand just the way she always liked. It only took thirty seconds, but it was as effective as the proverbial thirty seconds over Tokyo—it devastated her. I was really glad. Hey, she had devastated me, and unlike her I didn't have a rich spouse to ease the pain."

"Empty promises and sweet talk are the most effective tools of destruction," declared an attractive Philadelphia attorney in her mid-forties. "When my ex-lover decided she wanted to get back together again after she'd left me to 'find herself' for the third time in three years—she usually needed to 'find herself' when some exotic other woman was also trying to locate her—I decided to give her a taste of her own medicine. After she proclaimed her unflagging devotion, et cetera, I agreed without the usual protest. I told her I couldn't live without her. I smiled, I hugged her, and I told her I would call her first thing the next day—that I needed to be by myself for a night to sort through these wonderful feelings and get my act together for her.

"I had no intention of ever speaking to her again, and when she called I let the machine pick up. I told the doorman not to let her into the building. I told friends that it was all over, but I never told her. She was left holding the bag of empty promises instead of me. Maybe she learned something. After the whole thing was played out and she stopped even trying, I felt an enormous and genuine sense of relief. Finally, there was a sense of closure. We were even. I could let it go after that, and remember the good early days without bitterness." The closure this woman achieved is precisely what those who seek revenge wish for: an end to their uneasy emotions. They might not think of this as revenge, but revenge it is.

When an ex-wife appears on a talk show and details in front of millions of Americans the ways in which her adulterous husband carried on his affair with her best friend (or sister or second-cousin or baby-sitter), she is without a doubt getting even with him whether or not she identifies revenge as her motivation. A *Donahue* program a few years back explicitly addressed this issue—the show was titled "First Wives Seek Revenge."

Time Heals All Wounds... But Meanwhile You Can Wound All Heels

It was a man's nightmare: a group of disgruntled women discussing their ex-husbands' failings in front of an audience numbering in the millions—with no attempt to disguise anyone's identity. They didn't tell their stories *of* revenge, they told their stories *as* revenge. "After one year of marriage and while I was pregnant with our first child, he rented the apartment in the basement of our home to his girlfriend. When I complained about the redhead in the sheer nightgown or the very short shorts and halter top who kept having plumbing problems that he had to repair at all hours, he accused me of being paranoid and having a dirty mind,'' one woman explained to the sympathetic laughter of the audience. Another revealed how her ex-husband and his new love got acquainted: ''They met on the job. She was my baby-sitter. Her name is Jackie and she probably fell in love with Bob when we took her to the beach with us to help care for our brood of four. She was around twelve years old, shy and ugly, with a big nose, tiny eyes, and stringy hair. Over the years, she hasn't changed, except that now her list of traits includes a kind of dumb–blonde aura, you know, the kind that reads soup can labels for fun.''

These were not women interested in being fair, but they nevertheless saw themselves as being interested in justice. In such a situation, a woman might think of herself as simply instructing other women; she might think of herself as simply getting some attention. But what she is doing is nevertheless an act of revenge, given that on some level she wishes to inflict emotional pain to the degree that she feels it was inflicted on her.

Clearly, the participants must have edited and revised their stories. They created self-satisfying dramas where they emerged as battle-scarred heroines and their former spouses emerged as the ruthless and heartless enemy. At least the women on this platform were not the lip-quivering, nail-biting emotional wrecks they might have been, or once were. They were given the power to tell their stories, *their* side of the story, and were thus able to put perspective on the pain.

Having proved to themselves that they could get beyond the moment of injury by being able to talk about, even to joke about, what they experienced, they could reclaim themselves and move into the future instead of being stuck in the past. Interestingly, the program turned into an expression of the methods and power of survival instead of an exercise in mean-spiritedness. It may have started as revenge, but it ended as a commemoration of bad feelings put permanently to rest.

chapter four

NINE TO FIVE

Settling Scores in the Workplace

"If I got a fair wage, I'd do a fair day's work. So far I've been in no danger of having to do a fair day's work."
—TWENTY-THREE-YEAR-OLD WAITRESS

"The boss leapfrogged to success, and I have the bad back to prove it."
—LILY TOMLIN, *Nine to Five*

MANY PEOPLE SAY THAT ACTS OF REVENGE OR FANTASIES of revenge allow them to get on with their lives instead of remaining stuck in the moment of the injury. What constitutes a legitimate provocation for revenge? What constitutes an overreaction? Who decides which is which?

Opinion was divided in 1992 when Robin Carson of Conway, Arkansas, decided to become an avenging cook. A cake decorator, Carson was charged with seventeen misdemeanors, one for each of the unsuspecting victims of her recipe for revenge. Apparently an unhappy patron complained about the ice-cream store that Carson's boyfriend managed. The disgruntled customer was offered a cake as a show of good faith, and he accepted. Carson's decorating of the cake, however, added a little more than the usual flowers and sprinkles. According to newspaper and police accounts, Carson was suspected of using laxatives in her concoctions, causing the client and the sixteen coworkers with whom he shared it to become ill.

At the time, this story produced a flurry of discussion. Should Carson actually be arrested for her prank, given that all the eaters were treated and released with no serious side effects? Was she the only one who should bear the punishment, since she acted on behalf of her boyfriend?

A radio talk show in Connecticut featured these questions and others and I remember driving dangerously slowly so that I could pay careful attention to the astonishing array of responses from listeners. "Do you have that girl's number? I want her to do some work for me," said a man who clearly could have built a house with the chip on his shoulder.

"It's terrible that she took her anger out on people she didn't even know," cooed a small-voiced lady, who continued, "Those poor folks at his job thought he was just being nice. How awful." A baritone voice declared, "This is an example of the breakdown of our society. What will happen now? The store will probably be slapped with a lawsuit, have to close down, and put a lot of employees out of work."

"Lighten up," said another caller. "She didn't kill anybody. She just made the guy uncomfortable. If he was a chronic complainer, then he probably deserved it. I deal with a customer like that where I work. He makes my life miserable; we all cringe every time he walks into the restaurant. The kind of guy who has to be paid off just to shut up deserves to have something to really complain about."

The calls went on for nearly an hour, with the host saying very little. He really didn't have to because the passion from the usually complaisant listeners infused the show with surprising energy. The calls seemed evenly divided between those in the audience who applauded what they saw as the humor of the story and those who disapproved of the cause and effect of Carson's actions.

Most of us will probably feel a little of both disapproval and delight. Our nicer selves will, of course, feel a sense of repudiation (perhaps informed by worry—after all, we don't want to have to hire food tasters to sample everything we eat), but we might also harbor a sense of secret approval.

How Sonya Keeps Smiling

Sonya works for a major airline, and she usually loves dealing with the public. She's been doing it for a few years now and is confident about her ability to deal with people in a crisis situation, to remain cheerful, and to please the passenger whenever possible. But when she was still new at the airline, she was working "in the front lines," at the check-in counter.

Sonya recalls one customer who quickly lost the benefit of the doubt: "There was a long line because one of the flights was drastically delayed. Most people were frustrated and anxious, but they dealt with the situation with a few mutters and moans. I knew this one man was going to be trouble when he started yelling from the back of the line, 'What the hell is going on up there? Can't you keep this line moving?' He came to the counter with his two suitcases and banged his fist down. 'Look, you people have already screwed me up. I demand that you change my ticket immediately and get me on another flight.' " Sonya tried to be as understanding and efficient as possible.

"I did what I could, calling other airlines, searching the computer for the next plane out. I thought he'd be happy when I finally got him a commuter flight to his destination. 'For God's sake,' he yelled when I told him. 'What are you, a moron? I wouldn't fly in one of those death traps. You must be out of your mind to pawn that off on me. Why do they let people like you make decisions?' " She calmly asked him if he would prefer to deal with her supervisor, but he said no, he'd "had enough crap."

"After at least another ten minutes of what I knew would be fruitless searching—and now the people behind him were really angry—he agreed to take the commuter plane," Sonya told me. "His last words were 'If everybody working for this organization is as incompetent as you, no wonder your airline loses money.' He then stormed off. I wished him a good flight as if nothing had happened.

"The little old lady behind him in line had heard everything, of course, and she sweetly asked how I managed to stay so polite and cheerful in the face of his abusive behavior. I told her the truth. 'He's going to Kansas City,' I explained, 'and his bags are going to Tokyo.' She laughed and told me that I'd done the right thing."

Why Fantasies of Workplace Revenge Are Like Fantasies of Workplace Affairs

Fantasies of revenge at the office easily equal fantasies about affairs at the office: Neither is a good idea, but they remain difficult to avoid when you're cooped up in close quarters with a wide range of personality types, energy levels, and standards of performance. In a world seasoned by ambition and flavored with complex interpersonal relationships, revenge is a dish difficult to refuse.

While shaking out your umbrella on a miserable Monday morning, have you ever imagined what it would be like to have your overbearing boss working for *you*? Have you ever dreamed of putting superglue in the cavity of his Mont Blanc pen? Have you ever fantasized about what it would be like to threaten to fire *her* if she didn't give you a message on time, or wonder how it would feel to send *him* out for coffee because you don't like the brew he makes with the office machine?

Have you ever wanted to throw out a memo sent to a backbiting, snippy coworker announcing that the time of an important meeting has been changed, forcing her to walk in late? Ever dream of spiking his mocha café au lait with Ex-Lax before he takes a three-hour trip in the limo with the supervisor? If you've ever had fantasies like these, however fleeting, then you've flirted with the idea of enacting your own version of revenge.

Even if you haven't indulged, perhaps you've delighted in the revenge plots of colleagues and peers. When you hear the story about the *Encyclopaedia Britannica* editor, fired abruptly, who rewrote a large number of entries on the computer before he left, substituting the names of his boorish bosses for some of history's worst villains, do you secretly applaud?

When you hear the old union organizer's tale about the company that hired a hundred out-of-town scabs to replace striking factory workers, and paid the scabs' train fares to the site, only to have them all disappear once they arrived (they were themselves union members from this distant town), do you feel like cheering? When you hear about a sexually harassed administrative assistant who somehow managed to broadcast her boss's next attempt at seduction over the speakerphone, playing it to the entire office, do you smile?

All work problems are not generated from corporate offices or by people behind big desks. Occasionally the lessons of the marketplace come at a young age, which is what happened to a former student, Paula, when she was baby-sitting at fifteen. "The family I sat for regularly had three kids between seven and twelve who they couldn't control themselves. They had a mean dog that yapped at my heels, but I wasn't permitted to put it in the basement or lock it up in a room. The entire time I was there it was awful, but the work was steady and close to my house, which was important because I couldn't drive. The mother called at least once every hour and was upset when she got a busy signal, which meant that I couldn't stay on the phone with my friends even after I wrestled the kids into bed and calmed the dog down. They had a lock on their cable channels so I couldn't watch any movies. The kids played tricks on me, like ripping up my homework once, but as far as I could tell, their parents never punished them.

"One evening the parents called to say that they'd be late. I had school the next day but I had no real choice, so I agreed. An hour later they called to say that they'd be even later. I asked very nicely if I could count on some overtime because of the situation. She told me I was ungrateful—that they treated me like one of the family and gave me steady work and how dare I be so demanding. I felt awful. Then I started to think about how reliable and reasonable I'd always been with them. I hadn't complained about the fact that they never gave me a raise in two years of sitting for them, that I always agreed to come on short notice if they needed me right away.

"To get back at them I went through the spice rack,

the pantry, the cabinets, and the refrigerator and unscrewed—almost but not quite to the point of opening—
every jar, bottle, container, and canister I could find. The
next time anybody went to shake the pepper onto their
eggs, the whole top would come off. When they went to
use the ketchup, ditto. I imagined her getting the whole
container of paprika into her stew. I don't think they figured out that I did it because they probably used the stuff
at various times, so it didn't look like a setup. Whatever
they thought, they never asked me anything. The next
time they called, I told them my price had gone up, that
we needed to set their time of return in advance, and that
except for an emergency, that time was not negotiable. I
felt better able to ask them for improved terms after I
'capped off' my evening.''

Have you ever had a boss, coworker, or client who
treated you unfairly? Didn't you wish for justice? Sometimes an act of personal revenge is the only justice in the
workplace. It often seems that justice for one—even
through unofficial avenues—can lead to better working
conditions for all. A desire to get even, to right some
wrong, or to deal with a pattern of injustice or demeaning
treatment can lead to surprising alliances, and, in its most
positive form, to change for the better.

Bad Intentions, Positive Results

Sometimes the desire for personal justice can lead to actual, objective, impersonal justice. A classically elegant
fifty-year-old female vice-president of a Fortune 500
company once told me such a tale in dulcet tones, remaining unapologetic and magnetic throughout the story.

"The best form of revenge is simply to make the truth

known,'' she said. "You can virtually destroy someone by merely relating what he or she has said or done, without changing a word or a gesture." One could hardly disagree.

In her case, she was working with a man who believed that a female employee's accomplishments were worth far less than those of her male peers. Before leaving this man's employment, the woman photocopied private files that showed that virtually all the women in the company were paid twenty to twenty-five thousand dollars less per year than their male counterparts. She mailed this information, anonymously, to every woman in the company, from the receptionist to the vice-president for human services. Armed with this heretofore hidden information, these female employees filed a grievance and won their case, all through this one woman's act of revenge. "I did it for me," she said with a smile, "but I was enormously pleased for them." Happily her own psychological need for retribution combined with an authentic desire for the righting of a long-standing and hidden wrong.

Revenge is most often regarded as an affair of the heart, but the workplace has become a primary site for the need to get even because of the growing emotional investment we have in identifying ourselves by and through our work, even as the economy requires the "downsizing" of many businesses.

Downsizing

"I was downsized recently," reported a forty-three-year-old computer programmer. "The way my company did it made me feel like John Wayne Bobbitt after his wife 'downsized' him." The analogy is one that permeated a number of interviews: Even women felt they had been "castrated," not only by being fired or laid off but by the abrupt, often heartless manner with which the dismissals were performed (with gross insensitivity and without regard for the years of service an employee had provided the firm). "And when you can't strike back, you get even," this wryly intelligent man said, justifying his own sense of outrage at what he saw as a great injustice. He felt no remorse when he deleted all the company's files under his jurisdiction and handed in blank disks on his last day at the office.

Ernest Brod, senior managing director of Kroll Associates, a New York–based corporate investigations and securities firm, wrote a piece titled "In the Layoff Era, the 'Get Even' Ethic," which was printed in the *New York Times* in 1992. " 'Don't get mad, get even' has become a war cry among laid-off employees and those who expect to be. In companies around the country, employees are refusing to go gently into the night." His examples offer an array of familiar strategies for revenge, including the following: "A chemical company's most valuable new formula was offered to a competitor; a multinational company's departed chief financial officer spent months visiting one foreign tax official after another, offering to blow the whistle on alleged tax evasions; a consulting firm's former officer sent bogus letters—on company letterhead—to clients, suppliers, bankers, and competitors that were written to reflect subtle changes in the relationships. By the time the victimized company had figured out what had happened, it was nearly out of business."

Getting even in the workplace is often regarded by outsiders with special glee because the category of "good-guy worker" versus "bad-guy boss" seems indigenous to American culture. There have been dozens of movies on the subject. *Working Girl* pitted good-girl secretary Melanie Griffith against bad-woman boss Sigourney Weaver; *Wall Street* matched bad-guy rich-boss Michael Douglas against erstwhile-ambitious young-guy worker Charlie Sheen; *The Hand That Rocks the Cradle* positioned the evil female avenger against the nice woman who destroyed her incompetent-physican husband's reputation.

One of the key issues in Jonathan Demme's movie *Philadelphia* was the main character's desire for justice in light of his unfair dismissal from his law firm after it became known that he carried the AIDS virus. While his adversaries and former bosses wanted to prove that all the hero wanted was revenge, what the hero actually wanted— and what the jury awarded him—was justice. This is not to say he was not vindicated personally, but the arena of the grievance was the public space of law. The main character wanted to give voice to the outrage he felt at the unfairness, not of his disease, but of the treatment he received by those who wanted to punish him for who he was and blame him for how he lived. His heroicism depended on his refusal to be silent.

"Pink-Collar Ghetto"

Gender is not as important as class or personality in these films, but in real life—and a few good movies—gender is viewed as a factor that is clearly crucial in the revenge plot. Of all the films about revenge in the workplace produced during the last fifteen years, one of the most effective remains *Nine to Five*. This blockbuster movie, in contrast to the others, concerns itself explicitly with how to get even with a boss and a system that works by degrading and misusing the people it employs.

Lily Tomlin is a single mother who has been routinely passed over for promotions despite her astonishing efficiency; Dolly Parton is the private secretary who must routinely fend off her sleazy boss's unwelcome advances; and Jane Fonda is a newly divorced, newly employed, entry-level office worker. *Nine to Five* has as its battle cry the assertion made by Tomlin: "I'm no girl—I'm a woman. I'm not your wife, or mother, or mistress. I expect to be treated with respect and dignity."

Set in the quintessential pink-collar ghetto, the film shows the three women as they set out to get revenge on their "sexist, egotistical, lying, hypocritical bigot" of a boss, who is given to such remarks as "You girls never got the chance to play football or baseball, the best place to learn what teamwork is all about" and "You mean so much more to me than a dumb secretary" and "Spare me the women's lib crap." They fantasize about how they'd like to get even: Tomlin by poisoning him, Parton by "changing [him] from a rooster to a hen in one shot," and Fonda by chasing him with a pistol and capturing him as he cowers in fear in the ladies' room. They all manage to live out these fantasies, in a reduced but still effective way, by the film's finale.

But once they put the boss temporarily out of commission, the most significant moment in the movie occurs when the trio realize that they can make some big changes in company policy. They come to the conclusion that personal revenge must be translated into public justice, righting the wrongs not only in their own lives, but in the lives of other men and women in their situation. They send out a memo in the boss's name instructing the organization about new strategies, including equal salaries for equal jobs, a day-care center on the premises, and the availability of part-time work for those who need it. (It is worth noting that the same demands continue to be made in many workplaces fifteen years after the movie premiered.)

Our heroines begin an alcohol awareness program that rescues and rehabilitates a typist who has been drunk since the first frame; they make the workplace accessible to the disabled. When the boss is finally removed permanently—having been transferred to Brazil to work on the rain-forest clearance project—the three women stand in his office, toasting to the fact that "this is just the beginning." Like its 1993 counterpart, *Thelma & Louise*, *Nine to Five* is about the triumph of those who were written off as incapable of defending themselves. *Nine to Five* makes clear that an inadequate day's pay and unfair working conditions will lead to an unproductive day's work. Driven to subterranean methods of revenge, workers who are disenfranchised will take what they deserve whether or not it comes with a stamp of approval from the head office.

Since the revenge extracted by Tomlin, Parton, and Fonda is comic, we are left with an ending that looks positively toward a newly refurbished future. At the end of a film such as *Nine to Five*, we can applaud without hesitation a group effort to expose an injustice in order to heal psychic, ethical, and financial wounds.

"Are Women Human?"

Mystery writer Dorothy Sayers addressed a group of working women fifty years ago, and the question she posed then still echoes in today's workplace. "I am always entertained—and also irritated—by the newsmongers who inform us, with a bright air of discovery, that they have questioned a number of female workers and have been told by one and all that they are 'sick of the office and would love to get out of it' " wrote Sayers. She went on to ask, "In the name of God, what human being is not, from time to time, heartily sick of the office and would not love to get out of it? The time of female office workers is daily wasted in sympathizing with disgruntled male colleagues who yearn to get out of the office. No human being likes work—not day in and day out. Work is notoriously a curse, and if women liked everlasting work, they would just not be human beings at all. Being human beings, they like work just as much and just as little as anybody else. They dislike perpetual washing and cooking just as much as perpetual typing and standing behind shop counters. Some of them prefer typing to scrubbing—but that does not mean that they are not, as human beings, entitled to damn and blast the typewriter when they feel that way. The number of men who daily damn and blast typewriters is incalculable, but that does not mean that they would be happier doing a little plain sewing. Nor would the women."

The Targets of Workplace Revenge

Workplace revenge has three primary targets: the boss, the coworker, and the customer. The programmer who deleted his files is representative of a worker getting back at the boss, and by proxy, the organization as a whole. His best work is lost along with his job. Revenge against a coworker can take the form of everything from secretly drinking the diet soda she brought in for lunch to tattling to the boss about her poor work habits.

One administrative assistant, a woman who returned to

the workplace after being at home with her children for a number of years, was particularly displeased with what she considered to be the gross inequities in her office. In a story I heard many times over, she was making just over minimum wage to do work that her boss claimed as his own on several occasions—in her case, she would locate and put together data which he then handed into his supervisor, claiming that he'd spent hours finding and sorting the material, which was simply a lie.

"I decided that if I was going to run his little office without getting sufficient pay or acknowledgment," this woman said, "then I would run it into the ground." She had, as is the case with so many returning workers, applied herself to her tasks with enthusiasm, energy, and diligence. "To get back at him for not responding to how hard I worked, I started taking it easy and doing only that which I was getting paid to do, like filing and typing. He was upset that I was no longer pinch-hitting for him, but I explained that if he wanted that kind of work, then I wanted the title change and the increase in pay that went with it. I was sort of glad that he'd made me angry, because if he'd been really nice to me all along, I probably would have been content with his praise. Believe me, cash is better than compliments."

In most cases, office anger simmers at a low boil. But for some workers, their employment identity is their primary identity, and they derive much of their sense of position in the world based on their rank in the organizational team. Since they are not always rewarded for their self-sacrifice, many of these workers will turn to revenge when they are treated poorly.

"At 96, Feuding Matriarch Opens New Business," read a headline in the *Los Angeles Times*. Reporter Larry Green wrote a fascinating story about a ninety-six-year-old grandmother in Omaha whom he described as belonging "alongside giants in the pantheon of entrepreneurial chutzpah." Rose Blumkin got her renewed burst of energy from her desire to open up a furniture store across the street from her family's furniture store. "She's doing it for revenge," argues Green, going on to explain that "Blumkin wants to get even with two of her grandsons, who, she says, forced her out as chairman of the Nebraska Furniture Mart, a $150-million-a-year furniture and carpeting empire she founded a half-century ago. It's a vendetta worthy of 'Dallas' or 'Dynasty.' " Blumkin is quoted as saying, "I wish to live two more years and I'll show them who I am. . . . I gave my life away for my family. I made them millionaires. I was chairman of the board and they took away my rights. They said I shouldn't be allowed to buy anything. No salesman should talk to me. So I got mad and I walked out." She also walked across the street and opened a new business venture to compete with and undercut her fancy grandsons."

Devoted, self-sacrificing employees often find themselves in the same position as self-effacing and devoted spouses—or grandmothers—particularly when the relationship is troubled. If workers come to identify themselves as part of a certain team, then to a great extent the team functions as a central force in their psychological makeup. When the team rejects them, they are devastated because they have lost more than an income: They have lost a very large chunk of their sense of self.

When people are threatened by the loss of their jobs or by a loss of status at work, every other deep insecurity they have gets called into play. The workers who are most desperately in need of being valued are therefore the ones in danger of not receiving this validation because of their inability to achieve a happy distance from their definition of themselves as a worker and their definition of themselves as a complete human being.

Work and Identity

Troubled individuals, who are unstable for other reasons, can be really bad news. Criminologists have called workplace homicides the fastest-growing form of murder in America. More than 10 percent of the seven thousand fatal injuries that occur in the workplace each year are homicides. During the nine-year period from January 1, 1980, through December 31, 1988, a total of 6,956 cases were identified as work-related homicides.

In his 1973 study, *The Anatomy of Human Destructiveness*, psychologist Erich Fromm offered evidence that some of the more extreme personalities who act vengefully in the workplace may well have the sort of personality disorder that leads them to believe that any and all actions are directed toward them. He describes these people as "those who have an anxious, hoarding, or extremely narcissistic character, for whom even a slight damage will arouse an intense craving for revenge.

"This type would be exemplified by a man from whom a thief has stolen a few dollars and who wants him to be severely punished; or a professor who has been slighted by a student and therefore writes a negative report on him when he is asked to recommend the student for a good job; or a customer who has been treated 'wrongly' by a salesman and complains to the management, wanting the man to be fired. In these cases we are dealing with a character in which vengeance is a constantly present trait." There is nothing to stop such a person from wreak-ing havoc in the lives of anyone unlucky enough to come into contact with him, however minor a role they may play on the stage of his generalized anger.

In a 1992 *Wall Street Journal* article concerning violent retribution in the workplace, psychologist Thomas D. Harpley, founder of National Trauma Services of San Diego, wrote, "Oftentimes, their life is their job. When their job is in jeopardy, their life is in jeopardy." Dr. Harpley works with organizations and institutions to defuse potentially violent situations by teaching employers "to be alert to warning signs, such as employees' sudden behavioral changes." These changes might include acting pleasant or pleased as well as suddenly acting depressed or angry.

Fortunately, most revenge in the workplace does not end in violence. But much of it does end in discomfort, usually for the boss, coworker, or belligerent client.

"They took away my job, and while I can understand that it was their right to choose their employees, the way they did it meant that they took away my dignity, too," commented a feisty thirty-six-year-old Texas woman who had once held records for sales in her division. "They made me leave the office within an hour, giving me little time to pack up my office into bags and boxes and to say good-bye or explain anything to my coworkers. I left after a disagreement with my boss, true, but I felt as if I were being exiled instead of just having my employment terminated. They would have shaved my head if they were permitted to by law."

Dignity and Fighting Dirty

A simple sense of dignity and self-esteem are what most workplace revengers are trying to regain. Claudia, a twenty-six-year-old administrative assistant, admitted to herself that she was unhappy after working for the same company for six years. She was passed over for a promotion at a particularly crucial juncture, and this kindled her feelings both of low self-esteem and disillusionment. Claudia believed that she was being punished on some level because of her reluctance to play handmaiden to her boss's whims, but she also felt that her boss had simply not wanted to bother putting through the paperwork. ''She—my boss—used to tell me, 'I'll go out of my way for you only if you'll go out of your way for me.' It sounds okay, right? But where I just wanted a fair raise for a year's good work, she wanted me to pick up her dry cleaning, take her dog to be groomed, and return clothes she had already worn to stores while saying that she had only tried them on at home. Out of my way for her? She would have sent me to the moon if they'd had sale clothes in her size.''

But Claudia felt stripped of her dignity when her boss publicly ridiculed her for not knowing the meaning of a word. ''I was taking the minutes, and she was stressing the word *verisimilitude* when talking about the design aspect of a particular brochure. Well, I'm a devoted reader and I got good grades in school, but I didn't know what the word meant and I spelled it incorrectly in the minutes. I should have checked. I accept responsibility for that mistake. But she came out of her office like a lion out of a cage, calling me a dumb blonde and telling me that it was stupid women like me who kept other women—I guess like her—from moving ahead. She did this right in front of everyone. I was horrified.'' By humiliating Claudia, her boss set herself up as a potential target for humiliation herself; one of the biggest problems with any kind of unethical behavior is that it removes the shield of perceived good intentions that protect most of us from other people's ill wishes.

Honor is a word not often used, but it can be argued that we traffic in "honor" every day of our lives. We present a face and a self to the world and, for the most part, we expect to be accepted and treated as a fully fledged member of that world. But it doesn't always happen. When we're treated with a lack of respect, we tend to become angry and aggressive, especially if we cannot foresee a time when that attitude will change. It's curious that the street slang of the last decade has focused on the dangers of "dissing" or "disrespecting" someone. "He dissed me" has become shorthand for an array of defenses for a wide variety of actions, covering everything from a punch in the nose to a drive-by shooting.

But even those who have not encountered the phrase on an everyday basis understand the emotion evoked by the words. In his provocative essay "Norms of Revenge," philosopher Jon Elster states that "the urge for honor, like the enjoyment of other people's envy, are universal phenomena. They can be controlled but not fully suppressed. They arise in the mind spontaneously but need not have any further effect if we can recognize them and avoid acting on them." Recognizing and avoiding these feelings are difficult, however, because of the very fact that most people deny having them. Claudia thought of herself as a kind and compassionate woman. She never would have cast herself in the role of a revenger, but after her core sense of self was threatened and debased, she found the voice of her anger. She wanted her sense of self back; she believed her boss had stripped her of something important.

In this sort of showdown, dignity or self-esteem is often seen as a sort of emotional version of a controlled substance. Suddenly, it seems as if there's only so much of it to go around. Conversely, what is lost by one is gained by the other. Claudia's boss may have felt embarrassed that *her* office made a mistake, but after all, it was Claudia who would take the fall for the misspelled word, not her. So, to use this issue as a measure of a superior intellect and better breeding is to shift the grounds of the incident far from the real site of her anger.

"I was brought up to be a nice girl," Claudia explained over lunch at a restaurant near the building where she now works. "But I was furious after this happened. I thought about her all the time. It was like being 'in love,' but instead I was 'in hate.' I didn't know what to do. I needed her to give me a good recommendation, and I certainly needed a job, so I couldn't alienate her completely. I decided to use her own tactics against her; she'd made me feel small and stupid, so I wanted her to know how it felt. But I had to protect myself."

Claudia was under the influence of a phenomenon explored by psychologist Karen Horney "The Value of Vindictiveness." In describing patients bent on vindication for their real and imagined troubles, Horney categorized one set of motivations and methods as the desire to humiliate, defining this as the need "to expose to ridicule; to cause feelings of guilt and inferiority; to make a person dependent and subservient; to defeat and to triumph over the defeated offender." In Claudia's case she was responding to her boss's attack, but then the person longing for revenge can always justify the act, if only to himself or herself.

Claudia decided that if the boss was so sure she was just a bimbo, she would start acting like a bimbo—especially when it came to handling her boss's affairs. In this case, the word *affairs* carries more than one meaning:

Claudia's boss was sleeping with one of the supervisors at the company. Without making her instructions explicit, the boss clearly expected Claudia to cover for her and to get her out of some pretty tight spots; this unofficial agenda was something Claudia no longer felt able to carry out.

"I guess I was just too dumb to understand the complexities of a woman of her rank," the twenty-seven-year-old said with a grin. "If one of the other account managers called and asked where she was, I'd say something like 'Oh, she said she would be in New Jersey for the day, but in fact the number where she can be reached has a 203 area code; come to think of it, gee, I'm just not sure whether she's at that meeting—the scheduled plans were definitely not in Connecticut.' I was all wide-eyed and pink-cheeked and fresh from the farm. She thought I was dumb? You should have seen how she looked in a couple of weeks, once I started telling people that I couldn't get them the letter they needed immediately because she had told me to return some shoes to Saks. Naturally, I sweetly asked them not to say anything to her about it for fear that I would get into trouble."

Claudia leaned over as she explained, "She had few allies to begin with—she had fewer by the time word got around about how she really ran her life. I never said anything genuinely indiscreet because I didn't need to. There was no need to deceive. All I did was tell the truth instead of covering up."

Open-Mouth Sabotage

This particular type of revenge has often been referred to as open-mouth sabotage, because it involves the simple process of saying aloud what everyone suspects but no one is willing to disclose publicly. It is often a very gratifying process because it involves at the most a sense of disingenuousness but does not involve any other kind of deception. It's the sort of ploy used by angry siblings when telling on their brothers or sisters: "Mom, if Mary said she was going to the library, why did I see her hanging out with a bunch of boys at the mall?" When Claudia widened her eyes and ratted on her boss, she was using a subtle version of open-mouth sabotage.

Think of any hero in a business movie—or a Tom Clancy or John Grisham best-seller—and you probably have a case of open-mouth revenge. When Jack Ryan, the hero of Clancy's *A Clear and Present Danger,* tells the unctuous President, "I won't do the 'Potomac two-step.' I don't dance"—in other words, he wouldn't lie to cover up the military disaster precipitated by the hidden political machine—the audience applauded. To an extent, Claudia was also turning down the invitation to continue dancing.

Claudia and her boss decided to call a truce. "She and I agreed, without really saying it, that I would leave quietly and quickly if she gave me good references. I got a new job immediately and I've been very happy since." I ask her if she has any regrets, or if she flinches when she thinks about her past action. Spooning some whipped cream off the top of her coffee, she smiles and says, "No."

I ask her if she would do this again in the future if things don't go her way. "Probably not," she says, thoughtfully. "At this point I have a stronger sense of myself and a greater degree of self-confidence. If somebody yelled at me now, I would either smile and leave or suggest that they sit down and get ahold of themselves because their actions are inappropriate. I'm not as afraid as I was in my first job. I'd never let myself feel that low again. No one could have that kind of power over me now.''

The Struggle of Mutual Dependence

Workers often resent the power their bosses wield indiscriminately, and bosses may resent what they see as their workers' excessive demands. Both are locked in a struggle due to their mutual dependence; like a bad marriage, a bad work relationship is both intolerable and difficult to leave.

Consider the following classic revenge joke about a surly New York waiter and his disgruntled boss. The waiter's constant display of arrogance, perpetual whining, and unrelenting complaints seem to have gotten him exactly the response he's been aiming for: The boss decides to give the waiter a big raise in his salary. The waiter, feeling very good about himself, brags to the rest of the staff that he finally wore the old man down, and won himself a rightful place above the rest of the herd. A week later, the boss asks the waiter to come into his office. ''You're fired!'' the boss shouts, slamming his fist down on the table with a grin. ''Fired?'' cries the waiter, astonished. ''How can you fire me after you just increased my wages? This is crazy. Why would you fire somebody after giving him such a big raise?'' The boss, opening the door to show him out, says simply, ''I wanted you to lose a better job.''

Freed From Good Behavior

So rather than leave, workers may find ways to ''get even'' and stay even. George Orwell's 1933 classic about the perils, joys, and tragedies of both employment and unemployment, *Down and Out in Paris and London*, describes a world of dispossessed workers who have "given up trying to behave normal or decent. Poverty frees them from ordinary standards of behavior, just as money frees people from work." Freed from the usual constraints—and with nothing to lose—the men and women described by Orwell "discover the great redeeming feature of poverty: the fact that it annihilates the future. Within certain limits, it is actually true that the less money you have, the less you have to worry." Like poverty, revenge also annihilates the possibility of getting on with life because it, too, feeds off the idea that there is no longer any pretense of trying to behave generously.

Revenge seeps into every aspect of life in Orwell's world. Offered a position at a Paris restaurant, Orwell is told he is being hired because he is English: " 'We will give you a permanent job if you like,' " explains the employer. " 'The headwaiter says he would enjoy calling an Englishman names. Will you sign on for a month?' " The headwaiter's prejudice will make Orwell a convenient locus for his attacks.

Once he began working in Parisian hotels and restaurants, usually on a day-to-day basis, Orwell heard endless stories about how his fellow workers extracted their revenge. The story related next is one of many he heard.

"Once I was in a restaurant where the patron thought he could treat me like a dog. Well, in revenge I found out a way to steal milk from the milkcans and seal them up again so that no one would know. I tell you I just swilled that milk down night and morning. Every day I drank four litres of milk, besides half a litre of cream. The patron was at his wits' end to know where the milk was going. It wasn't that I wanted milk, you understand, because I hate the stuff; it was principle, just principle." Even in his desperate straits, this man is determined to secure justice. He raises his vengeance from the personal to the political.

As is the case with so many who take revenge, though, he must pay for his actions. "Well, after three days I began to get dreadful pains in my belly, and I went to the doctor. 'What have you been eating?' he said. I said: 'I drink four litres of milk a day, and a half litre of cream.' 'Four litres!' he said. 'Then stop it at once. You'll burst if you go on.' 'What do I care?' I said. 'With me principle is everything. I shall go on drinking that milk, even if I do burst.' "

In another incident, Orwell relates the tale of a waiter who "told me, as a matter of pride, that he sometimes wrung a dirty dishcloth into a customer's soup before taking it in, just to be revenged upon a member of the bourgeoisie."

The idea of sabotaging the business community blossomed in the 1920s and 1930s when Orwell was writing, but its seeds had been planted even earlier. In a book from the beginning of the century, *Sabotage: History, Philosophy, and Function,* Walter Minn advocates the overthrow of capitalism through the organized use of sabotage, setting up a dynamic in which "the mass of workers are already propertyless. No tie binds them to our so-called civilization. Sabotage, for protection as well as for revenge, appeals to them. They have nothing to lose and much to gain by its use."

As if he were prefacing Orwell's stories about kitchen work (or preparing us to read Upton Sinclair's classic novel *The Jungle,* about the unregulated food industry in the early twentieth century), Minn throws down the gauntlet to those who work preparing food in poisonous envi-

ronments so that a few can profit: "Let the cooks tell how
food is prepared for the table: how foul meats are treated
with chemicals. . . . Let the dishwashers, waiters, and
other hotel and restaurant workers tell of conditions under
which dishes are 'washed' and the orders 'prepared.' "
Clearly, this is yet another call for open-mouth revenge
against an unfair or unethical situation.

The problem appears to be growing in contemporary
business settings, according to several studies published
in international journals devoted to business. "Sabotage
as a labor relations reality is becoming increasingly evident in many industrialized countries. When labor-
management relations deteriorated at a French mineral
water bottler, the workers added soap to the water storage
tanks," write Robert Giacalone and Stephen Knouse in
Excuses: Masquerades in Search of Grace. It is not surprising that a number of books designed for the business
community have been written on this topic. Revenge in
the workplace is not inevitable nor is it always a negative
factor. Several studies have shown that small acts of revenge can actually make the office more palatable to disgruntled employees.

Stealing Post-It Notes

Small acts of deceit and wickedness are so familiar that
they hardly look like either to the naked eye. By stealing
pens or Post-it notes, by making long-distance calls from
the office phone, by taking long lunches or leaving early,
mildly frustrated workers find ways of revenging themselves on a company by providing themselves with perks
that the job doesn't officially offer. This behavior may not

even be conscious, but instead a sort of internalized self-regulating response.

A study published in the *Wall Street Journal* indicated that workers who took it upon themselves to get even with their employers in small ways were, in fact, relatively happy and efficient compared to their more honest co-workers. More extreme and damaging versions of getting even with the company range from destroying or falsifying records, creating computer viruses, and sleeping with the boss's spouse or child. These incidents, when they do occur, are quite dramatic, but they are, in fact, rare.

Occasionally the punishments inflicted by revengers are filled with imagination. In such cases, when we laugh or gasp in disbelief at someone else's anger and misfortune, we're showing our true colors, choosing up which team we're on. Rarely are any observers neutral.

"It's Not Enough to Win; Your Enemies Must Fail"

Illustrating the inventiveness of someone who has an enemy, and illustrating the maxim that "It is not enough to win; your enemies must fail" is a classic revenge joke concerning a grateful genie recently sprung from years of captivity inside the bottle. Eager to be of service to her new master, the genie offers him three wishes. "This sounds too good to be true!" cries the happy recipient. "Well, there's a catch," explains the genie. "You'll get your three wishes, but your worst enemy will get twice what you get." Disappointed at first, the new master suddenly smiles when he thinks of a way around the situation. "I'd like to be a millionaire," he declares, and is immediately surrounded by gold, jewels, and fancy cars. "But you must realize that now your enemy has twice this wealth," says the genie ruefully. The man just smiles. "That's okay. Now for my second wish, I'd like to have a harem of insatiable and gorgeous women who adore and desire me." "Whatever you say," shrugs the genie, and suddenly there are dozens of beautiful women who can't keep their hands off their new lover. "But remember," warns the genie, "your worst enemy has twice as many women who are twice as alluring." "That's okay," grins the man. "And what is your third and final wish?" asks the genie, deeply puzzled. "For my third wish," replies the man, with a satisfied smile, "I'd like *one* of my testicles to disappear."

One Mad Mouseketeer

A 1990 *Wall Street Journal* article titled "Sweet Revenge Is Souring the Office" cites a seasoned Disney employee who felt a need to get even after she was passed over for a promotion she felt she deserved. Using tactics familiar to anyone who has worked in an unpleasant situation, the woman began taking much longer to complete her projects. When her employer, who was under great pressure to improve the efficiency of his office, wrote a negative job evaluation, "without even talking to her, and placed it in her employment file, she responded with a lengthy memo and sent copies to the division's top brass. She also made nasty comments about his actions behind his back."

The article goes on to quote the woman in question as admitting that her actions were "vengeful," and done on purpose. "But I felt totally justified. I knew it would hurt my boss and destroy his credibility," she asserts. And destroy his credibility it did, according to the *Journal*.

"All hell broke loose," she recounts. Within months her boss was fired—and she got his job.

The same article describes an executive recruiter "who, apparently still angry at his former big bank employer for assigning him to an undesirable location after he turned down a foreign assignment, never loses an opportunity to raid that bank in his headhunting forays." Both of the *Journal* stories showcase the everyday nature of revenge at the office even when it is disguised as something else.

Often the sheer maniacal drive for success can mask a desire for revenge. How many times since childhood have we wanted to succeed, simply to thumb our noses at someone who has bet against us? I heard a story about a major writer who had to be talked out of dedicating his book to a high-school English teacher who had given him a D and written him a poor letter for college. This novelist swore that he would have gone into the shoe business with his father if it hadn't been for the galvanizing force of his anger at that time. Did he therefore thank this English teacher? "I hope he drops dead" was his less than literary reply. Nevertheless, a sense of rejection can spur people on to achievements that an otherwise more complacent life might have denied them. We become inventive when we have our backs to the wall.

Dirty Pool

In another article reported by the *Wall Street Journal* (which admittedly does on occasion read like *The World of Revenge News*), fifty-six-year-old Philip Leslie, co-founder of Leslie's Poolmart Inc., states that his goal is to ruin his ex-partner's firm: "I have vowed to make them go belly up." Building a new pool-supply company, according to the report, "complete with dozens of former Poolmart employees and a business strategy that draws a big bull's-eye over his former firm," Philip Leslie systematically set out to vanquish his former partner once he was ousted from the business.

Indeed, according to this article entitled "Desire for Revenge Fuels an Entrepreneur's Ambition," many of the employees left to join Leslie's firm. "Over the years, he was loyal to us, so we wanted to be loyal to him," says Benjamin Vasquez. Leslie did not stop there. His new stores are "near enough to Poolmart stores to be direct competitors," and in addition he started a competing mail-order business. Not surprisingly, Leslie contacted the *Journal* to tell his story during Poolmart's stock sale. Frank Dunlevy, a managing director of Montgomery Securities, lead underwriter for the offering, tells a reporter, "It's no accident that Mr. Leslie is talking to you at this time." True enough, says Mr. Leslie. It is one more opportunity "to try to pound the day-lights out of these guys," he says. According to many theories on anger, it is natural to feel a heightened sense of resentment and anger when you're in the company of the same problematic personalities daily, whether at home or at the workplace.

In his widely quoted 1966 work *On Aggression,* social psychologist Konrad Lorenz explores the so-called "polar disease," also known as "expedition choler," which, he argues, "attacks small groups of men who are completely dependent on one another and are thus prevented from quarreling with strangers or people outside their own circle of friends." The implications for the workplace are clear. Lorenz suggests that we respond differently to those with whom our lives are inextricably bound. "In such a situation," he goes on to say, by way of illustration, "as

I know from personal experience, all aggression and intra-specific fight behavior undergo an extreme lowering of their threshold values [and] one reacts to the small mannerisms of one's best friends—such as the way in which they clear their throats or sneeze—in a way that would normally be adequate only if one had been hit by a drunkard.'' Lorenz is concerned with how we can overreact when spending time in close quarters with another individual.

When Lorenz's theory is applied to the Poolmart story, the implication is clear. You have to be aware of the level of personal and professional commitment, even passion, held by those with whom you deal at work. Anyone close enough to be hurt by you might well be close enough to hurt you back.

A story told by comedien/activist Florynce Kennedy illustrates this point, and it goes something like this: A woman sits in her dentist's chair. He prepares her for the procedure, getting out drills and picks, rattling around while she sits there getting more and more nervous. Suddenly, as he bends over and asks her to open wide, he feels her hand reach out and grip his testicles, gently but firmly. He looks down into her smiling face and she says sweetly, ''We're not going to hurt each other, are we, Doctor?''

The way we respond to tales of getting even often reveals otherwise hidden or buried patterns of thinking and behavior that can give us a window into our own deepest definitions of self. These stories can be very affecting because they touch particularly primitive chords.

chapter five

PUNCH LINES

Getting Even by Laughing Last

"Lord, grant me the serenity to accept the things I cannot change, the courage to change the things I can, and the wisdom to hide the bodies of those people I had to kill because they pissed me off."
—ANONYMOUS

"Mine is a most peaceable disposition. My wishes are: a humble cottage with a thatched roof, but a good bed, good food, the freshest milk and butter, flowers before my window, and a few fine trees before my door; and if God wants to make my happiness complete, he will grant me the joy of seeing some six or seven of my enemies hanging from those trees. Before their death I shall, moved in my heart, forgive them all the wrong they did me in their lifetime. One must, it is true, forgive one's enemies—but not before they have been hanged."
—HEINRICH HEINE, QUOTED IN FREUD'S *Civilization and Its Discontents*

TO WANT REVENGE IS THE MOST HUMAN OF ACTIVITIES—
it's one of the few things people do that animals do not
(among the other activities that animals do not perform
involve applying artificial fingernails and singing out loud
to Aretha Franklin's "Respect" on the car radio). Many
of the world's best revenge stories have an element of the

comic attached to them, in part because—like many funny stories—they happen to Other People.

If we are having crumbs put into our morning coffee as revenge for never cleaning the office microwave (were we ever told that we were supposed to clean the office microwave?), we rarely see the joke as we're chugging down the grit. Revenge seldom seems fair when it's directed toward one's self, just as slipping on a banana peel is rarely funny when you're the one landing on your rear end. Nevertheless, revenge and humor can go together like the rows of teeth on a zipper. And laughter can prove effective as a tool, a weapon—and a lesson.

"Gotcha"

Using humor as revenge can be an elaborate game of "gotcha"—the emotional and verbal equivalent of tag. Let's say that Frances thinks teasing you about your weight will help you shed some pounds. Let's say she makes remarks such as "Pretty soon you'll have to start wearing tent dresses made out of real tents" while flashing a classic only-kidding smile as she watches you put a pat of butter on your mashed potatoes. (She, of course, is eating what looks like a bowl of AstroTurf garnished with a side of wood chips.) You sit across from each other at the staff cafeteria, and while your first instinct is to spill your coffee onto her lap, you decide instead to play the game she has set up.

You, offering an equally alluring smile, say something along the lines of "Sweetie, when my Thanksgiving turkey starts to look like you, I know it's time to throw it away" or "Funny how you're always so interested in what goes into my mouth. Isn't yours getting enough attention?'' Instead of being the object of the scene, you put yourself in the position of the subject. By answering back you become a player, not an instrument to be played upon by someone who thinks she knows your tune when in fact she is way off-key.

As a form of revenge, humor does not necessarily have to be shared or public to be effective. You can enjoy the joke being played on someone who wishes you harm even if no one else joins in. When one forty-year-old high-school teacher told me her favorite revenge story, she made the whole table laugh out loud at what had for a very long time remained her private giggle.

''I was getting a series of obscene phone calls at home late in the evenings,'' she said. ''This was several years ago, before I was married and before I had an answering machine—you know, when life was less complicated but less easy. Anyway, a heavy breather would telephone around midnight about twice a week. I called the cops but they didn't bother with it very much because he wasn't being threatening and because it wasn't happening all that often. But, of course, I was frantic about it. I tried hanging up but he would call right back. I couldn't just let it ring because my fiancé lived on the West Coast and often called around that hour as well. And *his* deep breathing sounded very different.

''One night I was so exhausted from a day of teaching and meetings and parent conferences that when the obscene caller reached me, I started to speak loudly and clearly, without pausing. 'I'm going to tell you about my day. I started with oral surgery to remove an abscess. There was a lot of drainage from my gums—which could really be in better shape—and then they had to spray it with all that iodine-type stuff, so that my face was puffy and red. When I got to school late I found that one of my best students had thrown up in the fire bucket—' and at that point he hung up. I laughed to myself for hours thinking that I grossed out an obscene telephone caller merely by describing my day.'' Her lesson was effective. He never called back.

Comic Revenge as the Sweetest Revenge

The fact is, comic revenge is really what most of us mean when we talk about revenge in the first place. Comic revenge is the dynamic behind not only half the sitcom shows and funny movies of the last thirty years, but of nearly every classic farce and comedy for the last three hundred years—maybe even the last three thousand. Comic revenge is the basis for National Lampoon's *Animal House*—where the grungiest guys on campus hilariously disrupt the sanctimonious rituals of the smug golden-boy, football-hero types—and for Shakespeare's *Twelfth Night*—where the smartest guys on the stage hilariously outwit the likes of sanctimonious and smug Malvolio (who, at the end of the play, declares, "I'll be reveng'd on the whole pack of you").

Comic revenge drives the plot of Walt Disney's *Cinderella*—everybody is delighted when Cinderella's vicious stepsisters can't fit their fat feet into tiny glass slippers—as much as it is behind the plot of Charles Dickens's *Nicholas Nickleby*—everybody is delighted when vicious schoolmaster Wackford Squeers is exiled in ignominy.

Much of the best humor has to do with power and the ways that some of the folks who have and use it shouldn't be allowed to have and use it—much like when folks have guns. Sometimes you feel as if there should be better laws governing the use of power, and then you realize that it's those people who *have* power who make the laws. That's the point at which you feel as if you need to laugh at the insanity of the system. Humor allows us to gain perspective by ridiculing the implicit insanities of our everyday world, and thereby to get back at and get even with the powers that be, by not letting them rule our inner lives. Getting the last laugh is a terrific—and usually healthy—way to get even.

"When one of my male colleagues gave me a pair of brass balls for a 'joke' Christmas gift, cheerfully presenting them to me at the office party with everyone watching," a forty-one-year-old female attorney explained, "I had no choice but to hand them back to him with a smile and say, 'I know your work. You need these more than I do.' Everybody laughed, and my victory was complete." In answering her adversary's joke with a joke, she emerged the winner. When the ball was in her court, so to speak, she was able to return it with a little extra spin that indicated her unwillingness to be the butt of someone else's unkindness, however, "cheerfully" it might be packaged.

The Laugh, the Bite, and the Kick

Comedy is important in the examination of revenge because laughter is as obvious a manifestation of refusal as a bite or a kick. Comic revenge is used from the playground to the boardroom, and is often one of the most effective ways of getting even. Rarely does truly comic revenge alienate anyone—often the target can be made to recognize a wrong and rectify it.

While on a book tour a few years back, I was told the

same comic revenge story by a number of crew people involved in various stages of television production. Apparently I was following in the wake of a well-known, best-selling mystery writer who had also been booked onto these programs. Unlike the rest of us doing this sort of work, this famous author was no longer willing to put up with the lack of preparation that one sometimes sees during a live interview; no doubt he felt he had earned the right (and the royalties) to command some sincere attention. He also found a way to get back at those television journalists who did not do their homework.

Most live television involves the use of a TelePrompTer—a television screen with a script that the host or interviewer uses to keep the program in motion. The best hosts use it as its name suggests—to "prompt"—but others rely on it exclusively, and read it line by line, all the while sounding as if they are the ones coming up with these fine questions and handy transitions. During a good interview, it is very common for the exchange to take on a life of its own, and only the least prepared host will need to read the screen question by question.

When the mystery writer was talking to a host who relied solely on the questions scrolling up the TelePrompTer, he made a practice of waiting until the words were off the screen before smiling and saying in his best voice, "I'm sorry, I didn't quite catch that. Would you please repeat the question?" Of course, there is no way to retrieve the question and if the host isn't paying attention, as sometimes happens, and especially if he or she hasn't even glanced at the author's book, as sometimes happens, then the embarrassment can be pretty severe. Apparently everybody working behind the scenes would try to control their laughter and give one another silent high fives.

The point the author made with this particular lesson

was that someone having a conversation with another human being should be thinking about what is being said, not merely mouthing sounds and looking interested. I heard this tale from makeup artists, camera operators, producers, and sometimes the hosts themselves. One thing was certain: The interviewers would actually read his books (or at least the dust jackets) before having him on again.

And they would have to have him on again, because he was simply too famous to ignore. He planned his revenge well, though probably would not have risked such behavior during his younger, more vulnerable days. But the most interesting part of this author's scheme was the fact that he highlighted an issue that many people working in the "community" knew was a flaw. His light and deft handling of it tickled their imaginations and no one, except perhaps some disgruntled hosts, thought worse of him.

Fighting Fair

Part of what makes this a tale of comic revenge is the fact that the author was getting even with someone who was, more or less, an equal. Because he was dealing with the public personality, the one in front of the camera, the one making more money than the rest of the team put together, his revenge was regarded as a fair response to a situation he found degrading. If he'd embarrassed the worker behind the TelePrompTer, on the other hand, or set up for ridicule the administrative assistant who invited him onto the show, then he would have seemed more of a bully and less of the clever avenger.

Herbie Bookbinder, the hero of Herman Wouk's coming-of-age novel *City Boy,* is one of those poor souls who finds himself at the mercy of a bully. Unable to defend himself physically and reluctant to squeal to his parents or teachers for help, Herbie discovers the glories of one public moment of triumphant revenge against his nemesis.

Lenny, the bully, humiliates intelligent and imaginative Herbie on a regular basis, taking particular delight in calling Herbie "General Garbage" during the rehearsals of a school play about the Civil War in which Lenny plays General Lee and Herbie plays General Grant. Lenny, big and dumb, loves the props for the play even though he has trouble memorizing the lines. Not surprisingly, Lenny is obsessed by the sword he must surrender to Herbie at the climax of the play; he won't let Herbie near it, and taunts Herbie in front of their friends about his sword-lessness. But Herbie secretly discovers "a feature of the weapon which Lenny had clearly overlooked. In his boastful flourishing he had pointed out every detail he had noticed to the envious boys," but did not realize that a small button kept the sword locked firmly into the scabbard. Herbie immediately grasps the idea that if he presses this button, Lenny won't be able to get the sword out of its sheath during the performance.

Herbie, kind and generous by nature, is tempted by the thought of revenge. "The small stout boy reviewed several incidents of the day in his mind: concrete against his nose, jeers at his black felt beard, 'General Garbage,' and the recent threat to render his head concave." Herbie decides to go for it: Wouk tells us that "he softly pressed the catch, locked the sword in its scabbard, leaned it against the wall, and strolled away to watch the assembly through the crack of the dressing-room door." When it comes time for Lenny's grand performance, with all the students and teachers in place for the stirring moment of

Lee's grand gesture, Lenny blurts out his line, "Sir, in yielding this weapon I give you the sword of the South, but not its soul."

But then everything grinds to a halt as Lenny tries to hand over the sword that Herbie has locked into place. It doesn't move. In front of a thousand people, Lenny "clapped his hand to the hilt, gave a vicious tug, and spun himself clear around. The sword remained fast in the scabbard." This offers Herbie a chance to achieve ascendancy over his enemy. " 'Never mind your soul,' said Herbie in a flash of inspiration. 'I'll settle for the sword.' " Wouk tells us "There was a deluge of laughter. Mrs. Gorkin was almost shouting from the dressing room, 'Unbuckle the belt!' Lenny lost his head, tugged and tugged at the sword, and began to swear. Mr. Gauss rose to take action. Herbie, emboldened by success, suddenly held up his hand and . . . reached over to General Lee's side, seized the hilt, and drew out the sword as easily as if it had been greased. The audience gasped in astonishment. Herbie turned to his orderly and blandly said, 'Give General Lee a cup of coffee. He seems to be weak from hunger.' "

Humor Harassment

When humor is used against an unequal partner, then the fight is clearly not fair. A joke directed at someone is rarely just a joke, even under the friendliest of circumstances. What is the best way to handle a witticism when it is really a thinly veiled attack? To put it more bluntly: What is the best way to respond to aggression—sexual or otherwise, directed at a woman or a man—when it is disguised as humor?

Let me admit that I collect great responses to bullying

remarks the way some women clip coupons. These re-joinders are useful, free, and can help you save what counts: time, energy, and sanity. My current favorites may be apocryphal, but they are nonetheless instructive for that. In the same way that fables are invented and yet contain truth, so do these. So while it's true that we can't always come up with the perfect answer, at least we should look to those who have as possible role models.

One of the stories I often tell when speaking to groups is one I still enjoy, although I first recorded it in *They Used to Call Me Snow White . . . But I Drifted* back in 1991. When Liz Carpenter worked for the Johnson administration, she wrote a book about her experiences working at the White House. The book was out for a while and did rather well. One evening she met Arthur Schlesinger, Jr., at a cocktail party. He came over to her and smiled and said, "I liked your book, Liz. Who wrote it for you?" Now, clearly dear Arthur meant this as his little joke. If she had stammered and blushed, he would have won the point. He could then say, "See, you just can't joke around with these women." If she'd pounded her fist on the table and threatened to call a lawyer, he could say the same thing.

Instead what Carpenter did was to say in response: "Glad you liked it, Arthur. Who read it to you?" All she did was take his format and adapt it for her own purposes.

Now, joking at the joker's expense is delightful re-venge. Rarely does life offer anything as satisfying as ar-riving at a position of triumph just at the moment someone else thought you were out for the count. It's a fine feeling to be awarded the last laugh.

The trouble is, most of us have been brought up to be so concerned with putting the welfare of others before our own that we are totally unprepared when a great comeback is needed. Over and over again, as I spoke to groups around the country, women would line up and want to talk about their response to Carpenter's line. They loved it, they wished they had said it, they would love to use humor this way themselves—but they would then catch themselves starting to feel guilty for even thinking about mouthing off that way. "I'd love to use something like that Carpenter line," one after another said, "but then I'd go home at night and worry: What if Arthur Schlesinger is secretly illiterate? What if his father is dyslexic? What if his kid uses *Hooked on Phonics*? Then I'd feel like I should volunteer for the Literacy Action committee four nights a week as penance for uncharitable thoughts.

But I firmly believe that powerful people who are jokers do not worry about their victim's response. This doesn't mean we have to become vicious versions of the worst bullying stereotypes, but it is an illustration of the expectation embedded in our culture that you can say what you want to people without power because they are not going to talk back. Freud's framework for the effectiveness of the smutty joke, for example, rests on the twinning of female shame and silence. If the female onlooker refuses to supply both of these reactions, the jokes fall flat. In the case of nasty stories—told by men or by women—this is a good thing to remember.

In the case of needing to draw attention and vindicate larger issues, humor can be used as revenge in matters that are personal as well as political. Texas political columnist Molly Ivins is a wonderful example of the maxim that writing well is the best revenge. Ivins writes about the absurdities of the Texas legislature, and leaves the "victims of their own stupidity" twisting in the wind. She tells a story about the legislature's refusal to move into the twentieth century. Apparently, the legislature refused to take an antiquated sodomy law off the books, because a neo-conservative politician called for a public (or open) vote at the last minute. It turns out that everybody who'd voted to remove the statute in private was too embarrassed or scared to back it up in public, so the law remains on the books.

Ivins said that, after all the fuss was over, and these right-wing guys were patting one another on the back, she wanted to run up to them and order the police to take them into custody because, as she put, "it is illegal in the state of Texas for a prick to touch an asshole." Telling the story to audiences all around the country offers a certain revenge on those who thought they'd won the day without anybody so much as noticing how badly they'd played the game.

"Easy for You, Difficult for Me"

Despite injustice and because of injustice, we need laughter in our lives. We choose to laugh at moments of crisis because the other alternatives, as one woman put it, are crying and throwing up and neither of those makes you look good. Poet Muriel Rukeyser said that "the universe is made up of stories, not atoms," and it's clear to me that she's right. The stories we tell ourselves and the ones we tell each other give us a way to rattle the cage door. Sometimes we can rattle it hard enough to allow for escape; sometimes we rattle it so hard it falls away altogether.

Then the next round begins. Oh, sure, it's easy for a secure and successful person who already knows the critic baiting her to come up with a snappy response, but what about the rest of us? What if you never even use a word like *snappy*? What happens if the only response you can think of is one that makes you sound like a whining nerd or a shrill hysteric? Because we fear exactly these two possibilities, we gulp down embarrassment and rage and remain silent. But we wish we hadn't. Everyone has a story. Once the subject is raised, there is an astonishing collective and bottomless desire to recite quite simply and in alphabetical order every instance of "humor harassment" we've ever experienced.

"With God as My Witness, I Will Never Be Shut Up Again"

I'll just do one, to get started: I'll begin with the first day of my first professional convention when I met a horribly well-known and mistakenly well-respected professor in the elevator. I was wearing a scarf from the college I had recently attended in England in much the same way that Linus carries his security blanket, and I was trying to Be a Good Girl and Be Nice, projects I have since abandoned. Anyway, this man looks at me and, with a sly and knowing smile, says, "You might look good in your boyfriend's scarf, but you have no right to wear it." In response I stutter out some devastatingly assertive line like "Um, well, um, I really did go to school there." To which he replies over his shoulder, as the elevator doors shut behind him, "You sure don't look as if you did."

Now, what am I supposed to think? This is an insult but he thinks it's a compliment? It's just an insult, straight up, no mixer? I guessed that it meant short Italian women were not supposed to get beyond the seventh grade. I guessed I should stop wearing the scarf. I guessed that, quite correctly in this case, he figured he'd get the last word because I'd be intimidated by his position of power, confused by what I was hearing, and scared into silence. He didn't have to think these things in words—he knew them the way he knew instinctively, let's say, which books were worthless without reading them.

Three elements—intimidation, confusion, and fear (mostly of sounding stupid)—keep many of us from talking back when it's appropriate. I would argue that one of the best times for talking back is when someone is using humor to ridicule, undercut, or shame you—especially (but not only) when their joking has to do with power issues. I wish I had come up with an answer in my case, but I didn't say anything as the doors closed behind him. I vowed, fist to the elevator ceiling the way Scarlett O'Hara held her fist to the sky in *Gone With the Wind*, that with God as my witness, it would never happen again. It has happened. Since then humor has been used against me—but not often. And rarely by the same person more than once.

In contrast to my speechlessness in that elevator so many years ago, I recently overheard an exchange between two elegant women, one of whom made Roseanne seem polite. It was at a cocktail party fund-raiser, and we were all supposed to be on our best behavior, making a nice show of ourselves for a good cause. I was doing my "best show" of mingling while really eavesdropping. That's when I heard one bejeweled woman say to the other, in front of a fairly large circle, "So, you say you're a writer now, Marilyn." She paused, smiled a rich woman's thin smile, and asked, "What's your favorite letter?" There were one or two raised eyebrows and eager looks. Without missing a beat, the other woman smiled back and met her adversary's heavily made-up gaze, replying, "Certainly my least favorite has got to be U."

Everyone in the little circle paused and then laughed. It was a fair fight, nobody was dreadfully hurt, and the evening could continue without incident. The sword-play aspect of the conversation allowed for the weapons to be put down once the game was over, at least publicly.

It might not even be necessary to give voice to your revengeful retaliatory remarks. One old friend claims that she fantasizes about revenge every day, "even though everybody thinks I'm little Miss Goody-Two-Shoes. Maybe that's how I can be nice to folks all day long. I think about how my bad-girl side would treat them, and I can laugh and let it go." Working at a police station as a secretary, she is caught up in often traumatic, unnerving situations where she has to keep her cool no matter what. She giggled, explaining that she felt funny even telling me one of her fantasies. With a promise of anonymity and gourmet coffee and pastries, she described a typical scene: "When one of the guys walks past me, as happened the other day, and asks me why a big, big girl like me has to sit in such a little, itty-bitty chair, I immediately think, 'For the same reason that a fathead like you has to stay in a crummy little job.' I'd never say something like that out loud, but when I think it to myself, I can at least get a laugh out of it."

In contrast to her silent laughter, I was told stories by several people who decided, after all, that it was indeed worth it to act out their comic revenge fantasies—usually after a prolonged period of waiting to see if the situation would improve. Nadine, one of the funniest, nicest women I've ever met, worked for ten years or so doing props for a major off-Broadway theater company, so she did not take kindly to the fact that, during one show's long run, the star objected to having Nadine handle her props. According to Nadine, "This woman thought she should be treated with more respect than the Virgin Mary. She was old enough to know better—she was actually older than the Virgin Mary; she'd been acting since the crust of the earth just started to cool—but unlike most veteran performers, she treated everyone around her like dirt. Day after day she'd complain about the job I was doing, and blame me for any and all mistakes—if she missed her cue, somehow I'd forgotten to arrange the artificial flowers just so and made her blow her line.

"One day I'd had enough. It was a Friday evening—always a big time—and she'd been screeching all afternoon. When she came into the wings to be handed an essential prop—a gun—I handed her a flashlight instead. There she was onstage in front of a full house, saying 'Now I've got you where I want you' and waving a flashlight at her leading man when she's supposed to be about to kill him. The leading man retrieved the scene by making something up, she came back into the wings and I handed her the gun, and despite the fact that I know she wished that it were a real gun so she could use it on me, it all went fine after that.

"The manager had me apologize formally, but I think he knew exactly what had happened and why. She complained less after that incident. I think she got the message that even an alley cat has claws."

A Chip Off the Old Block

Since, as the nineteenth-century writer Henri-Louis Bergson observed, a person is "generally comic in proportion to his ignorance of himself," this lack of self-knowledge is clearly the niche where comic revenge is most at home. A graduate of Yale recently told me a story about the revenge that her dorm decided to perpetrate on one of its more arrogant, self-absorbed, too-hip-for-words members. She laughed as she revealed the details, and explained that this particular revenge scenario was regularly mentioned any time any of her former classmates gathered together to discuss the better times of their college experience. How was their revenge funny? She explained.

"Chip had been applying for internships with various legal firms. He's a very aristocratic guy from a rich family and he thinks he's destined to be a hero out of a Grisham novel; you can probably guess that he didn't have too many admirers. At one point Chip carried his superpower act too far and alienated one of his few friends by refusing to allow him to wear his tux to a formal, even though this guy had lent Chip stuff and been a very good friend. The former friend decided it was time to take Chip down a few notches and let him know he wasn't God Junior."

As she continued, her voice became quietly conspiratorial, as if the planning of the revenge plot were being re-created in the telling. "His former friend asked a buddy with a very deep voice to call Chip and offer him a job in Manhattan with phenomenal pay and good benefits. It was totally outrageous, but because Chip thinks so highly of himself, he bought it without question. He was so excited that he immediately bragged to everyone, including his father, who asked about the firm and then told Chip that no such firm existed. Chip dialed the number the deep-voiced guy had left, and got a pizza parlor in the next town over. He was furious but he never figured it out. It never occurred to him that he was being taught a lesson in humility, because he didn't even understand the word." I asked her if she thought the plot proved effective as revenge. Her answer was interesting. "It didn't cause Chip any more embarrassment than he handed out to other people on a daily basis, and it made a lot of us feel better to think that somebody caught him 'out' in his snob's game of 'money tag.' ''

What intrigued me about her response was the fact that the little gang had revenged itself on the unlikable figure and they were satisfied by their actions, despite the fact that Chip thought it was a prank perpetrated by an unworthy and envious enemy. According to the young woman from New Haven, Chip was no worse off because of what happened. Yet other people around him were relieved of a certain amount of emotional tension and could get on better with him, and generally perform better as a group.

Unlike many other forms of revenge, comic revenge can liberate the spirit without having to shame the perpetrator. It can, curiously enough, be an effective form of revenge even when the object of the resentment remains unaware of its source. Just knowing, somehow, what they would think if they only *knew* can be a delicious and gratifying experience.

Healing Old Wounds

In Carol Burnett's brilliant memoir of her difficult and complex youth, *One More Time*, she devotes a section to the time she worked as an usher at the Warner Brothers Theatre in Los Angeles. For sixty-five cents an hour, she was made to wear an outfit that was "a combination of early Yvonne De Carlo and Buckingham Palace Guards [and] a Shriner-type hat. Mine was too small." The manager, Mr. Claypool, was given to chasing the pretty ushers around the theater and, as Burnett describes him, "He was also nuts. He never gave us verbal orders. He gave us hand signals, his very own personally made up hand signals.'' The kids working at the theater were not permitted to speak in words, but were instead fully expected to turn their hands at certain angles (palm up, palm down, index finger out, pinkie in, etc.) to indicate information. When Burnett once made the mistake of asking out loud for permission to get a drink of water, she was yelled at (in words) by the boss, who insisted that in the future she should ''snap your fingers until you get my attention, and when you do, you open your mouth and point to the back of your throat.''

She was fired, not for using any inappropriate hand signals (personally, I would have held up one finger in a very recognizable pose early on) but for trying to refuse admission to two customers who wanted to sit down right before the end of a Hitchcock movie. Her boss actually ripped the epaulets off her shoulders before throwing her out of a job she was counting on to give her an income for the summer.

Her revenge came many years later when the Hollywood Chamber of Commerce asked her where she wanted her ''star'' put on Hollywood Boulevard. ''I said, 'Right in front of where the old Warner Brothers Theatre was, at Hollywood and Wilcox.' That's where it is,'' she writes, ending the chapter with a triumphant ''Up yours, Claypool.'' It makes you want to applaud.

Burnett's example illustrates the fact that her revenge is really the achievement of symmetry at long last—something that had been imbalanced has been set right. The young girl in the Palace Guard outfit has been vindicated; her story can be reconfigured with the knowledge that it all worked out in the end (sort of like knowing that at the end of the Hitchcock movie the villain will get his just deserts). Clearly, the fact that Burnett devoted a fair amount of space to this incident was a testimony to the decades-long grip it maintained on her imagination. *And the triumphant end of the saga is an indication that the comic telling of her story offers both a release and a sense of closure. It certainly does for the reader. If Burnett hadn't gotten her sidewalk star in front of that theater, we would have had to go back and wring the guy's neck.

A recent Calvin and Hobbes cartoon neatly summarizes the same dynamic. The school bully terrorizes Calvin into relinquishing his spot on the swing, and then calls him a sissy for not putting up a fight. He is twice Calvin's size and there isn't even an argument. Alone and pouting in the right corner of the last frame, Calvin declares, ''Years from now, when I'm successful and happy . . . and he's in prison . . . I hope I'm not too mature to gloat.'' He should take comfort from Burnett's story.

It's an emotion and a wish most of us have nurtured at one time or another, this desire to have the hand of fate deal the card we cannot play at the moment. But to be able to achieve this, while keeping a sense of humor, is the real crowning glory.

Sticks and Stones vs. the Well-Aimed Word

Sticks and stones might break your bones, but everybody knows that words can also knock you out for the count. What can you do when you're the subject of hostility that's only thinly disguised as humor? Anger, resentment, bitterness, and fear frequently appear under the initially disarming guise of ''just joking around''—until the object of the joke sees the punch hidden in the punch line. It's the sort of feeling you get when you've been laughing along at a funny story only to realize that the story is being told at your expense. It's as if you're being asked to pay for dinner when you thought you were invited as a guest. Desiring revenge for such treatment is as much a sign of healthy self-esteem as a sign of pain. "One reason writers write is out of revenge," argues Cynthia Ozick. "Life hurts; certain human ideas and experiences hurt; one wants to clarify, to set out illuminations, to re-play the old bad scenes and [say] the words one didn't have the strength or the ripeness to say when those words were necessary for one's dignity and survival. . . . And that's a good thing, isn't it? So that in the end one is left with a story instead of with spite."

"Comedy = Pain + Time"

Humor does not purge our sense of distress at a kind of cultural captivity, but it does emphasize a sense of injustice and incites many individuals to further action. The humor of the disenfranchised is often anarchic and apoc-alyptic; those who have always considered it dangerous were right to do so. Both men and women use humor to get even within situations where the right words can ac-complish what swords cannot—a change of heart and mind, as well as a change in perspective. But, as the old saying goes, "Comedy = Pain + Time."

Humor works by bending or breaking the rules; it al-ways has. But at this moment in our culture we are un-certain which rules apply. This is one reason that our relationship to humor is at an important point of what can be best called the "conflagration," of destruction and, lit-erally, the recreation.

Stand-up comic and actress Rosie O'Donnell did a wonderful routine that illustrated the possibilities of humorous revenge right after the Clarence Thomas hearings in Washington.

"After he just sailed right through that appointment," O'Donnell explains, "the other women and I, who were working on this project, decided to sexually harass every guy on the set—the grips, the electricians, the actors, the associate producers. We went up to them and said, 'Hey, baby, bring that butt over here. Bend over, let's see how good you look. Yum, yum.' We did this all week long—until we realized that they *liked* it. I'm here to tell you that sexual harassment doesn't work the other way around." O'Donnell's setup for revenge is clever, but perhaps more poignant is the realization that joking about something as serious as sexual harassment can underscore the seriousness of it, rather than divert attention away from it. Rather than offer a respite from the tension inherent in the situation, the routine highlights it for the audience.

Performer and writer Alan Sherman used the same methods back in the early seventies. In *The Rape of the Ape* (with APE standing for "American Puritan Ethic"), Sherman suggested a version of O'Donnell's reverse psychology in order to settle some formidable scores. Like O'Donnell, Sherman points to the fundamental injustices of a system that made reparations necessary, and, like O'Donnell's, Sherman's prose contains an unnerving wistfulness about wanting to see the playing field made level so that all players have a fair shot at the goal.

"We must give the country back to the Indians; anything short of this would be welching. (My guess is the Indians won't want it back in the condition it's in)," Sherman begins. "Congress will appropriate funds to pay the Indians 200 years overdue rent with an option for the next 200. . . . Congress will remove the words 'merciless In-

dian savages' from the Declaration of Independence, re-
placing them with something like 'previous occupants' or
'those nice-looking fellows with the beaded jockstraps.' ''

Realizing that Native Americans are not the only group
deserving a little vindication, Sherman goes on to suggest
that ''Americans descended from slaves will be legally
awarded whatever their ancestors were deprived of. . . . If
the record shows that their ancestors spent a total of 124
slave years, the new law will entitle them to 124 years of
extra election votes, which they may cast in one election
or spread around as they see fit.

''As another alternative [African-Americans] will be
entitled to choose from a list of former slave holders, and
may hold their descendants as slaves for up to 124 years.''
Sherman's comedy is clearly laced with a sense of righteous anger, and it is no less funny for this edge.

Removing the Gag

Our appreciation of humor does not depend on whether
certain jokes and stories are ''politically correct''—although clearly Sherman's and O'Donnell's could be regarded as p.c. (especially if, as was once suggested, the
term *p.c.* can mean ''perfectly courteous''). We might
well laugh at jokes that express a desire to get back at
those who take themselves too seriously, and yet it is important to question whether we laugh at particular forms
of humor because of rage and fear; if someone makes an
offensive, hurtful, sexist, or racist joke, do we feel com-
pelled to laugh whether or not we are genuinely amused?
When humor is used foremost as a way to bludgeon or
gag the opponent, it is a dangerous tool. Such ''gags''

have for too long served exactly that purpose: to mute the powerless and vulnerable.

We must learn to use our humor and our collective power to undercut the effectiveness of the "gag" that would be put on us—or anyone less powerful than us. There has always been a laugh track, but sometimes that laugh track is misleading. For example, it is not as dangerous to say "I hope you will not find this funny because it degrades people" as it is to say "You must laugh at this, even if you find it degrading." That's the worst form of "politically correct" policing—the most insidious, covert, and potent—and that's what women, people of color, the poor, the uneducated, and other groups outside the walls of privilege, have had to face far too often.

The point is not to alienate others, but for us to focus on our own concerns and needs, to establish our own values apart from what we are conditioned to believe is humorous. These values may or may not coincide with those already established by our dominant culture, and yet we must work on making decisions based on choices that *are* really choices instead of following a script. Learning to laugh at what we find funny sounds easy, but isn't always because we've been following along with the laugh track for too long.

Both men and women can choose to use humor in such a way that it can heal rather than hurt. Telling our stories—to ourselves and to others—in such a way that we can laugh at the absurdities and incongruities of life can help us survive the worst of trials.

Nora Ephron ends her brilliant novel *Heartburn* with a list of reasons why it's absolutely essential to "turn everything into a story," a response to a friend who questions why she has to give a funny answer to even the most serious questions. "So I told her why," says Rachel, whose husband has just left her for another woman. "Because if I tell the story, I control the version. Because if I tell the story, I can make you laugh, and I would rather have you laugh than feel sorry for me. Because if I tell the story, it doesn't hurt as much. Because if I tell the story, I can get on with it."

Revenge, Laughter, and Release

Revenge and laughter have always had a great relationship, because both depend in a sense on the process of release. We want to choose laughter at moments of crisis, at moments when we are confronted with our own anger, because the other alternatives are just too sad to contemplate.

Once again truth is often the best revenge—and the most comic. Successful practitioners of comedy, and wielders of humor, will often mask their satire by appearing to describe faithfully a series of events. This is a method to which the heroine in Charlotte Lennox's *The Female Quixote* is devoted: "When actions are a censure upon themselves, the reciter will always be considered a satirist." One stand-up comic bases her entire routine on simply acting out all the behaviors cataloged as successful flirtation ploys. After reading the exact lines from a popular woman's magazine, she merely does what the article suggests—but she does them all simultaneously.

She begins by batting her eyelashes, then places her hand suggestively on her hip, then tilts her head to one side while looking playful, then runs a finger up and down her arm, then licks the corner of her mouth while letting her tongue show just a little bit, then kicks off one shoe, then tosses her hair off her face—and by the end of the routine she looks as if she needs heavy medication. The women in the audience, meanwhile, are hysterical. All the comic does is strictly follow the magazine's advice, but she ends up performing a piece of enormously entertaining social satire that unmasks her audience's frustrations at trying to be the eternally seductive female at every occasion. The laughter is, I believe, a small moment of revenge on the Madison Avenue image of femininity itself. To laugh at something intimidating is to diminish its grasp on our imagination.

From the Latin Vindicare...

"I looked up the word *vindicate* at one point in my career," Jim tells me as we sit at his kitchen table in New Hampshire, "and I saw that it came from the Latin word *vindicare*. Now, *vindicare* has several meanings—it means 'to punish' but it also means 'to set free.' "

I was up there in one of the wilder parts of New England because this man had just had another beautiful kid added to his family and because he told me we could talk about revenge. As a journalist he'd worked at a number of newspapers and magazines in his day, before deciding to work freelance from home. This is the story of an old score he had to settle.

"I knew that I needed to punish one guy who'd been attacking me for years in print even though I'd never thought of the word *punish* before reading that dictionary definition. I needed revenge because I needed to be set free before really heading out on my own.

"He was a solid-gold neoconservative, yellow-power-tie, anti-woman hardhead, and despite all the talk about the so-called liberal media, this man had a large and powerful following. He had stuff like 'Death Before Dishonor' pinned to his office door and I remember walking past that once thinking, Okay, I can arrange that. But I'm not the violent sort and I knew that I could never do the 'Let's step outside and settle this like gentlemen' routine. I knew I had to find a clever and better way to take this guy down, otherwise it would never work; my need for revenge would become a joke in and of itself, somebody everybody laughed about in the john.

"I figured that since he was always making fun of my educational background—I went to an inner-city school and a state college, certainly respectable enough—that he was insecure about that aspect of his own life. I've discovered over the years that people try to hit you where a punch would hurt them; they show you exactly where their own soft spots are by projecting them onto you. So I did a little checking into his background.

"Turns out that he was admitted to his preppy little university only after his uncle put some heavy pressure on some pals on the board of trustees to slip him in— there were big donations made. Basically his family bought his way into this college. I have a few contacts, and I managed to get a copy of his transcript from the first two years. He never got above a C and he failed several courses. This from a man who kept making the point in print that we all have to rise or fall according to our merits, and that in a true democracy intelligence, strength, and integrity will triumph. I guess he just left out the part about inherited money and power. I waited until the right moment and attached the transcript to his office door the day his editorial attacking funds for public education went into print.

"By the time he made it to his office that morning, half the staff had seen it for themselves and the other half had heard about it. Everybody was laughing their asses off because he'd been so pompous and holier-than-thou all along. It was a lot of fun, and all it involved was telling the truth. The truth is not only often stranger than fiction—it's much funnier, too. The truth gives you all sorts of avenues to reach vindication. I got my release, and he got a much-needed dose of reality.''

Certain forms of comedy can invert the world not only briefly but permanently, stripping away the dignity and complacency of powerful figures and refusing to hand back these attributes when the allotted time for ''carnival'' is over. Comedy can effectively channel anger and rebellion by first making them appear to be acceptable and temporary phenomena, which can be purged by laughter, and then by harnessing the released energies, rather than dispersing them. Turning the world upside down can prove that the world has no one rightful position after all. Suddenly we can see that we have created our own systems of balance based on nothing more than the continuation of what has gone before, that reason and nature are, well, neither reasonable nor natural.

Lessons and Learning

Some methodologies for getting even are more acceptable than others. For instance, a student at Pennsylvania's Geneva College decided to program his computer to telephone university administrators before dawn as a reprisal for their negligence in dealing with a faulty dorm fire-alarm system that had disturbed his sleep for months. It was a case of a red-eye for a red-eye; sleeplessness for sleeplessness. This form of revenge dealt with technology and seemed both clean and instructive. The alarm system was fixed with alacrity because, in part, the administrators had experienced what life was like from the student's perspective.

"Teaching someone a lesson" is at the heart of much of the revenge that can be called successful, if we define successful revenge as having positive long-term outcomes. Perhaps because of the student mentality, many of the campus mythologies I've heard have a distinctly didactic edge. "In the dorms there's a lot of conflict about quiet hours and noise late at night," explained a friend's eldest daughter. "My roommate's boyfriend came home late one night from a bar and was very loud. Several people on his floor were upset at how inconsiderate he'd been—this wasn't the first time this sort of thing had happened.

"They didn't do anything immediately, but instead waited until they knew he had a big mid-term coming up. The night before the exam about six people called his room, at intervals of about twenty minutes, until he unplugged the phone. Then one of them went outside and started throwing rocks at his window. It was interesting because nobody wanted to disturb the other people in the dorm, which would make the 'revengers' as bad as the villain, but they still really wanted him to know how it felt to be awakened. So they had to act like jerks. Finally they taped a letter to his door saying something like: How does it feel when you can't get enough sleep? Pissed off? Then don't be so——loud yourself."

Using a Comeback as a Way to Get Even

The ability to laugh at the chains that hold us is a sign that they do not control us even if they do confine us.

Those groups that have traditionally been denied power have always used laughter as a way to carve out a space for themselves in what can be a hostile world. When a heckler calls out to black feminist activist Florynce Kennedy, "What are you anyway, a lesbian?" she calls back, "I sure am, if you're my alternative." Her retort acts as her revenge. Every comic has a menu of responses to deal with hecklers, ranging from the gentle reminder ("You've obviously forgotten to take your medication tonight. We understand") to the bid for fairness ("Now, do I bother you where you work? Do I come and shake the Slurpee machine when you're on duty?") to the particular ("Forgive this guy—he's never seen a live woman onstage without a piece of Plexiglas in front of her").

The hecklers who assume that the performer will be distressed or flustered are now dealing with their own discomfort. This is a good definition of revenge that works simply and intelligently. We should all have a menu of appropriate but nevertheless comic responses when someone is trying to get the better of us.

The comic revengers are triumphant in plots ranging from Aristophanes to Atwood. According to Linda Anderson's *A Kind of Wild Justice*, comic revenge can be defined in part as "a group effort by which various members of society indicate their disapproval of a character's antisocial (but generally not illegal) behavior, and unite in an effort to punish and change it." After a display of successful comic revenge we are left with a sense of hope for the future, and not with merely a motley crew of disgruntled individuals bent on getting even at any cost.

Anderson goes on to explain that "comic revengers are seldom driven or commanded to revenge; rather, revenge is an action they choose to take. . . . They assume the task of revenge not with the single aim of destroying the victim, but the multiple aims of providing aid to one or more innocent parties, limited punishment and reformation of the victim, and the restoration of harmony in society.''

By using humor as a form of revenge, victims are able to move away from anger and toward a sense of self-possession. Those who use humor as a way of getting even or teaching someone a lesson are doing more than simply venting their own anger because they must necessarily transform their efforts into something creative and inventive. They have to think about a positive aspect of a negative feeling, and even that can help them retrieve and retain a balanced perspective on a difficult matter.

Comic revenge is not about losing control of your emotions, it's about regaining control over a situation.

The Right to Use Humor

One colleague, a distinguished full professor who also happens to be a tall blonde who wears red suits, was interviewed recently on a TV program about her work for the labor union. After the opening introduction, the host of the program led with the comment ''I never imagined you'd be so feminine.'' She was startled and flustered, like a horse facing a snake at a crossroads. She didn't want to go on, she didn't want to retreat, but she was certainly conscious of the danger. The snake isn't to blame for its snakehood, but that doesn't mean it has to be forgiven for biting you. What's the best answer? In the same bright, friendly, and surprised tone, she could say, ''And I didn't expect you to be so masculine!'' By simply turning the line around, she could make him hear the implications of his remark. No doubt he meant his surprise to be a compliment, but the subtext to his remark goes something like "Powerful women are supposed to look like Sumo wrestlers." There are big assumptions about gender and power behind the interviewer's little joke and these should be addressed.

So what are effective revenge options? Refusing to be silent is, I think, the first step. Silence and apparent humility have not worked as well as we might have liked. Hostility is still cross-dressed as humor. It is therefore important to answer back, not to let the victimizers assume that they will have the last word. We have to use the aggressor's moves against him or her in one fair, deft, and swift motion. Think of it as verbal karate, where the aggressor's force is used by the assailant to overcome the attack. Think of it as stealing the punch from the punch line.

When actress Judy Holliday was being harassed by a casting director who kept making insinuating remarks, she apparently removed the foam-rubber inserts from her bra and handed them to the gentleman, saying, "I believe it's these you're after." Now, I can't imagine doing that at the office next week, but I love thinking about someone somewhere having the guts to make it work.

What else can we do? We can be unapologetic when we're funny. When, as happened to a friend of mine recently, the office manager of your HMO is attempting to bully you into seeing a male physician because the women in the practice are booked up until 2030, use Carrie Snow's line: that going to a male gynecologist is like going to a mechanic who doesn't own his own car. I learned this sort of humor shorthand when, as a member of one of the first classes of women at Dartmouth College I was kiddingly told for four years, "Boy, I wish I were here during my grandfather's days. There were no women students then." Finally I learned to answer simply,

"When your grandfather was here there were no indoor lights. Things get better." People making a joke won't stick around to hear a logical argument, but if you speak up fast enough and offer one line, they can't avoid hearing you. Laughing, of course, does not mean we walk away feeling as if all our problems have been solved. On the contrary, humor serves to focus our anger at injustice, oppression, and stupidity. We walk away armed with a new grammar for our revenge—humor and anger are a powerful combination.

The Way the Cookie Crumbles

Even others can profit from our humorous revenge. A student, more familiar with the road stops on the information highway than I am (let's just say that I've been known to confuse a hard drive with a paperweight), handed me a printout that she'd accessed on the university mainframe. The printout indicates that it's from "Donna Anderson" and it is dated March 15, 1994. It concerns this woman's revenge against a famous and fabulously elegant department store known for its high prices and pretensions. "My daughter and I had just finished a salad at the cafe and decided to have a small dessert. Because our family are such cookie lovers, we decided to try the store's trademark cookie. It was so excellent that I asked the waitress if the store would give me the recipe and she said with a small frown, 'I'm afraid not.' Well, I said, would you let me buy the recipe? With a cute smile, she said, 'Yes. It'll be two fifty.' I said with approval, just add it to my tab.

"Thirty days later I received my Visa statement with a $250.00 charge listed under 'Cookie Recipe.' Boy, was I upset! I called the store's accounting department and told them that since the waitress had just said 'two fifty' I had no idea she meant it was in the hundreds of dollars. I asked the person I was dealing with to take back the recipe and reduce my bill and he said he was sorry, but all recipes were final sale. He said they kept them so expensive because they didn't want just anybody getting hold of their special recipes.

"I waited, thinking of how I could get even. I said, 'Okay, you folks got my $250.00 and now I'm going to have $250.00 worth of fun.' I told the customer service department that I would see to it that every cookie lover I met—and even ones I didn't—would get their recipe for nothing. The customer service representative said, 'I wish you wouldn't do this,' and I said, 'I'm sorry, but this is the only way I can live with the idea of giving your employers such an extravagant sum of money that they cheated me out of.' So here it is, and please pass it along to anybody who loves cookies!" The letter ends with the exhortation "This is not a joke! This is a true story. I paid for it, and now you can have it for free."

The phrase "I paid for it, and now you can have it for free" should be attached to all the best kinds of comic revenge. That one person had to act out the revenge might, in the best-case scenarios, help others to avoid the traps that were set and to be able to make better progress toward the ultimate good. Humorous revenge can represent a careful and considered reaction to a complex and untenable emotional situation. The experience is not exactly the most positive one on earth, but on the other hand it can indeed have positive long-term benefits.

Revenge and the Happy Ending

Personal revenge is frequently informed by (one could say adulterated by) the desire for a more political revenge as well. Consider the character of Ruth created by Fay Weldon in her wicked comic novel *The Life and Loves of a She-Devil*. While Ruth hates romance writer Mary Fisher, her rival, for the havoc of Ruth's own life, she is equally driven to extract revenge, not for herself alone, but for *all* the readers of romance fiction.

Ruth hates the fact that Mary Fisher writes about impossibly perfect happiness, and so makes her readers despise their own ordinary lives, and that she has led countless women around the world to believe that they will be rescued by a handsome rich man who will fall in love with them at first sight and never leave their side. Ruth's revenge is not just an act of personal anger. "Mary Fisher did a wicked thing: she set herself up in a high building on the edge of a high cliff and sent new light beaming out into the darkness," writes Ruth after she has destroyed the lives of her estranged husband and Mary. "The light was treacherous; it spoke of clear water and faith and life when in fact there were rocks and dark and storms out there, and even death, and mariners should not be lulled but must be warned. It is not just for myself that I look for vengeance . . . I don't forgive her novels." The last line is what transforms Ruth's series of revengeful actions into comedy, and calls forth every reader's applause.

There are some people who are at their best when they are at their worst. Up against an emotional wall or up against a powerful enemy, some men and women, in their desire to right a wrong or act on a grievance, are able to find a sense of strength and will they did not know they possessed. Suddenly they have the ability to make a lasting impression on a system previously impervious to them. For them, feelings of revenge and the need to get things back on track can lead to real improvement in their lives and the lives of those in similar situations.

There remains a fascination for the revenge plots contrived by other people, even ones with whom we have no personal connection, precisely because they are acting out what is very probably repressed in our own psyches. This is especially true concerning milder, comic forms of revenge, which are often enormously attractive, even to the most angelic among us.

chapter six

EMOTIONAL TERRORISM

Passive-Aggressive Revenge

*"She intended to forgive. Not to do so would be un-Christian; but
she did not intend to do so soon, nor forget how much she had to
forgive."*
—JESSAMYN WEST, "THE BURIED LEAF"

*"To see an enemy humiliated gives a certain contentment, but this is
jejeune compared with the highly blent satisfaction of seeing him
humiliated by your benevolent action or concession on your behalf.
That is the sort of revenge that falls into the scale of virtue...."*
—GEORGE ELIOT, *The Mill on the Floss*

I USED TO THINK IT WAS JUST *MY* FAMILY, GIVEN THAT
emotional terrorism is something I remember from age
three onward. I remember The Aunt Nobody Liked who
always said things like "This is a nicer roast than the one
you made last time. But maybe it's just a little, I don't
know, tasteless? Do you want my recipe for next time?"
Then there was The Uncle Everyone Feared, who would
get self-righteously indignant about the slightest opinion
if it dared to differ from his own. If you made a comment
about the weather and he disagreed, for example, he
would get very silent, pack up his long-suffering family,
and drive back to the suburbs. He would speak to no one

in my family for months until he was suitably placated.

There was the cousin who always "accidentally" ripped the nicest doll clothes I had, and another who always insisted on offering to help me with my homework in front of all the grown-ups when he knew full well that all I wanted to do was sneak away and watch cartoons. The cousin who brought his gum-chewing girlfriend to family dinners for the sole purpose of annoying his mother throughout the holiday season was also a charmer. He didn't dare annoy his mother all by himself because then she might stop cooking for him, so the gum-chewer became a focus of lingering resentment between them. Luckily for everybody involved, he wasn't angry enough at his mother to marry the girl just for spite.

There were uncles who smoked cigars that made aunts cough, there were aunts who insisted on helping to clear the table and inevitably spilled something on the floor, and there were cousins who played with the cat until she bit them. My favorites were the ones who always insisted on fixing a broken appliance only to break it past repair, or the ones who offered to hang a painting only to destroy half the wall with their hammers. It seems to me that this went on weekly, a veritable opera of miscommunication or an Olympic-level passive-aggressive contest of wills.

Frankly, I no longer think my family was too unusual. I've heard hundreds of stories about the little, everyday ways that people snipe at one another or ambush one another, all the while convincing themselves that they're just being nice. It's polite guerrilla warfare, where noble gestures are exchanged like gunfire and helpful statements tear the heart apart like shrapnel.

Other People's Families...

I hear stories that make me realize once again that we are more alike than we are different. My friend Kimberly's mother, for example, has become the subject of many a conversation about passive-aggressive retaliation against an unfair world. This woman is seeing a shrink, but she isn't talking to him at the moment. He doesn't know this yet because he's on vacation. Kimberly's mother is angry because her psychiatrist doesn't take her fears of death seriously, evidenced by the fact that he will not override her usual physician and order a complete hospital stay full of tests to discover the actual origin of her imagined illness.

Kimberly's mother longs for the hospital because what she really wants is doctors and flowers (male doctors and cut flowers), next to the bed. She wants an illness because what she really wants is a date, but since she's sixty-three and still married, she can't get one. (It's my opinion that she couldn't get a date anyway because she tortures everyone around her and men have a way of sniffing out that torturing trait like pigs to the truffle.)

So this woman calls her daughter to complain and to weep, and Kimberly listens as if it's her family job, which is what it has been since she was eleven and started to become a threat to her mother's sense of her own youth. Her mother calls everybody "gorgeous" because that's what she wants to be called, and she's afraid she's dying because she wishes everybody around her would drop dead.

She's the original Ms. Projection, claiming everybody is what in reality *she* is. She gets paranoid about her friend's not calling her after a dinner party, claiming to be worried that she made an offensive remark, when in reality she's mad as hell that the guest didn't bother to help in the kitchen and just sat in the dining room while she schlepped plates back and forth like a maid.

So, even though she's mad, she can't accept that image of herself and becomes fearful instead. Fear is, for Kimberly's mother, an old friend and useful ally. She worries through the night, counting the hours until she can telephone and say those famous words, "Did I wake you? I'm sorry about last night," thereby getting a stake into the friend's heart before the friend is even awake, the way a vampire-killer gets Dracula while he's still in the coffin. The friend, who has no idea what's going on and is sincerely confused by this early-morning conversation, is then left to try to make sense of it for the next several hours. Meanwhile, Kimberly's mother now hums around the house, straightening small objects that litter the shiny surfaces and feeling more in control.

"I'll Just Sit in the Dark"

A Malayan proverb cautions, "Don't think there are no crocodiles because the water is calm," and perhaps this should be needlepointed onto pillows or hand-painted onto refrigerator magnets so that we can remember its wisdom. Just because there is no frantic action, it doesn't mean that everyone is happy, and just because there are no bombs going off doesn't mean there isn't revenge in the air.

The mother whose endless headaches prevent her son from enjoying his dinner date may well be taking revenge on him for leaving her alone. "No, go ahead and enjoy yourself. After all, I'm only an old woman and I'll just sit here in the dark." Such words act like a stiletto stabbed into the heart of the child who hears them.

A woman may allow her roaming husband to return home after an affair, but then spend the next thirty years subtly getting revenge through small, momentary, and modestly insistent references to his past indiscretions. She forgives him every single day, thereby subtly reminding him of his injury to her and routinely forcing him to re-create his guilt and embarrassment. She's killing him with a sort of poisoned kindness, watching as he drinks every drop. She can't be faulted directly because, after all, it was nice of her to forgive him.

I must admit that I have a sort of emotional "allergic reaction" to this kind of revenge, preferring sugar in my gas tank any day to a sigh from a loved one who whines, "No, no, nothing is wrong, not really. Nothing you'd think was important anyway." That makes me want to hang myself, which is, of course, its desired effect.

In college I was assigned Ibsen's classic play *A Doll's House*, and I remember that I could hardly keep myself from shaking at my response to the man who believes he's being good when he's in fact at the heart of a destructive and miserable marriage. This man uses forgiveness the way others might use a left hook to the jaw. We hear the "benevolent" husband explain what forgiveness means to him: "For a man there's something indescribably sweet and satisfying in knowing he's forgiven his wife—and for forgiving her out of a full and open heart. It's as if she belongs to him in two ways now: in a sense he's given her fresh into the world, again, and she's become his wife and his child as well."

Wouldn't a duel at dawn be more fair? Wouldn't a

confrontation be more honest? Wouldn't poisoning the orange juice at breakfast be a kinder way to start the day?

"Forgive Your Enemies..."

Not that forgiveness doesn't have its place in revenge. As any number of wits have pointed out, the best revenge can involve being terribly kind to your adversaries. Indeed, a version of the line "Forgive your enemies. You'll feel better and it'll drive them crazy" appears to have been said by every aphoristic writer from Oscar Wilde to Andy Rooney. There's a subtlety in this method that can be very sweet indeed, but it takes a sense of distance and a sense of control that's difficult to achieve while angry or hurt. To be able to absorb the hurt without actually reacting badly is to be triumphant, surely, but the lack of reaction has to be genuine for it to work.

Turning the other cheek must be done without wanting to hurt the person who's hitting you; otherwise the point of the lesson is moot. One kid I knew from Brooklyn illustrated this when I overheard him tell a buddy, "Yeah, I turned the other cheek when he came after me this time, but next time I'm gonna punch the bastard's lights out."

The Faces of Passive-Aggressive Revenge

This level of self-determined revenge, though, is rare among passive-aggressive types. Most are content with not answering a direct question, with not taking your phone calls, with agreeing to be on the committee and then not doing any work, and with never meeting a deadline. Passive-aggressive revenge appears in as many forms as there are ways to say "Up yours," yet it maintains a facade of politeness. A passive-aggressive Valentine's Day present is a box of diet chocolates and a guide to fat content in food; a passive-aggressive Christmas present from a relative across the country could be a box of stationery complete with stamps and a note saying "Please write." These might be regarded as nice little reminders by the people who offer them, but unless you've asked for a fat-free cookbook or you don't live near a post office, they are the equivalent of an emotional elbow in the ribs.

I feel that I can speak with hard-won authority on this issue. A boyfriend from the early days of graduate school once gave me a copy of *Webster's Dictionary* as a birthday present because he thought my spelling could use some work. From someone else, this might indeed have been a thoughtful gift—from him it was a "gotcha" because he considered himself a much better student than me. My revenge was to skip the spelling lessons and finish my Ph.D.; the last I heard he is still in the master's degree program. Spelling well is obviously not the best revenge.

A frustrated worker might silently put up with a maddening employer by unconsciously sabotaging every project through poor performance or the awkward handling of minor but important tasks. "If I don't give my workers a reasonable salary, paid vacation days, a reasonable number of sick days, a full hour lunch, and a decent overtime wage, they aren't going to give me their loyalty or their best efforts," agrees one factory overseer. "They'll screw off if they feel like they're being screwed by the company. It's human nature."

An administrative assistant who hands in phone messages a little late on a daily basis is using a passive-aggressive form of revenge. A worker who takes unnecessarily long bathroom breaks, coffee breaks, and lunch breaks might be signaling his dissatisfaction with his work environment. So might the typist who gets every fourth letter wrong but can't be fired because her uncle owns the company.

Many psychologists regard a child who is "accident prone" as systematically acting out anger toward parents who otherwise pay insufficient attention so that the body itself becomes the site of revenge upon others.

There are those for whom a wound that they can show to another is as good as wounding the other themselves. "See how hurt I am?" they cry. "If you loved me more, I wouldn't have hurt myself." Also regarded as self-inflicted and self-directed acts of buried rage are bulimia and anorexia, frequently diagnosed as patterns associated with repressed anger in young women. But young men are not immune. (Just listen to the passive-aggressive's unofficial anthem, Bob Dylan's "Don't Think Twice, It's Alright," if you need confirmation of this point.)

As D. H. Lawrence wrote in his classic novel *Sons and Lovers*, "Recklessness is almost a man's revenge on his woman. He feels he is not valued, so he will risk destroying himself to deprive her altogether." Lawrence was referring to the way his hero rides a bicycle dangerously fast down a dark hill, but his remark also could apply to the man who, in repressed anger, drives his car dangerously or walks through a bad neighborhood late at night.

Suicide is, of course, the most extreme twinning of passive-aggressive anger and the need for revenge. The wife who leaves a note on the dining room table for her husband that reads "Your dinner and my head are in the oven," is taking her revenge as well as taking her own life. Destroying yourself so that someone else will feel bad is surely too high a price to pay for satisfaction, and yet many psychologists rank suicide as one of the most aggressive acts of revenge that can be committed by a human being against those closest to him.

Mrs. Beeton and Miss Manners

There are also kinder and gentler forms of passive-aggressive revenge, such as the one found in *Mrs. Beeton's Book of Household Management*, the classic Victorian handbook of etiquette that was the standard governing behavior in countless households for several generations. Even dear Mrs. Beeton condones passive-aggressive revenge when the situation demands it: "It is generally established as a rule not to ask for soup or fish twice, as, in so doing, part of the company may be kept waiting too long for the second course, when, perhaps, a little revenge is taken by looking at the awkward consumer of the second portion."

To an extent, even the perfectly correct Mrs. Beeton can counsel using passive-aggressive behavior because it works below etiquette's radar—most social screens cannot detect incoming fire. There's a sense that something is amiss, perhaps even a distinctly uncomfortable atmosphere, but there's no way to fault anyone for its effectiveness. This is at the heart of all passive-aggressive revenge: working below radar.

Judith Martin, also known as Miss Manners, is a contemporary arbiter of social rules. In her widely syndicated column, Miss Manners has often been heard to vaunt the delights of perfectly acceptable passive-aggressive revenge when the situation demands it. The examples she offers pose rather more delicate problems than the matter of soup. Miss Manners is proper but never coy; she addresses the important issues without subtlety. "If you are rude to your ex-husband's new wife at your daughter's wedding, you will make her feel smug. Comfortable. If you are charming and polite, you will make her feel uncomfortable. Which do you want to do?'' and ''Many relatives who do not get along use etiquette as a weapon with which to fight. Choose your weapon'' are two excellent examples of her expertise in perfectly polite passive-aggressive relations.

Perhaps Miss Manners's best recipe for revenge is couched in the response to a woman who knows that her husband is having an affair with a close friend. ''If you really want to be evil (and why not—it will make you feel better), you might make vague statements with a radiant face that make [your friend] believe, without you saying so, that you are spending time with a man who makes you look more thrilled than your husband apparently did.'' This will pique her; but she will mention it to your husband, to salve his conscience. . . . It will also pique him. Two people in this state of mind are not going to enjoy each other for very long.'' Charming and deadly, Miss Manners's schemes are poised on the border between wicked and delightful—a difficult place to find, but a great place to be.

Beware the Solicitous Insult

The complexities of passive-aggressive revenge are sometimes daunting when they appear as a show of concern. There's always a colleague who sees you in the hallway and says, ''You look tired. Is everything okay?'' Now, you might be wearing your best new suit, happy and relaxed from a terrific weekend sailing on the lake, but suddenly you feel a little down. Maybe he's right. Maybe you're tired. Maybe you didn't have such a good time after all. Maybe the suit makes you look old. He walks away whistling, having had his revenge—albeit unconsciously—for your looking too good for a Monday. He does it every week, and he does it to most people, but it's still effective because it seems as if he's only being nice. He's played an expert version of passive-aggressive "gotcha" and won.

Unless you can identify his little remark as the attempt to get even with you for enjoying life more than he is, then you might well internalize it and think you've done something to generate the comment. With passive-aggressive revenge, all you have to do is be having a better time than the revenger. You can become a target to some unhappy people if you merely happen to like your life.

"It takes your enemy and your friend working together to hurt you to the heart; the one to slander you and the other to get the news to you," commented Mark Twain. Sometimes the people who seem to be trying to do you the most good are the ones who end up—consciously or unconsciously—getting even with you for an earlier imbalance. "I never fear my enemies because I know where they stand," remarked one senior government official I met at a party. He looked around the room at his congenial coworkers and, smiling, said, "It's my friends who terrify me."

A former student of mine, a woman now in her mid-twenties, told me, "It was my best friend from college who called to tell me that I was not being invited to the mini-reunion held by a woman who used to be part of our group at school. When Janet phoned to say how sorry she was that Maggie was cutting me out because Maggie thought I was too arrogant, I burst into tears. I'd always thought Maggie and I were on good terms and I was very unhappy to hear that she thought badly of me. But then I reflected on how eager Janet had been to tell me the news, and thought about how she'd always been on the outskirts of the circle. That's when I thought, Janet's getting back at me because I was more popular in college than she was, and even though that explanation sounded arrogant even to me, I was sure I had hit it on the head. I thought about calling Maggie and seeing whether I could swing an invitation but decided against it. I didn't like the cattiness of the whole episode, but it also made it clear to me that my good friend Janet had a grudge against me that could mushroom like an H-bomb.''

Eating Well Is the Best Revenge

My anger takes over when I'm feeling out of control in my life; for others, anger is what they use to control the world around them. Laura was one of the few girlfriends who actually came to me to talk about revenge. After all, she argued, she had already accepted responsibility for her part in a disastrous relationship, and had no trouble ''owning'' her feelings—in other words, she knew the vocabulary but I could see by the expression in her dark eyes that her emotions hadn't quite caught up yet. But I did listen carefully, and it seems that she was speaking for any number of women who felt betrayed by the man—or woman—in their lives. Laura, a research chemist, understands how the very universe is constructed, but she, too, has trouble dealing with the chemistry of her own anger.

''No woman over thirty has gone through a relationship without feeling fat,'' asserts my friend Laura as she eats another cannoli, ''and nobody goes through a breakup or even just a really bad time without wanting to make him pay. Wanting revenge is as natural as having a bad hair day, and for most women it's no more dangerous.''

Laura's point about the inevitable twinning of revenge and love is a good one, as we've seen in Chapter 3, especially in the light of the fact that revenge is awakened, like a sleeping sea serpent, by profound pain and fear. If we love deeply, it is not surprising that we grieve just as deeply if that love is taken away. It might also follow that we want to exact recompense and restitution, even if that feeling is illogical. ''How can he make it up to me that he thought my work was less important than his, and that he was going to put the relationship on hold?'' asked Laura. ''I'm thirty-eight, and I'd like to have kids. What am I supposed to do, go to court and sue for the five years' worth of more mature dates that I could have had? The trouble is that emotions are not admissible evidence,'' she said, sipping espresso. ''It feels like somebody syphoned off my sense of self-esteem and self-worth and I want to get it back by getting some of his. I feel as if I've been mugged, but the frustrating part is that the mugger doesn't actually know the scope of his crime—he thinks I'll just get over it in time.'' Having known Laura for a number of years, I was aware that she'd have to do something—anything—first so that she could feel back in control of her life.

We decided that she should follow the advice of Euripides, who declared, ''There's nothing like the sight of an old enemy down on his luck.'' Laura waited until she knew that her old lover was going through a tough time at work, and she went to his usual restaurant with a fabulously attentive man, sat at a table in his direct line of sight, drank champagne, looked beautiful in a dress he once wrongly said didn't suit her, and waved gaily from across the room as he hunched over another tense business lunch. She reasoned that the worst that could happen was that she would feel drawn to him again, but she decided to risk it.

"Just seeing him looking nervous made me feel better. I remembered how awful it would be for days at a time when he was in some financial crisis, and I was delighted to walk out of the restaurant knowing that I didn't have to be the object of his bad temper. I could put the episode behind me because I felt like I orchestrated the last scene, and that his final image of me wouldn't be of a tear-streaked frightened face. More important, I needed to have him looking after me as I walked out the door, instead of the other way around."

The Late Revenger

Most passive-aggressive actions are easily seen by those who are affected by them and rarely acknowledged by those who commit them. Certainly they are common forms of revenge, especially for fastidious types who can't bear to think that they might harbor such unkind sentiments. Psychoanalyst Willard Gaylin defines passive-aggressive behavior as that in which "the aggression is always couched in behavior that can easily be rationalized as nonaggressive (even presented as a service), and there is a vague and indirect quality to this form of aggression that resists frontal attack."

He goes on to argue persuasively that "these passive-aggressive individuals even deceive themselves into thinking that they harbor no aggressive feelings. They are amazed that they are so often misunderstood. They do not understand why everyone is always so angry with them.

'What in the world did I do?' is emblazoned on their escutcheons. They are preeminently the whiners, the guilt vendors, the martyrs, the sighers and the sufferers of the world—and the latecomers.''

Gaylin's discussion of chronic lateness as a passive-aggressive act is worth repeating in detail because it lays out a map for most manifestations of this form of revenge. ''Some latecomers deny their aggression, claiming simply to be chaotic people. If that were so, the pattern of lateness should indicate this chaos. They should be ten minutes late one time, a half-hour late another, two hours late a third time. If their latecoming is based solely on disorganization, then you have a right to expect that they be ten minutes early sometimes, one-half hour early another time and two hours early a third time. . . . Latecoming is a typical example of passive-aggressive action.''

While not all passive-aggressive action is revenge, it is usually a pattern constructed to make a person's worth clear to others who, the person fears, might not recognize his or her importance. Often this is done in direct response to a perceived slight or insult.

A man who is yelled at by the boss may come home only to yell at his wife, who will in turn yell at her child, who might in turn take out his anger on the family pet. It is human to vent anger downward, often away from the causal and powerful catalyst. The displacement of anger creates a chain whereby the least articulate and most fearful member of a household or community becomes the scapegoat, the one upon whom all blame is heaped and who bears the burden of punishment for wrongs he or she has not committed. For those who appear to be perpetually on the receiving end of such anger, the only possible forms of revenge are passive-aggressive in nature.

Beware Best Intentions

Unlike other forms of revenge, passive-aggressive behavior is particularly insidious because the people committing it often remain blissfully unaware of the true force of their impact. They think they are doing what's best for everyone, or, at worst, they believe they are inconveniencing others just the "teentsiest itty bit." I quote that phrase because it was a favorite of a woman I once worked with, whose passive-aggressive revenge was to speak in baby talk until you wanted to stuff a diaper into her mouth to shut her up.

At a dinner party, I witnessed a wonderfully acrobatic passive-aggressive routine between a young couple. We were talking about the newest crop of actors and actresses, and they'd obviously been keeping up with current cinematic trends. One aspect of their exchange intrigued me. The well-groomed young man always said "film" and never said "movie." His wife always said "movie," and it seemed to me that she deliberately chose to say the word "movie" in reaction to his use of the word "film." He seemed annoyed at her, "correcting" her opinions on more than one occasion. After a few minutes of this, she turned to the assorted company and, smiling, announced, "This is our version of 'Let's Call the Whole Thing Off,' you see," referring to the Cole Porter classic. "But we don't need to sing it in front of all of you." Gracefully turning to her husband, she said, "It's okay if I say 'movie' in mixed company. It's an American word. You don't have to think any less of me." It was all done with such exquisite lightness you could hardly tell they were actually having a marital argument in the middle of a formal dinner party. These were two people destined to be together.

A colleague told me, at great length, about the way his eldest son perfected a method of tormenting him beyond all patience: The kid pretended never to hear something the first time it was said to him. Everyone in the family had to repeat everything they said at least twice, sometimes even more, until he responded. They had his hearing checked, took him to every doctor in town, including a psychologist who suggested that they write down what they wanted to communicate. "I'm supposed to cover the goddamn house with Post-it notes?" was my colleague's response. The kid had the household in turmoil, which is, presumably, exactly what he wanted. After his first semester at college he returned home for the holidays cheerful, independent, and a good listener. The problem never surfaced again.

Aggression and revenge need not even express themselves in words or be recognized by the perpetrator of the act to hit their mark: A hooded glance, an ironic smile, a sarcastic gesture, a disdainful tilt to the head, a certain condescending look can all be slings and arrows to those who are aware of them.

Sure, I'll Do the Laundry...

"I never considered it an act of anger or revenge," says my friend Suzy, "but there was a time when we were first married that I did manage to destroy every piece of my husband's clothing by either washing or ironing it badly. I didn't want to let him know how much I resented having to leave my hometown because he got a new job. I thought I was being a good newlywed by not complaining, but when I think back on it, I can see that I did find ways of making him pay for how unhappy I felt. We were rarely relaxed in each other's company because I always wanted praise for my good-wife act, and he didn't realize that. Not that I was a great advertisement for household tasks. There was the day when I inadvertently dyed all his white underwear and socks pink because a pair of my new colored tights 'somehow' got mixed up with his laundry. Then there was the time I put too much starch in all his collars and gave him a series of nasty rashes on his neck. I shrunk his sweaters and hemmed his trousers unevenly—yes, I guess I was pretty unhappy.

"Eventually I wised up, got a job of my own, and things improved. We sent our clothes out to be laundered and dry-cleaned and I learned to tell him when I was upset by using language instead of laundry." The sort of low-level depression that engulfed Suzy at the start of her marriage is a version of low-level rage turned inward against the self and manifested in trivial, apparently coincidental actions, all of which have negative effects on the target of the unidentified rage.

"But it is a sad fate to be required without respite to repel an enemy instead of working towards positive ends," declares mystery writer—and sage—Dorothy Sayers. "And very often the housekeeper submits to it in a kind of madness that may verge on perversion, a kind of sadomasochism. The maniac housekeeper wages her furious war against dirt, blaming life itself for the rubbish all living growth entails. When any living being enters her house, her eye gleams with a wicked light: 'Wipe your feet, don't tear the place apart, leave that alone!' She wishes those of her household would hardly breathe; everything means more thankless work for her. Severe, preoccupied, always on the watch, she loses joie de vivre, she becomes overly prudent and avaricious. She shuts out the sunlight, for along with that comes insects, germs and dust, and besides, the sun ruins silk hangings and fades upholstery; she scatters naphthalene, which scents the air. She becomes bitter and disagreeable and hostile to all that lives.'' Sayers, fond of emotions pushed to the extreme as any mystery writer must be, comments simply, ''The end is sometimes murder.''

Revenge of the Weak

One of the reasons women seem to be more obvious practitioners of passive-aggressive behavior can be explained by the theories developed in ''Neurotic Dependency in Successful Women,'' an article by psychologist Alexandra Symonds. Explaining why women are more likely than men to negotiate the complexities of personal relationships by using tears rather than anger to drive home their points, Symonds argues that women ''were not allowed to fight for themselves on the basis of strength, since this was not feminine, but instead learned to fight on the basis of weakness. They learned that men will do things for women because they are too weak and helpless to do for themselves. . . . Everyone, men and women alike, has trouble with direct aggression, but women are trying to deal with it for the first time as adults while men have faced this problem since early childhood.''

In other words, the passive-aggressive woman fits neatly into the form-fit mold provided by a society that often rewards women for sadness (''You're beautiful when you cry. I'm sorry I was out late'') while punishing them for anger (''How dare you accuse me of being inconsiderate! That's what I get for marrying a shrew'').

Those who appear to cave in emotionally often become so adept at it that they resemble fighters who take a fall at a rigged boxing match. They seem to be down for the count but you can't tell for sure.

Both men and women can become expert self-sacrificers and use this as a method of revenge. Ironically, practitioners of this behavior have been known to sacrifice everyone but themselves. They become the "poor souls," inevitably on the losing end of any transaction, even as they wield power by painting themselves as victims. In Elizabeth Bowen's powerful novel *The Death of the Heart*, we learn that "sacrificers . . . are not the ones to pity. The ones to pity are those that they sacrifice. Oh, the sacrificers, they get it both ways. A person knows themselves what they're able to do without. . . . Incurable strangers to the world, they never cease to exact a heroic happiness. Their singleness, their ruthlessness, their one continuous wish makes them bound to be cruel, and to suffer cruelty. The innocent are so few that two of them seldom meet—when they do meet, their victims lie strewn all round."

Passive-aggressive behavior is used primarily by individuals in emotionally or socially weak positions. More reluctant than most to recognize, never mind admit, their anger and resentments, they rarely consider themselves capable of initiating an insubordinate act. "I could never hurt a fly," says the delicate and traditional woman whose children live in terror of her—not because of her spankings or her anger, but because of her tears and melancholy moods. She can be as controlling as the most domineering harpy, and perhaps even more effective at getting her way in the long run.

Who Pays for Dangerous Passive-Aggressive Actions?

A mother who repeatedly tells her children about her un-happiness with their father, for example, is creating an act of aggression against her husband even if that is not her intention. Her children will learn to despise the man who hurts their poor mother; her passivity works like a knife in the destruction of the good image they may have had of their father. Her tears are her revenge; her children's hatred of her husband is a vindication of her perception. "Suffering is used to make others feel guilty," declares psychoanalyst Karen Horney, with an "emphasis on needs, appeals to pity and to sacrifice." Such people see themselves as victims of abuse, and look for confirmation of this from others.

Subjecting those around them to their insatiable desire for attention, affection, or reassurance, such people may well be getting even with a world that refuses to grant them acknowledgment unless they occupy the role of vic-tim. The gravest problem, of course, is that the children are the ones who pay most dearly for this particularly insidious and far-reaching form of revenge. It is not the husband who is most damaged, but the children who feel enraged and despairing in the face of what they can only recognize as their mother's sadness. In using them to fur-ther her revenge, whether she sees it that way or not, such a woman is the most destructive of individuals.

Surprise: Men and Women Differ

Conditioned by society to follow certain gender-specific dynamics, men and women react differently to pain.

Where a woman might be more prone to using guilt to manipulate a situation, a man might be reckless and self-destructive as a form of revenge. The man who, after an argument with his wife, drives at ninety miles an hour around dark curves might well be thinking, See how you like it when I'm in the hospital because of you. The man who drinks, smokes, and overeats might be revenging himself on a woman who doesn't treat him the way he thinks he should be treated.

"When a man wants to reveal deep emotions, he seldom uses speech," quips Alfred Gingold in *Fire in the John*, his witty reply to men's-movement literature. "He resorts to other forms of expression, such as the hives you get at the sight of your boss or the stutter you develop on the third date." In *If You Can't Live Without Me, Why Aren't You Dead Yet?* Cynthia Heimel quotes comic Richard Pryor: "When a woman's heart is broken, she cries and shit. But men don't cry, they take a walk and get run over by a truck. Don't even see it." Heimel comments, "But we women, in our constant struggle for equality, are now aping this stiff-upper-lip routine, with much the same results." In other words, a woman who sees herself as "independent" or "as tough as a guy" might begin to believe that self-destructive behavior is a suitable method of revenge. One thing is certain: Acting dangerously can never bring peace of mind; there is no triumph in crashing your car into a telephone pole in an attempt to make somebody feel bad. No one will feel worse than the driver. Self-destruction is synonymous with self-abasement and no sense of satisfaction can emerge from such an act.

For the most part, classic practitioners of passive-aggressive behavior engage not in life-threatening activities but in ones that are annoying and disturbing. Passive-aggressive experts refuse to lend their voices, energy, or sense of commitment to a cause, but instead gain a sense of power by refusing to participate. Their revenge is to refuse to play rather than to refute the premise of the game—they merely threaten to take their toys and go home.

Getting Even Without Getting Caught

In *How to Avoid Love and Marriage*, Dan Greenburg and Suzanne O'Malley offer a range of passive-aggressive revenge options: "Your husband steadfastly refuses to help out in the kitchen. Following several ugly fights on the subject, he has vowed to do his share of the cooking from now on. He invites his boss and several business associates to dinner but, conveniently, he has to go out to run some errands when it's time to begin preparations for the meal." Having set the scene, the authors suggest that there are two ways to deal with the situation to act out a perfectly constructed passive-aggressive marital fight guaranteed to last for days.

In Option A, you can "refuse to ask him for help. In fact, refuse to acknowledge that he is even there. Throughout the dinner party, never speak to him directly, but use one of the guests—preferably your husband's boss—as an interpreter: 'Mr. Whiner, could you please ask my husband if it would be too much trouble for him to pass the butter?'" In Option B, we are told, "You know your husband will never be ready to do his share. Don't do your share, either. When your guests sit down at the dinner table and your husband asks, 'Say, hon, what's for dinner?' explain that you were just about to ask him the same question." The humor in the passage reflects the customary dynamic of such exchanges. Few couples could read the passage and not laugh at the absurdity—and familiarity—of the sentiments expressed even if they've not spoken the actual words themselves.

"I was the husband of a woman who took our marriage as a kind of pass/fail course," recalls a university professor in his mid-sixties. "We were married in 1981 and divorced in 1988 and they were the longest seven years of my life. She had been a student of mine, which was probably the first mistake, and she was the sort of spoiled, pouty, pretty type that got her way by sulking seductively in the corner. This is not to say that she didn't do what was absolutely necessary to look good on paper—she had a part-time job in the library, she cleaned the house, cooked most of the meals—but in seven years she never told a funny story, never made a friend, never initiated an activity, never bothered to do anything to make our relationship work.

"The less she did, the less I wanted to be with her, which in turn made her do progressively fewer things. She wanted to be pampered, but she didn't want to be a partner, and her revenge on me was to stay a little girl. I probably deserved her muffled anger because I should have known better than to marry someone nineteen years my junior. She needed to be with people her own age. Her passive-aggressive behavior brought me to my senses and I left to move into my own apartment. We were divorced, she went back to finish her degree, and I married a woman closer to my own age and background. When we argue, we really argue, and it's much healthier to square off against an equal."

In an uncanny reversal of this relationship is a couple who seem to thrive on their mutual and chronic passive-aggressive habits. "She talks and I don't listen, but this is the secret of our marriage," says the husband. "If I paid any attention to what he said," replies his wife, "I would have left a long time ago." There's revenge here, perhaps, but also a lot of reciprocity.

Withdrawal and Revenge

It's clear, then, that the label "passive-aggressive revenge" could be pasted on a wide range of behaviors. But it should be emphasized that passive-aggressive behavior isn't necessarily a sign of defeat, or of a weak will. On certain occasions, withdrawal is a more effective means of revenge than it is a means of birth control. When he was asked by one of the most prestigious university presses to assist in creating a reading list for a well-established, well-known, and highly paid scholar who was putting together an anthology of major works to be marketed to the general public, one assistant professor—the low man on the academic totem pole—agreed to do it for a modest fee. The contract he signed obligated him to produce an annotated bibliography and granted him an acknowledgment in print for his work. It turns out, however, that they wanted him to do all the work on the book and receive no credit beyond a mention of his help on the bibliography.

As his interaction with the press grew more complex, he understood that his role was to select the texts and edit them, leaving the older man (who was being paid a five-figure fee while the assistant professor was getting a three-figure fee) to simply write a brief introduction. When he brought the matter up to his editor, the woman replied that the book would sell only because the established scholar's name was on it—it hardly mattered what was between the covers.

Infuriated, not only by the way he had been misguided and mistreated but by the dishonesty at the heart of the project, the assistant professor decided to back out of the deal altogether. He broke the contract, paid back his small fee, and negotiated a contract under his own name with another press. His highly successful book came out two years earlier than the established scholar's book and sold twice as many copies. The erstwhile assistant professor, now a full professor with his own set of worries, sees his withdrawal from that corrupt process fifteen years ago as the turning point in his life. He attributes his success to his initial desire to get even with those who had taken advantage of his youth, inexperience, and talent.

Check Your Bags

In a hotel in Seattle I had a long and interesting conversation with the young woman who came to clean my room. A student at a local college, she worked as a maid in this rather posh establishment in order to pay her tuition. Cheerful and pleasant, she smiled when I told her the subject of this book. I didn't expect that she'd have any stories for me (clearly, I thought, she'd be like one of the heartbreakingly nice kids in my classes who don't understand why Ahab just won't let the whale alone), but I asked her anyway. As it turned out, she had a whale of a tale of her own, one that changed my hotel habits for good.

"Most of the guests are wonderful, but every once in a while there's one who can spoil my whole day," she told me. "A guest who berates you, who doesn't like some other service at the hotel, such as room service, but takes it out on you instead, or one who simply barks orders as if you were their personal slave—these people can ruin the small amount of pleasure there is in doing your job well. I know it's my business to make sure the guests are satisfied with their stay here, but there's no pleasing some. When a guest goes overboard with rudeness, I've developed a strategy that allows me to get on with my day. I hide some small item of theirs somewhere in the room. I'll deliberately misplace something when I'm cleaning.''

She is quick to explain that she has never done anything actively bad, a common cry from the passive-aggressive revenger. ''I've never stolen anything, but I've *moved* a heck of a lot of stuff. Nothing valuable or important—I'd never touch a watch or a passport—but little things that drive them crazy. I'll take their dental floss or their lipstick and put it back in the suitcase. The pajama top that they left on the floor for me to pick up, I'll push it a little further back until it's hidden under the bed. I'll half-hide their remote-control devices, putting them away underneath something near to where they left them. It makes me feel better to think that I made them uncomfortable. They think of me as somebody without a brain or feelings, and I use both to get even with them.''

I gave her a generous tip when I left, in part for her honesty in telling me her story, and in part because I counted my undergarments and they were all there.

The Vulnerable Vultures

Those who face the fact that they harbor a need for revenge are generally less dangerous than those who nurse those feelings unaware. ''The weakest and most timorous are the most revengeful and implacable,'' writes philosopher Thomas Fuller. When faced with the mouse that roars, it is difficult to disagree.

Catherine, an executive at an insurance company, found this out the hard way. "One of the women in the office was always making me cups of tea and asking me about how my kids were doing. She appeared to be a good, kind soul, a little timid but very considerate, and after a time I opened up to her. I told her that one of my sons had been arrested on a drunk-driving charge, and that I was distressed over this.

"Years passed, and as I moved up in the corporation, she stayed where she was and we lost touch. I didn't see myself as leaving her behind or breaking off our friendship but clearly she did. Ten years after the drunk-driving incident, when my son was running for a local political office, she telephoned the town paper to report that he had a record and suggested that they look into it. The reporter called me and told me who gave him the information. I was stunned. When I confronted her, she told me that she'd been wanting to hurt me for years for abandoning our friendship. The friendship obviously meant more to her than it did to me, but I was absolutely unaware that I'd caused her any pain because she never said a word."

When it appears as passive-aggressive behavior, revenge shifts from its usually conscious ground to that of the hidden, buried, and secret turf occupied by the darker, less available psychological processes. This is one of the reasons passive-aggressive behavior is as difficult to change as it is to be near. The best ending to a painful episode might well be to be able to shake hands and leave with the understanding that the matter has been put to rest. But, as someone once commented, anytime you bury the hatchet, you mark the spot—just in case. Perhaps we should keep Cynthia Ozick's good advice in mind: "In saying what is obvious, never choose cunning. Yelling works better."

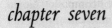

chapter seven

CAN'T GET NO
SATISFACTION

Anger, Revenge, and Justice

"A little rage, a little revenge, clears the air and cleans out the system. It's emotional roughage."
—ANONYMOUS CALLER TO A TALK SHOW, 1993

"The thousand injuries of Fortunato I had borne as best I could; but when he ventured upon insult, I vowed revenge. You, who know so well the nature of my soul, will not suppose, however, that I gave utterance to a threat. At length I would be avenged; this was a point definitely settled—but the very definiteness with which it was resolved precluded the idea of risk."
—EDGAR ALLAN POE, "THE CASK OF AMONTILLADO"

IT'S TOUGH TO TYPE WITH A CLENCHED FIST, BUT I'M trying. I wanted to write about anger while I was actually mad at something, which means I couldn't start working on this chapter for a good, oh, ten or fifteen minutes. If anger were mileage, I'd be a very frequent flyer, right up there in First Class; if it were food, I'd have to be hauled around by a winch. If anger were sex, I'd have my own 900 number.

But anger is like none of these things. It's an itch, an

allergic reaction to some little piece of life's pollen blown your way. Anger is personal. Somebody else might not even notice what's bothering you, but the grievance sets your heart racing and your eyes watering and your face blushing. Anger is more particular than sexual attraction or greed. Anger is the quintessential individual-signature emotion: I am what makes me mad.

In my case, this makes me a trucker whose vehicle is making love to the rear end of my Volvo or an automatic teller machine that summarily eats my bankcard without telling me what exactly I've done to offend it.

Why else am I mad? Should the list be in alphabetical or chronological order, or would it be better to organize my current revenge list by height, or perhaps geographical location? Today, for example, I am furious at everyone and everything around me. I started off by getting mad at myself. I forgot to put gas in the car yesterday, which means that I need to go to the service station before heading in to the office, which means I'll be late for my first meeting. I'm mad at the foolish woman I was yesterday who didn't plan for the efficient and considerate woman that I woke up as today. I'd like to go back and yell at me. (When this wish to tell myself off in different voices becomes too frequent, I'm going to book into the Sybil School of Behavioral and Chemical Therapy.)

I'm mad at my husband. I come home after getting a thirty-dollar haircut which, I was assured, makes me look glamorous, thin, sophisticated, and adorable (none of which I looked when I went in to get the haircut). My husband greets me not with adoration, but with the less-than-glamorous-and-delightful news that the cat threw up on the good rug. I am not thrilled with the cat, whom I resent only slightly less than my husband at this point. My haircut and I clean up after my indifferent pet, who sits grooming herself in disdain and contempt, as if to say, "I never need a haircut. So much for being higher up the food chain." (No doubt she is mad because her bowl contained only cat food and not Mouse du Jour. Mind you, this is a cat who is herself an expert on revenge. She has, for example, mastered the art of eating one entire houseplant for every day we're gone on holiday. She regards flower gardens as salad bars, but only when she's furious.)

Returning to my haircut: I re-enter the living room and dare to use the terrifying phrase "Notice anything different?" on my spouse. My husband, wildly scanning his imagination for possible answers as if he were being asked a tough question on the marital S.A.T.s, suggests that perhaps I've changed my makeup. I mention that I'm not wearing makeup. He says that counts as a change and so he has answered correctly and has to get full marks for the response. I tell him I got my hair cut. He asks me what he should say about it.

I leave the room and count to 5,987, return to where he is reading the paper, and proceed to tell him that he might say something like, "Your hair looks nice." He says, "Your hair looks nice. You should see how it looks if you put on makeup," at which point he returns to reading the paper. I leave the room and count to $9 \times 5,987$, which is a very high number, and contemplate a life of celibacy. I think about how his suits would look if I sewed leather patches all over them—not just on the elbows.

I'm considering how to be best revenged at a colleague who has sneered, "Well, if I wanted to stay home and write *popular* books, I'd consider myself a traitor to the academy." I'm also trying to deal with the student who stormed into my office making vague threats because she has somehow calculated that by getting a C+, a C, and a C− on last term's exams, she deserves at least a B "because I showed up to almost every class and took a lot of notes.''

I'm not feeling all warm and fuzzy about the old friend who has told me that he's getting divorced because ''After she turned forty, she just couldn't make me feel the same as she did when we were first together.'' I grip the phone until my knuckles are white and yield to the temptation to tell him that he hasn't exactly become Mel Gibson in the passing years. I feel good about my little humorous-vengeful statement, but then I hear him smile—a neat trick, when you come to think about it. All smug and happy, ignoring my remark, he says, ''Oh, but it's different for a man.'' I am mostly angry that he is right. As Cynthia Heimel has pointed out, in the space of five years Sally Field went from playing Tom Hanks's object of desire in *Punchline* to playing his mom in *Forrest Gump* because Field hit the age wall in the film business. And all the while I'm thinking that it's a really good thing that gun control laws exist and apply to me personally. Because if there's anything that makes me want to take revenge, it's exactly this kind of frustration. (A friend of mine who lives in a small suburban town plagued by armed robberies grew fearful enough to suggest to her husband that they buy a handgun to protect themselves. The husband thought for a while, but then decided it would be a bad idea. ''You can't keep ice cream in the house for more than two hours without eating it,'' he pointed out to her. ''You think it would be a good idea for you to own a gun?'')

In the opening line to a clever article titled ''Anger: Your Best Power Tool,'' Judith Stone writes ''I got in touch with my anger. We met for lunch. Things went well. It moved in.'' In contrast to Stone, I've spent much of my life trying to stay out of touch with my anger; the trouble is my *anger* keeps trying to get in touch with *me*.

"I'd change my name and phone number if it meant my anger would have a harder time finding me," I tell Ellen, who nods in sympathy, having just yelled her way out of her third job this year.

Getting Angry and Getting Mad

"Having a temper is like having an old boyfriend—you want it to stay as far away from you as possible and you want it to stop interfering with your life," she murmurs in agreement, explaining that "anger is nothing you need or desire, but it's there anyway." We are in perfect agreement, but the real question is: How should we deal with it? Is it truly best for all anger to be handled as if it were nuclear waste, to be disposed of as quickly and silently as possible—only to surface later in some mutant manifestation of its latent power?

It's tough for me to get angry without getting mad. "You lose all sense of perspective!" one ex-lover wrote in his good-bye note. I'm told that I first roar, then weep, and then inevitably end up apologizing. Those apologies are the worst part. There's usually a feeling of sheepish humility, a sense of embarrassment at having let myself go, of giving way to emotion. "If you get angry at your husband and slam down the phone," my assistant tells me, "it doesn't take more than twelve minutes for you to become a shuddering ball of penitence and fear." Every time seems new to me, but my friends tell me I have a pattern. The litany of questions starts, and they're always the same ones: Will he ever forgive me? Will he like me again? Why would he put up with a woman who behaves so badly? Why can't I be nice? Why do I get so mad at the thought that I have to learn to be nice?

"How do those *other* women do it?" Ellen wails. "You know, the ladylike ones who remain silent and smiling at the cosmetics counter for what seems like a good four or five days without getting a glimpse of their free sample. After seeing fifteen minutes of a one-hour lunch break go down the drain, I begin to mutter to the poor soul standing next to me something about needing to buy more eye cream to take care of the wrinkles I've acquired during the time I've spent waiting on this line."

"I know, I know," I interrupt, to finish the scene I know so well: "She'll smile gently at your sarcastic remark, this good soul, and you'll bite your tongue and swear inwardly that you'll be like her."

"Yes, that's it," agrees Ellen. "Every time I tell myself that I won't be bitchy, I'll behave."

But then, says the little devil on my left shoulder, *I'll* spend four days waiting at a counter without being served. I'll stop insisting on a good table in a restaurant when I'm eating alone that evening because I'll be too nice to ask to be moved away from the family of seventeen. I'll stop insisting that my husband be faithful or a boss be fair because I'll feel as if an angry response is unwarranted. Maybe I'll get to the point where I'll listen to pubic-hair jokes without screaming or calling a lawyer or taking the case in front of a congressional hearing if the guy telling the pubic-hair joke ever comes up for nomination to the Supreme Court.

"To be angry is to revenge the fault of others upon ourselves," intoned Alexander Pope in what I can only imagine was a sanctimonious English accent. Easy for him to say (even though it could be argued that half his poems were written as revenge). When I'm in a bad mood

I want to tell Alexander to go soak his bewigged head. Not only is anger *not* an unfamiliar emotion; anger is my buddy, my life's companion, my chum.

Once again, Judith Stone has an interesting point to make about women's anger. Stone quips, "I'm a good girl on my mother's side" and goes on to explain that in her early training, "like so many other women, I'd learned early to say 'No, of course I'm not angry!' when I meant 'I'd like to mambo on your spleen in spikes.'" Fearing that she would alienate everyone around her if she let rip into rage, Stone ends her article by discussing the ways in which everyone can best use their anger.

I worry about losing the best that anger can offer as well as the worst, throwing out the right anger with the wrong. Since we're taught from our cradles onward that a temper in a girl is much worse than a temper in a boy— like all the other things women have had to learn for ourselves—it is not surprising that we need to get a sense of how to do it without overdoing it.

"So," I ask Ellen, "where do we draw the line?"

"Remember when you got as angry at the clerk who gave you the wrong change as you did at the boyfriend who called his other girlfriend long-distance from your office phone?" she asked. The very memory made me grab the table for support. "You should have made a distinction between the two." Now she tells me! "The right thing to do with the clerk is simply point out that he or she has made an error, and the right thing to do with the boyfriend is simply pour WD-40 in his Grecian Formula."

Anger as a Magnifying Glass

The key seems to be perspective. Anger, like revenge, generally can be a positive force and do some good without unnecessarily hurting anyone. In her best-selling book, *The Dance of Anger*, Harriet Lerner declares without apology that "anger is a signal, and one worth listening to." Most of the time, when anger tries to get in touch with me, I'll just leave a message saying I'm having too good a time to return the call. At other times anger becomes too great an indicator of important issues to be overlooked.

Anger is like a magnifying glass: Depending on your perspective, it either distorts everything or makes everything clearer. Anger is one of the last remaining emotions that can make us feel ashamed of ourselves. It's embarrassing to be angry, and so many of us have learned how to hide it effectively that we sometimes manage to hide it even from ourselves. But anger doesn't disappear just because it's not seen; every closed eye doesn't mean a peaceful sleep. Anger—whether it's hidden or out in the open—is at the heart of the desire for revenge. My anger takes over when I'm feeling out of control in my life; for others, anger is what they use to control the world around them.

Paradoxically, anger is also an emotion that can make us feel unashamed and even stronger after we feel defeated and humiliated. It can help to restore a sense of self-worth, because anger is an indication that you merit judicious treatment. It's also an indication that you believe the world is not chaotic, not unreasonable, and not random in its distribution of goodies and whacks. Anger indicates that you think life should be fair.

When life isn't fair, we get angry. Perhaps I should narrow this down a bit: When life isn't fair to *us* or to those we love, we get angry. When life is unfair to others, we get philosophical. It's pretty easy to deal with the gross inequities of the world when you're dealing with them from a distance. Anger is a response that draws on the immediacy of experience, although it must be emphasized that historically the best and most productive anger does move beyond the personal into the political and the social. When, for example, individuals are angry enough at an injustice perpetrated by the society of which they are a part to take it personally, they can affect great and lasting change.

Anger, like smoke, curls around the edges of many civil rights demonstrations; anger informs and always has informed some of the most important debates and movements in this country. To believe in a cause with passion is to risk encountering anger—in one's self, in one's opponent—but the risk is sometimes worth it.

To say we are willing to fight for a cause might not be literal, but the figure of speech is telling: When we put ourselves on the line for an idea, there is at least an implied threat that the overthrow or defeat of our position will raise a response—that we will become angry, and perhaps angry enough to literalize the metaphor. We might actually have to fight in order to win. When it comes to matters of belief, we might find that we would rather fight than switch. Anger is inflexible. Perhaps its inflexibility is what makes it one of the seven deadly sins.

It's undeniable that inflexibility can be a weakness; after all, anger makes us lash out at our loved ones, makes us bitter and self-destructive, makes us miserable company. But righteous anger's unwillingness to compromise can also be a strength. And the same can be said of anger:

It can mark a blind and foolish refusal to negotiate with life's realities and disappointments, but it can also mark a triumphant turning point.

"Anger stirs and wakes in her," writes Toni Morrison in *The Bluest Eye*, a novel about an abused child's coming of age. "It opens its mouth, and like a hot-mouthed puppy, laps up the dredges of her shame. Anger is better. There is a sense of being in anger. A reality and presence. An awareness of worth." This last point is perhaps the most important one: If you allow yourself to get angry at an injustice committed against you, you underwrite your emotion with a sense of self-worth. If you get angry at an injustice committed against others, you underwrite their value with a sense of your own worth. Anger can offer a sense of indignity to replace a sense of shame.

The All-Revenge Wedding

Some of the revenge stories that get passed around like chain mail involve precisely this sort of replacement of shame by rage. One story that I heard from women in New York, St. Paul, *and* Toronto—who all swore that it happened to someone whom a friend of theirs actually knew—involves just this sort of gratifying movement from embarrassment and self-doubt to justified anger and appropriate revenge. The details of the story changed very little from one city to the next. A young woman without a pedigree is about to marry into a fairly aristocratic family. Her fiancé, a man of some means, generously offers to foot the bill for the wedding and she gratefully accepts, given that she has very little money herself. (She was described as a freelance writer, a medical student, and a dancer by the respective narrators.) It all seems like a fairy tale until she discovers that her betrothed has been sleeping with her maid of honor.

The bride-to-be decides, uncharacteristically, not to do anything about it. The one or two friends who are certain that she knows are surprised by her lack of action, but they keep their shock to themselves. They think that their friend must have decided that the financial security was worth the humiliation. The wedding day comes and everything goes beautifully until the minister asks, in front of the assembled congregation of several hundred guests—most of whom are on the groom's upright and conservative family's side—whether anyone has a reason that these two should not be joined in matrimony.

The bride turns away from the altar and addresses the guests, saying, "I know why we cannot be wed. He's sleeping with the maid of honor." Walking out of the church into a waiting taxi, she leaves him with a red face, an angry and ashamed lover, and a huge bill for the nonexistent wedding reception.

It's no surprise that this story, whether urban myth or something closer to an actual incident, gets repeated as the sworn truth: It has all the elements of positive revenge. The young woman did not sit around wondering what she did wrong to "drive" her fiancé into the arms of another woman; she did not exonerate those closest to her by blaming herself for their selfish actions. Her anger clarified the impossibility of her situation and allowed her to leave with her self-esteem intact after a severe setback. One imagines that lessons were learned all around.

Turning Over a New Leaf

But not all acts of getting even can be committed with such deliberately balanced methods and consequences, especially when they involve truly powerless individuals. "I lived with my brother and his wife when I was growing up," began one caller to a radio program where the topic of discussion was revenge. I was on the other end of the line and immediately sensed the hurt and anger in the voice of the woman who was speaking. She was an adult, and the incident she was relating happened many years ago, but the skid marks were still on her soul.

"My brother was a decent man, taking me in after our parents died, but his wife was awful. She was cold and aloof, and made sure I knew that I was living off their charity. One day in fifth grade I dared to bring two friends home from school, and she humiliated me in front of them by saying that while she had to provide food and lodging for me, she wasn't under any obligation to provide it for the whole town. I was afraid to tell my brother because I thought he might side with her and I didn't have anywhere else to go. It was awful.

"About a week later I was just sitting in their formal living room and I got the idea to tear out one page from every book in their library. It took me almost a year, but I think that I got to every single volume. I used to wad up the pieces of paper and carry them in my pocket so that I could touch them and tell myself that I found a way to get back at her. Somehow it calmed the fury that had nowhere to go. It's taken me fifteen years of therapy to admit that I ever committed that secret crime. The irony is that I am now a librarian. I spend my time taking care of books."

Much has been written about anger, mostly about how to work through it, but working through anger is like working through a three-thousand-piece jigsaw puzzle of the aerial map of Antarctica: It's an invigorating idea in the abstract but almost impossible to do in the natural span of an ordinary lifetime. Besides, "working through" anger might not necessarily purge the emotion; sometimes facing the anger and the need for reciprocity against an injury can underscore a long-standing grievance.

In fact, the knowledge that you will seek from revenge can help you to put your rage aside. "I knew a man so accustomed to revenge that he didn't even have to carry the small change of anger around with him," said an elderly gentleman, referring to a gangster he knew in his youth. But clearly revenge should not be associated only with men in fedoras; sometimes the good side wins, motivated in part by healthy anger and the desire for revenge at the right time.

Getting the Message Across

When an unidentified neighbor of Taylor's bought a van equipped with a new gadget that actually shouted, in a deep voice, "You are too near this vehicle" and parked it outside her apartment building on a busy Chicago street, Taylor thought she would lose her mind. The voice alarm went off constantly, and as a freelance writer whose office was just outside the first-floor window, Taylor was interrupted in her work during the day and in her sleep at night. She left notes on the van's window, asking the owner to please disarm or at least *fine-tune* his or her alarm system so that it would not shout every time someone walked past it. Nothing changed. She asked the police if they could do anything but they couldn't. She asked the folks on her floor for suggestions, but apart from ones involving crowbars and other glass-breaking objects, she was left to figure out a peaceful way to get her point across.

One night when she was preparing a mass mailing for the next day's post, she looked at the dozens of sheets of mailing labels and had an idea. On these labels, instead of printing addresses, she printed messages saying: "Please do not ignore this. Please stop your car alarm from waking us all up. Or: Your alarm is too sensitive. Please have it fixed." She took the sheets of sticky labels down to the van and, page by page, plastered them all over the vehicle's windows. The labels did not come off in sheets, but individually, so that the owner would have to scrape them off one at a time. The van did not reappear on her block, and Taylor only hoped that it had found a quiet home in a peaceful parking garage.

Anger on Behalf of Others

"Nothing makes me madder than to see the powerful step on the weak," growls my friend Peter, who is a partner in a law firm. "I rarely get angry on my own behalf because I know I can take care of myself, but I'm very aware of the fact that I'm in a privileged position. I do a lot of pro bono work because when a client comes in who has a legitimate grievance and can't afford to pay to get justice, my sense of anger kicks in. Like when a day-care center was being threatened by a landlord who wanted to break the lease to bring in a dance studio he could get more money from. The co-op nursery got the full benefit of my anger against the landlord. My wife says that I inevitably make the other side sound like the Antichrist, but I like my anger and I enjoy settling those kinds of scores."

The belief that some version of fate will take care of the vulnerable and punish the wicked is the linchpin of the myth that promises that, as long as you trust that good will triumph, everything will work out on its own. In general, therefore, people are expected to remain part of— that is, they believe they should be part of—a system that will always make everything come out even in the end, that will balance the scales without anybody having to put his thumb down on the edge to make sure the scales are balanced. No one is more angry at injustice than someone who once believed that justice was guaranteed.

"They kept talking in front of me as if I wasn't there, or as if I were an immigrant who didn't understand English," growls Marco, an engineering student at an Ivy League school who happens to be African-American. "When I was trying to get a car loan from a local bank in this fairly provincial town where my university is located, I was a victim of the kind of prejudice I had rarely experienced so overtly before. My parents would have been happy to buy me the car, but I wanted to get a Fiat and I didn't want my father's opinion—I decided to be independent, and I suppose I wasn't properly prepared to deal with the more deleterious aspects of bureaucracy. I'm a product of prep schools, and I guess I've dealt with a more subtle and rarefied kind of discrimination, but this was like something from a sixties movie starring Sidney Poitier. They were asking one another questions about my finances that I should have been answering.

Finally I asked if I could use one of their phones. In front of the loan officers I'd been talking to I put in a call to my uncle, an official at the Treasury Department in Washington. I explained the situation and asked if he would speak to the loan officer directly. She got as red as her nail polish and was stammering by the time she finished the conversation. I don't usually pull rank, but I was prepared to embark on a reign of aristocratic terror by that point. I got the loan and a letter of apology. Anger can be cleansing, useful, baptismal.''

Car Tales

This is only one of many examples of revenge stories I've heard involving cars; most of the others involved cars already on the road. When National Public Radio host Faith Middleton opened the phone lines to hear about revenge fantasies, the switchboard was overwhelmed by car tales. In part this might have been prompted by the fact that both Faith and I had opened the program by talking about how we each independently came to the conclusion that a collective act of revenge should be perpetrated against the drivers of tractor-trailers who tailgate their smaller brethren until we are too terrified to drive on the interstate. Callers spoke of fantasies involving paint being sprayed automatically onto any vehicle coming within five feet of a car—preferably, paint in bright indelible colors spelling out ''I am a moronic driver.'' One caller who identified himself as a perpetual pedestrian wanted to arm himself with spray guns of paint—or paint remover—to mark those cars that went plowing through designated walkways and well-traveled intersections without taking into account the fact that a slow-moving pedestrian might be making his innocent way across the road.

One CB aficionado called to say that when trucks passed him at dangerously high speeds he would invent a ''smoky report'' indicating a police presence that inevitably slowed them down. When asked why this seemingly preventative measure was an act of revenge, the caller made it clear that he always said that the police had been located a few miles back—just where these drivers had been going seventy or eighty with an overload of freight. Apparently this made them feel rather anxious.

Venting their frustrations and laughing about their angry fantasies seemed to make the participants feel good rather than bad about the world. After what had been a long, rough trip to the radio station, plagued by those who learned their driving skills at the Mad Max School of Automotive Courtesy, I, too, felt relieved of the burden of some anger, having spread it out on the bread of a collective experience.

When the fantasies recounted on Faith's show didn't involve cars, they seemed to involve politicians. Faith hoped that Rush Limbaugh would one day wake up in heaven only to find that God had put Whoopi Goldberg in charge. Other suggestions included finding pictures of Newt Gingrich in a pink gown, and having Thelma and Louise preside at a new hearing about Clarence Thomas's nomination to the Supreme Court. (Interestingly, Eleanor Smeal, president of the Fund for the Feminist Majority, actually welcomed the fallout from the Clarence Thomas appointment. Smeal suggested that, during the Hill-Thomas hearings, "The Senate did more in one week to underscore the critical need for more women in the Senate than feminists have been able to do in 25 years").

Instant Revenge

Anger lurks in the background, perhaps informing actions and patterns of behavior in ways that cannot be charted because their cause remains hidden and therefore unexamined. Often the anger is then turned toward the self, or toward even more powerless companions. But when anger leads to revenge, it often moves in the opposite direction:

It moves upward, against the more powerful.

Louise, a secretary who has done excellent work for her New York employers for well over ten years, told me a story of how she lets the "muckety-mucks" know that they should be nice to everybody. "Some snotty consultant from out of town wanted me to get her two tickets to see Beethoven at Lincoln Center. She was very curt and very condescending. So instead of calling the orchestra, I phoned the theater across the street from Lincoln Center and booked her two seats to see a kids' movie about a dog, which also happened to be called *Beethoven*. I had the tickets messengered to her hotel with a note that said 'Welcome to New York, where you're treated as well as you treat others.' " Explaining that "if you can't strike back when it hurts, you then end up lashing out at other people who don't deserve it," Louise was confident that her bosses would back her in her action. That she's usually the most generous and helpful person in the office is well known. When bothered past the point of acceptability, however, Louise declares, "I act fast and get my anger out of the way."

Those who have been abused or treated with an undeserved harshness often grow up feeding on anger and cutting their teeth on rage. Perhaps the best example of the disowned and spurned offspring was created by Mary Shelley two hundred years ago. The monster in *Frankenstein* instantly aroused the reading public's interest and sympathy, and the creature still commands print and screen attention. Kenneth Branagh's film version is a recent treatment.

"If I Cannot Inspire Love..."

The monster is enraged, not at his circumstances generally, but at the neglect and rejection shown by his creator. He enters the world believing in goodness and only the vile way he is treated leads him to want his revenge. "I was benevolent and good; misery made me a fiend. Make me happy, and I shall again be virtuous," pleads the monster to Frankenstein. "How can I move thee? Will no entreaties cause thee to turn a favourable eye upon thy creature, who implores thy goodness and compassion? . . . My soul glowed with love and humanity; but am I not alone, miserably alone? You, my creator, abhor me; what hope can I gather from your fellow creatures, who owe me nothing?"

Denied companionship and compassion, the monster turns to raw vengeance. "I will revenge my injuries," he vows. "If I cannot inspire love, I will cause fear. . . . If any being felt emotions of benevolence towards me, I should return them a hundred and a hundredfold; for that one creature's sake I would make peace with the whole kind!" But there is no possibility of commiseration, and so Frankenstein becomes the target for the bottomless rage of his creation. "Are you to be happy while I grovel in the intensity of my wretchedness?" the monster wails. "You can blast my other passions, but revenge remains—revenge, henceforth dearer than light or food! I may die, but first you, my tyrant and tormentor, shall curse the sun that gazes on your misery. Beware, for I am fearless and therefore powerful. I will watch with the wiliness of a snake, that I may sting with its venom. Man, you shall repent of the injuries you inflict." Shelley's novel creates an embodiment of revenge, and gives voice to the buried and unresolved anger that is the hallmark of human existence. In his misery and his longing for vengeance, the monster is very human indeed.

What the most recent film version of *Frankenstein* has in common with another classic revenge tale is actor Robert De Niro. In Martin Scorsese's successful remake of the movie *Cape Fear*, De Niro, along with Nick Nolte, presents one of the most raw and unmediated obsessions imaginable. De Niro's character, Cady, is imprisoned for a violent rape in part because defense attorney Nolte did not provide a fully adequate defense on his behalf. Once-illiterate Cady leaves prison having learned to read well enough to understand the finer points of the law with which he now intends to torment the man whom he regards as his betrayer. He wants restitution for his lost time and lost life. When offered money by the lawyer, Cady chides him: "So, shall we itemize? What shall be my remuneration for being held down and sodomized by four white guys? Four black guys? Shall my compensation be the same? What is the formula, sir?" Distraught over the world's abandonment of him, Cady decides, like Frankenstein's monster before him, to teach those who have betrayed him lessons in loss.

Like the monster, Cady is wildly beyond being able to forgive and forget, and focuses his rage on the one man who could have once helped him. The two become obsessed with each other, bound in a rage as mutual and gripping as the most passionate romance. They are enthralled by each other; they cannot escape the entanglements of their hatred any more than Romeo and Juliet could have escaped their love. "I'm the best thing that ever happened to you," hisses Cady. "I bring meaning to your spiritless life. . . . Well, you know what the Good

Book says about a rich man's chances of getting into heaven. . . . So I've come to divest you of some assets. Remind you what *wretched* means. You are going to learn about loss, Counselor. . . .''

Rage and Sympathy

As loathsome as Cady and the monster are, they nevertheless remain archetypal figures who elicit from their audience great sympathy as well as great outrage. The rage felt by these beings, rejected and despised even by those who by rights should be their allies, surely touches us where we ourselves are most vulnerable. Their rage is the rage of every child whose bedroom door is shut against the light by a parent too tired or too frustrated to offer comfort, the rage of the teenager whose belligerence betrays a fear of abandonment more than a sense of independence, the rage of the offspring ignored, damaged, or abandoned by a loved one. They reflect, in other words, a part of ordinary human experience. No one has been adequately loved at all times, and therefore no one has escaped some version of the anger embodied by these two larger-than-life figures.

Something that should not be overlooked, however, is that there is a concept of responsibility for the initial hurtful action. Only when someone seeks to harm us specifically do our most profound desires for revenge surface. Someone who meant us no harm, who hurt us inadvertently, or who could not help but act a certain way does not usually call forth our rancor.

We don't yell at old folks who accidentally prod us with their canes; we don't accuse babies of throwing up on our suits for spite. A lesson can only be learned by someone who can grasp the underlying point; retaliation depends, in part, on the response of the other person. If you stub your toe on a chair, you might swear but you wouldn't put a curse on it—or any piece of furniture, for that matter. If your alarm clock fails to wake you up for an important meeting, you don't blame it personally, and you probably wouldn't spend a whole lot of time figuring out how to get even with your Bulova. But if your roommate doesn't wake you up for an interview, and instead goes to the meeting herself hoping to land the job, a little retaliation might not be out of order.

When faced with acts or words edged with cruelty, indifference to justice, or gross unfairness, even the kindest souls might find themselves considering revenge. "There was one kid who used to wait for me by the bus stop every day on the way home from school," recalls an editor in his mid-thirties. "He was a bully straight out of central casting—he seemed to be about thirty-five, but he was probably only eighteen or nineteen. Still, that's pretty old to still be in school. He was bigger than me, and much more intimidating than I could ever be, and really I had no alternative except to let him beat me up or walk the mile or so and avoid the bus. Sometimes he'd get at me in front of a bunch of other kids or a girl I liked, and the physical pain was nothing compared to the emotional agony. I didn't dare get back at him in any way that would permit him to identify me, but I needed to vent some of my anger. I went camping one weekend and brought back a bag of assorted animal droppings—not a fun thing to do in and of itself, believe me, but it was for a good cause—and I mailed it to him. I don't think he ever found out that it was from me, but whenever I saw him hanging around trying to look tough and cool, I could at least think, Yeah, you look really cool now, but I know that one afternoon you came home and opened a box of wild animal droppings and you didn't know who it was from. Actually, this guy probably didn't even know *what* they were, he was that stupid. I didn't have as much anger afterwards because I knew I had at least made him very uncomfortable. It was small-minded and dumb, but I was glad I did it.''

The Power of Collective Outrage

If you want to study or understand someone's outlook, you must observe what arouses a deep emotion in him or her, and anger is one of the deepest emotions of all. All of our life's experiences have an integral emotional environment, and anger often brings the most central of these emotions to the surface, acting like an irritation that raises a rash, or like the friction that produces an image on a piece of paper placed over a tombstone's engraving.

"My anger was like a slow and stately ship traveling across the abyss of the relationship I was in," intones David. "I loved Peter from the moment I met him, and for six years he loved me back. One day he simply stopped—or that's how it appeared to me. He moved out a week after he declared that we were no longer right for each other, leaving me with full payments on the mortgage and all our bills, as well as a broken heart. Soon I found out that he had moved in with someone I had considered a mutual friend who lived on the other side of town. When I could no longer stand being Mr. Nice Guy, I bought a can of spray paint and waited until after dark on a night I knew they'd be out. Well, I had no idea how truly difficult it is to do graffiti properly. I got the first few letters across the front of their white-brick Georgian building—'BAST'—but I couldn't fit the 'ARDS' on the same line and had to put it underneath. As I drove away I thought about it and decided that it would bother them more the way I'd done it since it was unsightly as well as vulgar and rude.''

Whoever wants to become acquainted with the most authentic self of another person should listen to the language spoken about the most typically masked emotions in their life, anger being paramount among these. In anger we demonstrate, explain, and reveal our deepest selves. To observe how we use anger, then, is to stand at an angle of vision that allows sight into otherwise hidden corners. It permits us to view the emotional and ideological landscape of our own lives and the lives of those around us. "I realized that I lashed out at people who exhibited weaknesses that I felt I had myself," admitted a young athlete. "I would go bonkers and want to kill a guy who talked about missing practice. I became the conscience for the team and it was my job to see to it that anybody who screwed off got 'punished,' until I saw that I was being used by the other guys. I didn't need that kind of anger. I even started missing practice a couple of times myself. It made me less pissed off at other people and let me lighten up. I was getting revenge only on myself when I was punishing them.''

"Anger as Soon as Fed Is Dead..."

Admitting our anger and our desire for revenge, even to ourselves, can give voice to important aspects of our personalities. It can also be the beginning of a change of heart and mind that can paradoxically lead to freedom from negative emotions. Admitting anger can be the first step in getting rid of it. As poet Emily Dickinson wrote more than a hundred years ago, anticipating today's psychologists, "Anger as soon as fed is dead / 'Tis starving makes it fat."

This leads to a basic but crucial question concerning the relationship between anger and revenge: Why do we often choose to bury our anger, only to use it later as a catalyst, under the thinnest disguises, for a series of actions apparently caused by a different set of circumstances?

Michael Corleone in Mario Puzo's *The Godfather* is set upon by bad cops who beat the hell out of him despite the fact that he is a war hero and an honors student who has not until that point been involved with his father's business. As his previously untapped anger emerges in a frost, not in a flame, Puzo tells us that "at all costs he wanted to hide the delicious icy chilliness that controlled his brain, the surge of wintry cold hatred that pervaded his body. He wanted to give no warning to anyone as to how he felt at this moment." Perhaps part of the instinctive mechanism for this burying of anger—either consciously or unconsciously manipulated—lies in the fact that, after all, we find fully flushed anger intolerable to sustain and difficult to make work for us. Anger is unwieldy. In its grip we fear losing control that might help us achieve justice. " 'Never get angry,' the Don had instructed. 'Never make a threat. Reason with people.' The word 'reason' sounded so much better in Italian, *rajunah*, to rejoin."

The Corleone family's methods for reasoning with someone have less to do with the foundations of Aristotelian logic than they have to do with the poured concrete foundations of buildings, but the point remains an interesting one. When the power of "reason" becomes synonymous with the power of irrevocable force to provide a response to any harm done, then only a masochist is unreasonable. The twinning of the two terms—reason and rejoin—is useful in understanding how those who traffic in revenge justify their ways and means. "You will understand my reasons for doing what I do" becomes the definition of a reasonable man.

We look for closure in order to put our anger to rest. "I wanted to leave my mark on my ex-girlfriend's life," says a young man who is clearly destined to break a few hearts of his own despite the fact that he is currently grieving after the loss of his first college romance. "Before I left, I taught her pet parrot to say 'Sammy loved me,' 'I want Sammy back,' and even a slightly garbled version of 'Meaningless affair' which sort of came out sounding like 'Pieces of eight.' "

Upstairs, Downstairs

"Three years I spent looking for the right apartment," explained Paul, a financial consultant in New York who prides himself on thoroughly researching and planning his life to the smallest detail. "I read over minutes from co-op board meetings to see whether I'd agree with their policies, I spoke to those inhabitants of the buildings who would talk about their experiences—in short, I did everything possible to make an excellent choice. The apartment I moved into was flawless: big, great views of the river, marble floors in the bathroom and kitchen, everything I wanted including an overall sense of elegance. I was supremely happy for about a month. Then the woman upstairs found a new companion. He was a musician, and astonishingly bad at his chosen craft.

"He was a saxophone player. He played constantly—she was away much of the day, and often away for days on business—and I was losing my mind. I did everything I could to ask them gracefully to make this hideous routine cease but they ignored me. Finally I enlisted the help of other annoyed owners, a few of my friends, and the building's superintendent (who, with the help of some cash in his palm, was eager to come to my aid). We made sure that their essential daily lives were as devastated as ours. The sax player's apartment turned out to be a hard place to live: Fuses kept blowing, their water was often on very low pressure, their mail was often delayed or lost. They asked those of us living near them if we had similar problems and we ignored their inquiries the way they had ignored ours. Their phone rang at all hours of the day and night, especially late at night about an hour after his playing had stopped. Needless to say, they moved out. The next couple who moved in are wonderful, and there's never been a problem in the building since. For a bunch of basically conservative individuals, we certainly learned the value of collective action."

Collective revenge within small communities is fairly common, especially when the community is created by shared living spaces or work environments. According to Vita, a graduate student who lives in a dorm suite with six other women, anyone who deliberately refuses to obey the agreed-upon rules of the community deserves censure if they cannot be convinced by persuasion. "One of the women wouldn't keep her own makeup and hygiene products in her room," Vita told me, "which is what we all agreed. If everybody left their stuff in the one bathroom we all shared, it would be chaos, so the rest of us respected this but she didn't. For a while we just picked her stuff up and put it on her bedside table. Then we started to throw it into a bag and leave it on her bed. Finally we started throwing it away. She was furious, but we all agreed that unless she stuck to the collective agreement this is what would happen. She got the message." While this might seem like mild revenge, it nevertheless represents a common form of group action concerning a member who considers herself beyond the reach of the usual standards. Such people are often the target of collective revenge.

Swimsuit and Sibling Rivalries

In a less typical situation among roommates, I heard a story from one of three sisters who worked in New York and shared a living space. Living in an apartment owned by their family, they were fairly comfortable except for the antics of the middle sister, who was particularly competitive. This sister was forever boasting about how she stuck to her diet and exercise plan while her sisters were less concerned with their appearance. She would tease them about their lack of suitors, and whined when she couldn't quite get the zipper closed on her size-six jumpsuit, asking them to help.

"When she bought a tiny two-piece bathing suit last summer," giggled one of the other sisters, "we immediately went to the store and bought the same one in a size four. We took the size six out of her drawer and substituted the smaller one; she couldn't tell the difference until she went to wear it. Of course, when we all went to the Hamptons, she was miserable because she was spilling out all over the place. She felt fat and stupid. It was how she made us feel, so we sat there in our bathing suits that fit us properly and smiled the smiles of the gratified.''

The largest collective action, of course, is the due process of law. When personal anger can be channeled into this fundamental device for achieving vindication, there can be the most satisfying revenge of all: public acknowledgment of a wrong committed against you. In his essay "An Explanation for Retribution," ethicist Andrew Oldenquist argues that "when revenge is expressed through institutional ritual and ceremony, the actions of individuals are transformed into the actions of a community; the private act of an individual becomes, through ritualization, the moral act of a collectivity. The indignation of the community is expressed in solemnity, black robes, and ritual, which is a transformation and sublimation of anger and invective. If all of this is so, revenge is not eliminated and replaced by something totally different, but only civilized, 'sanitized.' In distinguishing retributive justice from revenge, we do not take the revenge out of retribution—this cannot be done.''

In Herbert Packer's "Justifications for Criminal Punishment," the legal scholar argues that legal resources are "as capable of serving as outlets for feelings of revenge as are undisguised pleas to make the offender pay. Indeed, these claims may be less defensible than straightforward pleas for revenge.'' Karl Menninger offered a similar opinion when he wrote decades earlier that "personal revenge we have renounced, but official legalized revenge we can still enjoy. Once someone has been labeled an offender and proved guilty of an offense he is fair game.'' Menninger adds an undeniably compelling point: "We approve severe penalties for those offenses which most of us feel little temptation to commit.''

The Bottom Line

Perhaps this impulse to delight in reprisals against those who commit deeds we are unlikely to replicate is behind the attention paid to a tale of revenge—*tale* being a particularly appropriate word in this case—that made headlines in 1990. The *Chicago Tribune*'s version of the incident, which took place in a bar near the St. Louis law school that both parties attended, stated that "emboldened by 'three beers,' [Charles A. 'Chep'] Hurth decided to make his move. He had chatted with [Maia] Brodie briefly earlier in the evening. Apparently at bottom for any pickup lines, Hurth showed his interest by planting a fierce bite on Brodie's buttocks. Not smitten in the least, Brodie felt nothing but shame, pain and embarrassment." One St. Louis paper ran as its headline "HE BIT HERS, SO SHE SUED HIS"; one wit commented that "in this case, you are what you eat."

Brodie took Hurth to court (both looking "like they had walked straight out of the *Preppy Handbook*," according to the *Tribune*) and won $25,000 in punitive damages. Perhaps the court was willing to rise to the occasion because Charles A. Hurth III had, as an undergraduate at Vanderbilt, tried his "toothsome come-on" at fraternity parties. One of them went on to date him, he testified. "He could not remember the woman's name." According to a piece in the *St. Louis Post-Dispatch*, "He told Brodie she should take his chomp on her rump as a compliment." Her revenge was to exercise the community censure to its fullest in the eyes of the court and the press. One hopes that, as a prospective lawyer, Hurth was discredited in the eyes of his peers and appeared a fool to the community at large. At the very least Brodie made sure that she walked away the winner, and that she made it safe for other women to turn their backs on Hurth without the fear of receiving one of his "compliments."

Perhaps the most striking feature of people's descriptions of their feelings of rage is the emphasis on the clarifying nature of the emotion: It seems to reduce everything to an almost primordial state where complex relationships or mitigating circumstances are out of the picture. The purifying fire of anger can make revenge easy to imagine and easy to exact. "Once I was mad, I was well on my way towards seeking justice," said one community activist. "And I wasn't going to allow myself to be sweet-talked with promises of better times coming. I wanted to get direct action now, and if that meant making trouble, I made trouble for whoever needed it most."

Revenge is the handiwork of the powerless. Those who are unable to prevent an action from occurring because they lack conventional power will not lack the power to revenge the action once it has occurred. This is one of the great tragedies of modern life and one of the most significant aspects of the argument concerning the function of getting even in the lives of many people.

Take an all-too-familiar example: A woman cannot prevent her ex-husband from beating her even after the courts have issued multiple orders of protection. She has abandoned hope that the courts will punish him for such actions. She is driven to feel, therefore, as if the only way to put her life into some balance is by killing her assailant. She learns through pain to "put up or shut up." She discovers the inconsistencies and contradictions of a world in which she can assume the power to punish but not to protect, since even threats of violence have not protected her in the past.

The desire for revenge churns up an unnerving conflict for those who long to put the whole painful episode behind them, even as they also long for the satisfaction of engineering a scenario that ensures the correction of an injustice, or guaranteeing retribution for a wrong committed. They want simultaneously to be forgiving and to see that their enemy is punished. Part of the anger people feel when they are in the midst of a revenge plot is anger at themselves for being unable to simply release the negative emotions and leave it at that.

Quiet Explosions

Stephen King has made a fortune and created a following by portraying the erupting anger of the dispossessed. In his characteristic plot, he presents readers with out-of-work writers, middle-aged, lonely (and therefore dangerous) men and women. Saturated with revenge, part of King's fundamental power comes from the visceral association of the reader with both the victims and the perpetrators of revenge. In *Carrie* we are introduced to a character who makes Medea look like Mother Teresa.

"She looked the part of the sacrificial goat, the constant butt, believer in left-handed monkey wrenches, perpetual foul-up, and she was," King writes, immediately creating both a sense of vulnerability and a sense of danger—Carrie is a girl with nothing to lose. Living with a mother whose sanity has long since deserted her, faced with the usual horrors of adolescence compounded by a bizarre and impoverished upbringing, Carrie becomes the target for everyone's ridicule until she discovers her extraordinary capacity and talent for revenge.

In one of her earliest discoveries of her telekinetic powers, she revenges herself on a local kid who ritually shouts insults at her. "Carrie glared at him with sudden smoking rage. The bike wobbled on its training wheels and suddenly fell over. Tommy screamed. The bike was on top of him. Carrie smiled and walked on. The sound of Tommy's wails was sweet, jangling music in her ears. If only she could make something like that happen whenever she liked." Discovering her rage and her powers of revenge, however, Carrie becomes possessed by them. "Carrie's whirling mind strove to find something huge enough to express her agony, shame, terror, hate, fear. It seemed her whole life had narrowed to this miserable, beaten point of rebellion. . . . It was time to teach them a lesson. Time to show them a thing or two."

When Carrie destroys the prom, destroys her vicious enemies, and wrecks the school gym, vowing to "get all of them. Every last one." She is the embodiment of the avenging outcast. She doesn't only burn down her house like other revenging heroines; for good measure, she burns down the school gym as well (thereby fulfilling the fantasy of many thousands of readers). Harnessing her anger and using her mind to punish those who have hurt her, she is a literally fantastic figure, able to make whatever she wishes come true. It is as if King creates Fannie Flagg's Towanda the Avenger's teenage sister, who limits her revenges to high-school matters.

Stephen King does not have a lock on the anger and revenge plot, however. *Paradise Lost*, by seventeenth-century poet John Milton, is still one of the best-known and most widely read pieces of revenge literature, even if King outsells him daily. In Milton, as in King, revenge is rarely portrayed as the act of a weak character, but is instead shown as an indication of intelligence, strength, and calculation. The struggle between Lucifer and God over the future of mankind's collective soul has become a pretty popular plot, but Milton's version remains one of the old standards. Since we all know how the story ends, it's clear that the three-hundred-year popularity of Milton's work depends not on plot but on presentation. Lucifer is an enormously seductive and wicked character—one Alec Baldwin or Jeremy Irons could easily play, for example—and he can be regarded as heroic at the beginning of his fight against the forces of good because of his intelligence, determination, and strength of will.

In a line so popular it has been quoted in innumerable movies and comic books—including one of the *Star Trek* films—Lucifer declares, "better to reign in hell than serve in heav'n." But as the poem progresses, we see Lucifer become progressively more obsessed with revenge until he is reduced to a hissing serpent, belly on the ground, stripped of his heroism and driven only by the need to destroy. Lucifer, realizing that he cannot win against God, must settle for revenge in place of winning, since that which is "not victory, is yet revenge." He will attract sinful human beings into his camp and "seduce them to our party" so that God himself will grow discouraged and wipe them off the face of the earth. "This would surpass common revenge, and interrupt his joy in our confusion, and our joy upraise in his disturbance," delights Satan. For a moment, seeing innocent Eve alone in the garden, he loses his focus and remains "stupidly good, of enmity disarmed," but he soon shakes himself back into his usual evil. In the end, even Satan must acknowledge, in another famous line, that "revenge, at first though sweet, bitter ere long back on itself recoils."

Of course, it isn't only the Dark Side that thinks about revenge. We hear in Psalm 55 the hope that God "shalt bring them down into the pit of destruction: bloody and deceitful men shall not live out half their days" and in Psalm 58 the detailed wish, "Break their teeth, O God, in their mouth: break out the great teeth of the young lions." Psalm 57 gives a fairly succinct biblical rendition of being hoist by one's own petard when the speaker declares that "They have prepared a net for my steps; my soul is bowed down: they have digged a pit before me, into the midst whereof they are fallen themselves," and the hope that the enemy will always be hurt by the boomeranging effect of his own evil designs: "Let them melt away as waters which run continually: when he bendeth his bow to shoot his arrows, let them be as cut in pieces." Are we to pity our enemies? Not exactly, since "The righteous shall rejoice when he seeth the vengeance: he shall wash his feet in the blood of the wicked." To see one's enemies punished becomes not only the satisfaction of the flesh, but food for the spirit; to see justice carried out on earth, according to the psalmists, will encourage the virtuous to see the benefits of their goodness and prove that God is not deaf to the prayers of His followers. "So that a man shall say, 'Verily there is a reward for the righteous: verily he is a God that judgeth in the earth.' "

Revenge as an Indicator of Deeper Issues

The revenger feels the thrill of embarking on a quest for the sake of righteousness. In achieving the goal, whether by harming his enemy or teaching him a lesson, the revenger usually regards himself as dealing with more than personal issues—he believes he is conquering injustice itself. For some, it becomes a game of wits: Once all the rules are gone, he is free to invent his own; he no longer feels the need to "play fair" because he believes he has not been dealt with fairly in the past. Revenge is a game for the defiant, the passionate, and the rebellious.

Often motivated by unconscious (or at the very least inarticulated) psychological needs and drives, many of which might be disguised as ways of achieving justice, the revenger can lose perspective concerning not only the real situation, but his own authentic aspirations. The specific need for justice can easily dwindle into the need for a general sense of personal potency. If the situation is resolved to his liking, the revenger might well take full credit for the success, whether or not he was actually instrumental in its achievement. Getting revenge can become the defining force in the life of an individual, who regards successful revenge as a primary affirmation of self-worth.

Anger deflects our attention from our own failings onto someone else's; it substitutes the pleasures of contemplating a range of actions we know we can implement for the desperate thoughts of what we could have done in the past; and revenge is unquestionably an intoxicating substance, one that makes us impervious to the slings and arrows of current misfortunes.

To take up this last point: Revenge is often regarded in the same light as a controlled substance, and an irresistible one at that. Revenge is the cocaine of emotions: highly seductive, exceptionally compelling, and remarkably unpredictable in terms of its effects on individuals. Revenge can be addictive when it's handled in large and repetitive doses. It can become the everyday method of handling any conflict, which, in the long run, is ineffective.

Hooked on Revenge

"You can get hooked on revenge," teases Larry, a handsome twenty-eight-year-old bartender/actor who wishes he was more easily able to let bygones be bygones. "When I was on the wrestling team in high school, I got my first taste of revenge. I had always been a small kid, and I was picked on in elementary school and there was nothing I could do about it. I knew that if my old lady complained to the principal, then I would catch it even worse. I began to build myself up in junior high and made varsity wrestling in tenth grade. There was a guy named Bruce on the team who had given me crap since third grade, picked on new kids and nerdy kids and whatever, and he was also on the team. Without really planning anything outright, I realized that I'd been holding in all this pent-up anger until tryouts for the first line of the varsity squad. I was up against Bruce, who was smiling at what he thought would be an easy match against this dork he'd been trashing for years.

"This guy was never so shocked in his life. I didn't hurt him, you understand, not physically anyway. I just outdid him on every maneuver. The coach was laughing by the end of the second minute. He was pinned under my arms like he was a begging dog. It was great. I beat the shit out of him and twenty years later I still feel like cheering myself on. After that I realized that getting the upper hand was a great feeling. Now I wish I weren't used to giving as good as I get. I could use some patience and a lower setting for my temper."

Larry feels hemmed in by his need for revenge. "There's no twelve-step program for me," he sighs, only half-jokingly. "I'm just getting by in my job because every time some drunk acts like a jerk, the muscles in the back of my neck get rigid. I clench and unclench my jaw all night long because holding a job in a service industry depends on treating every customer with respect. I have trouble working with other actors because each time I sense a vicious competitive drive, I revert to my earlier ways and I think about beating the guy up. I think about taking him onto the mats, and I think about taking his lover onto the mattress. I'm notorious for stealing my rivals' significant others, and this is not because I'm promiscuous by nature, but because I'm vindictive by nature. I'm not sure I can ever break this habit and I'm afraid that it will get me killed. One way or the other, this will lead to my self-destruction."

Larry pauses, shy and sheepish for a moment, polishing wineglasses and placing them in precise order on the shelves. I am struck, as we speak, by his love for getting things precisely right. Every glass sparkles in this dark bar. "I know it isn't a healthy sense of competition which drives me. I don't want just to win—I want to teach my opponent a lesson. And that's the line I cross every day from competition to revenge. It feels good in the short term. I like beating somebody at a game they're sure they'll win, but the feeling doesn't last."

Even the intoxication of revenge becomes difficult to achieve or sustain once it's reduced to a mere habit. When revenge becomes compulsive, or more typically, obsessive, it eventually affords decreasing satisfaction to the perpetrator. This is one reason that successful revenge is often quick and to the point. When it falls into a pattern of repetition, it loses its flavor and becomes a hollow ritual without resonance.

"The Thunder Rolls"

Tellingly, one of America's favorite recording artists is country singer Garth Brooks. In concert, Brooks sometimes adds lyrics to his megahit songs, and the additional verses always seem to include revenge scenarios. In his 1992 hit "The Thunder Rolls," he tells us the story of a woman who waits up through a storm for her man, hoping it's the weather that's making him late again. The song ends with the recognition that the perfume on his clothes is not hers. It's a fairly conventional scenario for a country song, but in the concert version of "The Thunder Rolls" we hear a new "live-only" last stanza. The betrayed wife reaches for a pistol to make sure that this is the *last* night she won't know where her husband's been.

The passion exhibited by the audience for the live version of this song seems to include as many male roars of approval as female. The frenzied approval of the last stanza crosses gender lines, and clearly everybody feels that it's okay for her to go for the gun, even, one presumes, the one or two members of the crowd who are themselves stepping out on their wives.

There's a tombstone from the mid-nineteenth century bearing the inscription "At Least I Know Where He Is at Night." The emotions are not new, even if the presentation of them in song form is still slightly shocking. The wife in Brooks's song moves from a position of passive receiver to one of active initiator. Presumably the audience's response is due to the surprise of finding that the victim is no longer willing to accept business as usual.

In another Brooks number, "I Got Friends in Low Places," the speaker is a loutish party-crasher who shows up at a splashy event where his old love is flying high with her new beau. The hero, however, doesn't mind leaving early because, as the title indicates, he has other circles of friends to visit. At first hearing it's a paradigmatic good-old-boy's rejection of any situation where cutlery will be used, but the concert version adds a twist: After Brooks does an introduction about how he would have handled the situation back home, the live version ends with the hero telling his new rival that he can put his party where the sun doesn't shine.

Implying that it was less than manly for the hero merely to leave for low places, Brooks, in concert, reestablishes the machismo of the protagonist. The speaker swears, uttering "Kiss my ass"—oooh, boy—before he leaves the party, and that tiny act is enough to send the audience wild. They scream as if Elvis himself were before them, goading them on. The final refrain ends the song with a bang, and since the thousands of voices could not have been dubbed, it's clear Brooks is cashing in on an appetite for retributive solutions to relationship problems.

Hit Lists

It would actually be quite reasonable to come up with a revenge song "hit list" that plays off all the various implications of the word. The list might include such recent successes as "Independence Day," another country song. This time, the lyrics concern a woman who sings about lessons learned in her childhood when her mother burned down the house of her abusive husband, lighting up the sky on July Fourth. "Talk about your revolution," she sings, celebrating a "day of reckoning" when all the weak will be strong and when the guilty will pay. She claims not to be condoning her mother's actions, but the fact that the refrain includes the line "roll the stone away" gives us positive images of resurrection that are difficult to ignore. Other songs focus on acts of domestic violence, such as "Janey's Got a Gun"; in this rock number, a girl kills her father to avenge years of systematic abuse. We've come a long way from "Lipstick on Your Collar."

The Lure of Murder Mysteries

In *Gaudy Night* by Dorothy Sayers, heroine Harriet Vane returns to her undergraduate college for a reunion. The opening chapters are full of ironic words about academic life: "The fact that one had loved and sinned and suffered and escaped death was of far less ultimate moment than a single footnote in a dim academic journal establishing the priority of a manuscript. . . ." Harriet's comments about the importance of scholarship sound a bit overblown: Do we really believe that a single footnote weighs equally with happiness, life, and death?

It is, in fact, because of a dusty, obscure piece of scholarly material that someone is out for revenge. Annie Wilson was married to a man who stole a letter from a small European library in order to have his dissertation accepted; the letter was the only existing evidence contradicting his argument. At length he was found out by a woman who now teaches at Harriet's old college. His career was destroyed. His wife seeks to avenge her husband's downfall, and his subsequent suicide, on all the women scholars at Shrewsbury College. Early on, Harriet, a successful writer of mysteries who herself was once accused of murdering her lover, says rather offhandedly to a group of her fellow collegians who wonder why she continues to write murder mysteries: "I know what you're thinking—that anybody with proper sensitive feelings would rather scrub floors for a living."

Now, Harriet is addressing lecturers and deans when she says this, and uses "scrubbing floors" as a general example of working at something that would not make the emotional demands of mystery writing. But when vengeful Annie screams at Harriet, "I wanted to see you all dragged into the gutter . . . it would do you good to learn to scrub floors for a living as I've done, and use your hands for something," she means it literally, and it is a central part of her motive in committing the elaborate psychological crimes that structure the plot. In Sayers, as in Alfred Hitchcock and most traditional mysteries, the vengefully wicked are duly punished once they have committed their acts of vengeance. But it is interesting to note that their acts of vengeance are necessary, not only to secure our loyal attention as they move the plot along, but within the stories themselves: At the expense of themselves, these characters are settling a debt. Anywhere from righteous to misguided to psychotic, they nevertheless regard their own anger and desire for revenge as justified.

Over and over while discussing revenge with people, I heard about a classic episode from the popular Alfred Hitchcock television series involving the murder of an unfaithful husband by his long-suffering wife. Apparently this story has captured the imagination of any number of Nick at Night fans. The wife kills her spouse with, I believe, a leg of lamb, then cooks the lamb and serves it to the officers who come looking for the murder weapon. Perhaps there is the cursory ending saying that she was finally apprehended for her dastardly deed, but since those endings are narrated by Hitchcock and not dramatized, they seem to be merely tagged-on caveats, the equivalent of the small print beneath a car ad saying "Professional driver on a closed road. Do not attempt." Interesting to think that the audience for Euripides's *Medea* could handle the villain getting away with murder, but that a 1950s audience had to be warned away from trying what they were seeing on their own.

Frustration and Revenge

People can be angry not just because they've been hurt or insulted but also because they've been poorly trained or unrealistically led to believe that something good would happen. People are often very angry and vengeful when they feel extremely disappointed, or when the last possibility of hope for something is removed. "I was trained to murder but not to live normally in ordinary society," explains one angry Vietnam veteran who has served time for breaking the windows of luxury cars and smashing in expensive storefronts, despite the fact that he didn't actually steal anything. "I wanted somebody to know how it felt to get your life smashed up for no reason—not even for profit. I wanted to do something as violent and as meaningless as what was done to me." Revenge against a group is interesting because the injury is different from what it is in a one-to-one situation. The vet's life was not hurt per se—he received no physical injuries—but his life was altered in a significant, unchangeable, negative way. Choosing to vent his anger on a group that represents the larger injustice is at the heart of this man's violence.

Choosing targets that have only minimally to do with the real reasons behind our anger is not uncommon in tales of revenge. This vet's logic worked in much the same way as Captain Ahab's did in Herman Melville's *Moby Dick*. For Ahab, a whale is the embodiment of all the world's wickedness. As a portrait of a man intent on "audacious, immitigable, and super-natural revenge," Melville's creation of Captain Ahab has few equals. Representing the voice of reason and balance, first-mate Starbuck asserts fairly early the work that "I came here to hunt whales, not my commander's vengeance. How many barrels will thy vengeance yield thee even if thou gettest it, Captain Ahab? It will not fetch thee much in our Nantucket market." Not understanding how Ahab could want revenge on "a dumb brute . . . that simply smote thee from blindest instinct," Starbuck considers Ahab more than unreasonable, declaring him to be "blasphemous" in his hunger for vengeance. Enraged, Ahab argues that "I see in [Moby Dick] outrageous strength, with an inscrutable malice sinewing it. That inscrutable thing is chiefly what I hate; and be the white whale agent, or be the white whale principal, I will wreak that hate upon him." Ahab places a high price on what he has lost to the white whale—his leg and, with it, his sense of wholeness—and prepares to do battle for the outrage perpetrated on him. "Talk not to me of blasphemy, man," shouts monomaniacal Ahab. "I'd strike the sun if it insulted me."

We learn later that "Moby Dick had reaped away Ahab's leg, as a mower a blade of grass in the field . . . [and no one] could have smote him with more seeming malice." Since this encounter, Ahab's relentless pursuit of the beast has consumed his entire life. "All that most maddens and torments," Melville writes, ". . . All truth with malice in it; all that cracks the sinews and cakes the brain; all the subtle demonisms of life and thought; all evil, to crazy Ahab, were visibly personified, and made practically assailable in Moby Dick. He piled upon the whale's white hump the sum of all the general rage and hate felt by his whole race from Adam down; and then, as if his chest had been a mortar, he burst his hot heart's shell upon it.'' Ahab plummets into the sea with Moby Dick in an unholy embrace at the end of the novel, thereby offering another vision of the way that revenge binds together the revengers in an irrevocable union. Ahab is undone by his all-encompassing rage, and the final catastrophe is that he takes others with him in his quest for vengeance. Ahab wanted Moby Dick to pay the debt he felt was owed him; it was a tragic bargain. The phrase ''pay your debt'' can be a provocative one, despite its clichéd usage, because it assumes that there exists a legitimate social contract that binds all of us equally.

Anger as an Index

For some, anger becomes a way of life, and the perpetually pissed off prefer that their sense of outrage remain intact. Nevertheless, there is an inherent power in facing anger fully, which serves several purposes: Even while the use of anger draws on emotions we might have felt since childhood, it simultaneously serves to estrange the familiar, allowing us to see what we ordinarily take for granted in new or different perspectives, leading us to discoveries. The anger that a stand-up comic feels in response to a house that gives him a hard time or won't laugh at his routines can be the basis for the humor he uses in his next gig—''When I was performing in South Dakota, a state where they're still excited about the wheel and the closest they get to a computer is the Etch-a-Sketch, they didn't get my jokes. . . .''

Anger and the desire to revenge what appears to be an imposed silence has often inspired writers, particularly writers who use humor. Wendy Wasserstein, author of the brilliantly funny and successful play *The Heidi Chronicles*, explains that ''I wrote this play because I had this image of a woman standing up at a women's meeting saying, 'I've never been so unhappy in my life.' . . . Talking to friends, I knew there was this feeling around, in me and in others, and I thought it should be expressed theatrically. But it wasn't. The more angry it made me that these feelings weren't being expressed, the more anger I put into that play.''

"Revenge Is Necessary"

We must finally recognize that anger is rarely arbitrarily assigned, any more than love or envy is arbitrarily assigned. Anger rules out the possibility of detached contemplation; even passing moments of anger are effective indicators of the emotional and intellectual states of the individuals who pass through them. It is a complex register of the shifts and changes in a person's relationship to his or her position in the world. When the desire for revenge becomes paramount, anger can lead to some enterprising and creative actions.

In *Conceived with Malice*, a brilliant consideration of the connection between revenge and literature, Louise DeSalvo uncovers and explores the buried territory of rage informing some of the greatest acts of creation. DeSalvo quotes analyst Otto Rank, who told his author-patient Anaïs Nin that ''revenge is necessary. To reestablish equilibrium in the emotional life.'' Nin, DeSalvo explains, was retaliating against her abusive father by means of her fiction. DeSalvo quotes the section of Nin's diary where the author herself confronts this idea: Nin writes, ''I did not go to the very end with my father, in an experience of destructive hatred and antagonism. I created a reconciliation and I am writing a novel of hatred.'' ''Nin saw her novel *Winter of Artifice* as her retribution against her father,'' according to DeSalvo, ''thought out, instead of wreaked upon others.'' As John Gardner said, ''Good fiction has come from the writer's wish to be loved, his wish to take revenge, his wish to work out his psychological woes, his wish for money and so on. No motive is too low for art.''

DeSalvo makes a convincing case for reading the works of many writers from the perspective of art-as-revenge: ''Because it can be read by many people, the novel is a public form of humiliation that can provoke profound shame,'' DeSalvo explains. ''The work of art, composed in private, can ruin reputations when it becomes a public document, if enough of its readers know the story behind the story.'' She goes on to discuss the reasons that art-as-revenge can be a positive experience: ''Writing releases rage less harmfully than if it had been more overtly expressed. In the process, the writer comes to accept the pain of the loss, rather than denying or escaping from it. Organizing and expressing experiences prompts a feeling of mastery, supplanting a feeling of victimization. The artist, strengthened through pain, achieves insight as a concomitant to healing.''

Anger and revenge might not erase the past, but if handled properly, they can permit you to get on with your future. Call the product of this process Quality Anger or Quality Revenge, perhaps, because it isn't petulant or selfish but rather driven by a sense of community and humanity. Anger and revenge can offer a sense of indignity to replace a sense of shame, and offer a voice—raised above others—which can finally be heard. Those voices are most effective when they are raised in unison, when they have mercy behind them, and when, instead of *only* roaring at the anger of old pain, they can also begin to sing about the glorious possibilities of a future where anger and revenge have a smaller house than laughter and hope.

chapter eight

ACHIEVING A BALANCE

"Roz can see that she will never be prettier, daintier, thinner, sexier, or harder to impress than these girls are. She decides instead to be smarter, funnier, and richer, and once she has managed that they can all kiss her fanny."
—MARGARET ATWOOD, *The Robber Bride*

"It's just not worth the effort to hold on to a grudge. While you're holding the grudge, your rival is having a party."
—DIANE CLEAVER, LITERARY AGENT

REVENGE, LIKE LOVE, IS ONE OF THOSE EMOTIONS WE'VE all felt—even if nothing's come of it. Sometimes fantasies of vindication can offer a newly revived vision of our own lives; like any outrageous dream of self-indulgence, such thoughts can clue us in to what is actually possible and desirable in real life. At times giving full rein to the fantasies of our darkest heart can act as a form of catharsis, and allow us to pay some emotional bills; in other cases, thinking about how to achieve justice can act as a catalyst for genuine and positive change.

On November 13, 1994, a British newspaper ran a lengthy op-ed article extolling the virtues of revenge. Frank Ronan opened his confessional piece with a line striking both for its simplicity and its strangeness. "The other day I murdered a Teddy Bear," Ronan began. "It was an act committed in the sort of mad, cold rage of which I had always hoped I was incapable, at least, capable of avoiding. I stabbed it, dismembered it and cut it to ribbons on the doorstep of the owner, and took the head away with me so it could never be repaired. The destruction of this object was, in all probability, the most hurtful thing I could do to the person who owned it, without incurring a prison sentence.'' Ronan adds, ''It was also, it transpired, the best thing I could have done to save my own sanity. Overnight, I was transformed from a suicidal wreck into a semblance of my old self.''

Surely these intriguing and disturbing images would be more at home in *Nightmare on Elm Street* than in a respectable morning newspaper such as *The Observer*? A grown man killing a teddy bear? Even a horse's head in bed would seem less weird to most readers. Yet it's clear that Ronan's views reflect not some eccentric and personal perversity but are instead representative of a universal need to get even in order to get over pain.

''There was a time, only weeks ago, when I would have argued against vengeance,'' explains Ronan. ''I thought that the conscience was to be indulged before all other sensibilities; that it was more important to be good and to be right than to have some good Old Testament satisfaction. What I had not understood was the psychology of being a victim and what it is to lose one's power.'' Having wrenched himself away from an abusive relationship, Ronan felt a need to do more than leave without a final gesture. ''By a lucky accident I achieved the perfect revenge. The object I destroyed was inanimate and of no value to anyone but the owner, but in some way I paid him back a small measure of the pain he had so liberally dealt out to me.''

In seeking closure, Ronan chose an act of revenge that was emotionally satisfying but nevertheless undeniably benign. No doubt his lover felt the loss of a beloved and irreplaceable object, but Ronan was able to inflict a degree of pain that stung most deeply by what it represented more than by what it actually achieved. "By that murder I not only stated that I had come to hate him just as much, but that that hatred was justified. With one melodramatic and symbolic but effective bound, I was free."

Throwing Away the Pain

Granted, the teddy bear was an innocent bystander. But what is most important here is Ronan's focus on emotional freedom that revenge has afforded him. Killing the teddy bear permitted him, however absurdly, to regain a sense of himself. He emerges from this small, concise act of revenge as man reborn, in a certain sense, to the joys of the future. His pain, while not altogether dissipated, has been moved from the foreground to the background. Instead of remaining a creature handcuffed to the pain of the past, reliving his suffering on a daily basis, he chooses to move away from suffering and into the possibility of gaining perspective on his situation—and toward the possibility of happiness.

"To the happy," writes Fay Weldon in *The Hearts and Lives of Men*, "all things come. . . . It is our resentments, our dreariness, our hate and envy, unrecognized by us, which keep us miserable. Yet these things are in our heads, not out of our hands; we own them; we can throw them out if we choose." Though we recognize that anger, resentment, and hatred are all fully human emotions, it is nevertheless true that our lives are better when lived without a regular diet of these feelings. When we feed too steadily or for too long on the worst parts of our lives, it becomes increasingly difficult to accept the more healthy fare of ordinary joy. Choosing to accept, understand, and transform the desire for revenge into a positive force can mean, paradoxically, choosing to forgive the one who inflicted damage in the first place.

Forgiveness does not rule out anger; you can forgive the person without forgiving the action, and indeed there are actions that remain unforgivable. "It is . . . valuable to note that when we forgive, we do not condone," writes philosopher Howard McGary. "When we condone an injury or wrongdoing we are in a sense playing down the seriousness of the violation." McGary's point is an important one because it allows us to see the difference between forgiveness and permission: You can forgive someone without implying that what he or she *did* was either acceptable or repeatable.

From Confession to Contrition

"I'm afraid to forgive my wife for her affair," a chronically unhappy friend confessed, "because I'm afraid that will give her all the permission she needs to go out and do it again." So instead of being able to put the past behind them this husband keeps his wound open, always reminding his wife of her error and the pain she caused him. As a result, they are both nervous, wary, and locked into an old and never-ending battle. Only until he can offer her forgiveness—and not see himself as a sucker for doing so—can their relationship move forward.

Repenting her actions fully, the wife returned to her husband with the full understanding that their relationship would never be forced to endure such hardship again. She explained that she understood the difference between confession and contrition, and that she was genuinely contrite. She explained, sincerely, how sorry she was to have hurt him and asked for his forgiveness. He agreed to resume the relationship, but forgiveness seemed as out of reach as a falling star.

If he could find one way of settling the score he might be able to leave his pain behind and move on to forgiveness. Counseling might help; so might asking her to burn every picture, note, and present she received from her lover in a ceremony over their barbecue. "He does a continuous autopsy on the relationship to find out what went wrong," sighs the husband's best friend. "I tell him that if he keeps cutting open the past, nothing can repair itself." Anything would be better than being stuck where they are, not being able to look at the past without pain or the future without fear. Choosing to forgive might well be the truly final gesture permitting a wound to heal. It can allow the last act to play itself out and lead to closure.

The Role of Forgiveness

"Many have thought that an important aspect of forgiveness is the role that it plays in not letting our resentment toward wrongdoing go beyond appropriate limits," McGary explains. He goes on to argue that if "rightful resentment goes for too long unchecked, it will be so consuming that the person doing the resenting" won't be able to get on with life in any meaningful way. Perhaps what is most important in this discussion is the understanding that forgiveness has much more to do with the person doing the forgiving than it does with the original wrong-doer. It would help the husband at least as much as it would help his repentant wife, for example, if he were able to forgive her. It would set him free, and allow them to establish new ground instead of continuously going over old territory.

Letting go of the pain inflicted by someone else does not have to be motivated by any desire whatsoever to allow that other person off the hook. To experience the process of forgiveness, a person need not be motivated by the wish to make the wrongdoer feel better. Instead, forgiveness can begin with the simple wish of wanting to move ahead into the future instead of remaining shackled to a single moment of pain in the past.

Forgiveness, however, might only be possible if on some level retribution or justice has been achieved; in this way, paradoxically, revenge and forgiveness are two parts of the same process. This might remind us of the old Spanish proverb that declares, "If I die, I forgive you; if I recover, we shall see."

Inherent in this saying is the idea that forgiveness is not truly forgiveness if it is coaxed or coerced. The slate cannot be wiped clean with a cloth still sullied by animosity or resentment; in order to achieve a fresh beginning there must be a sense of a threshold crossed, of being able to stamp "paid" on the debts stockpiled by the suffering and anger of the past. Getting even can mean getting on with a life that is not informed by anger, resentments, or old, unsettled scores but is instead about perspective, justice, and the possibilities of forgiveness.

Giving a Name to Revenge

Being conscious of the desire for revenge can also, as we've seen, help someone from acting on that desire. We skirt the whole notion of revenge, whistling in the dark to keep the very idea away, yet we often draw closer and closer to it without recognizing precisely what we are doing until it is too late. A woman leaves her husband without realizing that she is trying to get back at him for emotionally abandoning her. A teenager crashes his father's car as a way to get even with him for favoring a younger sibling. A secretary steals from the petty cash box because she was insulted by her boss but couldn't speak up. Revenge exerts a formidable attraction because of its atavistic nature, and yet our culture keeps it hidden or translates it into only its most acceptable—and by extension its most diluted and unsatisfactory—forms.

No matter how civilized we are or how much we have controlled our instinctual life, it is simple human nature, on occasion, to feel the need to take revenge against someone who has harmed us. The most potentially dangerous situation for the majority of people is when this feeling slips into our emotional lives without our being aware of it. The need for revenge is a silent, unrecognized, and shadowy part of life that interferes with everyday actions, especially when we don't name it or notice consciously that it's there. Like an undetected virus, it can weaken and eventually destroy if not caught early on—or not dealt with appropriately. Left to its own devices, unchecked or unmeasured, revenge can go wildly awry.

Better, then, to be like my former colleague Virginia. When she began teaching at a small community college in the South, she ran into some stonewalling from older faculty members who branded her as lightweight and frivolous because she spent her time actually *talking* to the students, scheduling regular conferences every week. She made a policy of leaving her office door open so that students felt welcome just dropping by. To her enormous surprise, one afternoon an enraged faculty member stormed over to her office and accused her of using the conversation in her office to distract the students who were attending his lecture. He charged her, loudly and publicly, of being no more than a nuisance. "My students are no longer paying attention to what I'm saying," he thundered. "They are too busy trying to hear what's going on down the hall." Instead of saying, as she had every right to, that it was not her polite conversation distracting the students but his threadbare ideas and dreary teaching methods that were boring them, she said nothing. Virginia, in fact, appeared to absorb his anger by closing her door. She seemed to be defeated.

But Virginia, it should be noted, was not one to take disrespect lightly. She was a professor of classical languages. Not only did she have a picture of Nemesis, the goddess of retributive justice, on her door, she also had a quotation from Publilius Syrus written out in fine lettering and posted directly above her office hours. It read *Ab alio expectes, alteri quod feceris*, which means "Expect to receive such treatment as you have given."

A few days after her colleague's harangue, Virginia bought a popcorn maker. Just in time for the beginning of her colleague's class, she began preparing vast quantities of popcorn. The hallway was suffused with the delicious aroma of buttered popcorn until the building smelled more like a theater than a college. She knew very well this would truly disrupt her colleague's class, but since she popped away with her door closed there was very little he could say. To accuse her of undermining his authority because of her popcorn-making behavior was perhaps too foolish even for this geezer, and he retired shortly thereafter. Virginia considered giving him a Pop-Till-You-Drop machine but she decided that her revenge was complete without the final flourish.

Taming Revenge

Revenge has played a role in the cultural, social, and psychological development of individuals over time in and around the world. "Revenge is universal" anthropologist Jon Elster affirms, although "norms of revenge are not." Elster argues that most cultures place "revenge on the same plane as hunger, desire, fear, and pleasure. These are all common to humanity, but the experiences and definitions will change with circumstances. The basic emotion or condition, however, remains very much the same." Arguing that "the urge for honor, like the enjoyment of other people's envy, are universal phenomena," he suggests that the desire for revenge may be controlled, but it will never fully be suppressed. We might as well address the idea, learn to live with it, and—most importantly—"domesticate it" in such a way that the most dangerous aspects of it will be disarmed.

When Eliza Doolittle sings "Just you wait, 'Enry 'Iggins" in *My Fair Lady*, she is doing just this: charting precisely the ways she will abandon her master when he is sick or when he is drowning, and then ends the song with a climactic fantasy of being invited to court and asking, like Salome, for " 'Enry 'Iggins' 'Ead." The song is comical rather than scandalous. We know that Eliza's affections for Higgins is paramount. She imagines her revenge because it permits her to vent her feelings without getting herself into any actual trouble.

The songwriters knew very well that Eliza was expressing a universal emotion in wanting to throttle her beloved—and they knew that such a dream could be put to comical use because by bringing it out into the open, they could diffuse its intensity. Sometimes we exact revenge from the people we love best, those closest to us. "Every animal revenges his pains upon those who happen to be near," Samuel Johnson noted, no doubt because our nearest and dearest are in the position to do us the most good—or the most harm. Even when they are not necessarily the cause of our grievance, all too often those closest to us receive the burden of our displaced anger. This is another reason that it is important to identify the true sources of our emotional discomfort—in order not to act out revenge on those who deserve and request only our happiness and solicitude.

Restoring the Balance

The difference between obsessive and cathartic thoughts of revenge is the difference between lightning and a lightning bug. Obsessive thoughts of revenge can never be anything except damaging to the person carrying them around. Just like a loaded gun in a suitcase, explosive feelings of revenge can backfire all too easily.

But as we've seen, small, often comical, acts of retributive getting even—righting an injustice or leveling an imbalance—can allow us to move in healthy ways away from destructive and self-destructive acts. Anger, frustration, and guilt, so often attributed to the working through of individual emotions, can usefully be grounded in a larger cultural context: We see that we are not alone, and we see the very good reasons we might be feeling oppressed not only by one individual but by the system as a whole.

And, as we've also seen, sometimes what begins as a personal act motivated by revenge can have long-reaching and positive ramifications, bringing an issue into focus or highlighting an injustice that is widespread. Taking up arms against a sea of troubles is not a contemporary phenomenon, and even appealing to the courts to settle a personal problem is not a trademark of the baby boom generation.

A Woman's Recompense in 1860

As the following report from an 1860 publication indicates, seeking help from the courts to balance the scales of justice can have an effect on the personal as well as the political. "A woman in Detroit has brought an action against her husband to recover wages as a domestic," the story begins. "It seems he procured a divorce from her eight months before. She knew nothing about it, and stayed with him, performing her usual domestic duties." Such a statement prompts two responses: How could a system exist in which a wife would not know her husband divorced her? And, if she performed *all* her usual wifely duties, shouldn't she get paid for both the day and the night shifts?

The Sibyl, a woman's magazine where the report first appeared, goes on to explain that the woman's husband had only "recently told her of the divorce, and she, much exasperated, seeks to punish him, or at least make him pay for the eight months of service, from which his own act had legally released her." Exasperated? Is that all? *Of course*, she thought to punish him, and while no record is made of the trial's outcome it is a hope dear to the hearts of any justice-minded individual that this lady received some sort of recompense for what she went through. One can only imagine what a woman put through the same experience today would do. But one thing is certain: Only through the courage and resourcefulness of people who, once injured, feel they have the right to redress a balance do laws and customs change.

And working within the system—even if that system is flawed or needs to be changed—is crucial. Psychoanalyst Willard Gaylin argues that "in our search for individual justice we must not destroy the sense that we are living in a fair and just state. All of us are prepared to accept individual inequities. We all know that life is not always fair. Still, somehow, we expect that generally the good prevails." Gaylin cautions against believing that only "outsider" or personal justice can satisfy an appetite for rectifying a wrong. "We must not attempt to purchase an elegant and individual justice for each person at the expense of the concept called social justice," warns Gaylin. "It would turn out to be a very costly exchange."

As we've also seen, people commit just about any act in the name of revenge. Some kill, others get pregnant. Some divorce, others marry. Some die, others stick fiercely to life. All could be regarded as revenge, depending on the context. A warped form of forgiveness itself can become a form of revenge, with the forgiver using kindness as a noose or a bludgeon, as a method of assuring perpetual control over the one who has transgressed. Ethicist Marvin Henberg observes that "like the weather, retribution is an everyday topic of conversation; unlike the weather, however, men and women actually do something about it. Such maxims as 'Don't get mad, get even' provoke guilty smiles of self-recognition. In ways both large and small, in grand schemes and in petty bickering, human beings find means of retaliating against those who have injured or offended them."

Nothing That's Really Sweet Is Really Simple

Sweet revenge is no more unobtainable than true love or the perfect job, but it should be kept in mind that sweet revenge is also *as difficult* to secure as true love and the perfect job. There are times when you might believe you have it right, only to discover that you've been tricked or thwarted into a situation that is more harmful than beneficial. The basic tenets concerning true love and the perfect job also apply to revenge: Everyone has a different definition of success; everyone embarks on a variety of plans to achieve it; and very few people will understand why it's so important for an individual to have success. And revenge, like love, can make us miserable or can give us a new sense of our ability to make a place for ourselves in the world. It can deplete or add to our lives; it can be comic or tragic; it can ease defeat—or enhance victory.

"My best revenge was to take this guy's controlling vice—greed—and turn it against him," chuckled a builder who'd worked long hours for low pay at a commercial job site, where he was renovating an old bank to house a new law firm. "You have to understand that this was an attorney who made more money than God, and acted like he was a pauper. He squeezed a dime out of everything and everyone. It was hell to work for him, but this was fifteen years ago and we were just starting out and needed the work, so I didn't dare complain even when he insisted on overseeing every screw we put into the wall to make sure we were using only the cheapest materials. One day he pushed all my buttons—arguing with one of my workers, making a lewd remark about a woman on our crew, and accusing me of overcharging him on the last invoice. I knew I had to do something or else walk off the job, and there were too many people depending on this work for me to screw them up because of my anger.

"Then I had an idea. A few weeks later, when we opened up a wall to get at the old electrical wiring behind it I pulled out a crumpled and dusty ten-dollar bill, and then I pulled out a twenty. 'Look at this,' I called over to him. 'It seems that there's money hidden away in this wall.' He rushed over and started pulling out bills. 'Open this wall up,' he demanded. 'But it's brick, and that'll cost you a bundle,' I explained. He said, 'Just do it.' So I called in my workers and we spent a long time carefully taking apart the wall. There was no money in it; I'd planted those bills. It was worth it to see his disappointment. If he suspected I'd set him up, he never confronted me, probably because he was too proud to think that a simple guy like me could have outwitted him. It was great."

If a desire for revenge cannot be fully suppressed, how can we best confront and deal with these untidy emotions? The solutions are as varied as the personalities and circumstances of those involved, and many of these solutions make sense on a visceral level, which makes them difficult to dismiss. A Chinese proverb, for example, advises that "if thine enemy wrong thee, buy each of his children a drum." With this gift, you ensure your enemy's headache and domestic disharmony. From Eastern folklore we've integrated a similar notion when we talk about owning a "white elephant."

The phrase "white elephant" comes from a practice of the Siam courts whereby royalty would present white elephants to overly sycophantic or aggravating courtiers who were then likely to be ruined by the expense of maintaining this gift. In such a way has the phrase "white elephant'' come to symbolize a possession that is both useless and costly. The act of giving a gift as revenge is an intricate matter, but not an infrequent practice. In contrast, sometimes acts motivated by twinges of revenge can turn out to be, in the long run, quite practical gifts. In other words, revenge can take many forms, including ones that appear like acts of generosity—or that genuinely *are* acts of generosity.

Wholesome Revenge

One respected teacher I worked with had a slightly malevolent way of dealing with smug or arrogant students who thought a little too highly of their own gifts. When he suspected that a student was simply caught up in the drive to obtain an improved G.P.A., without caring if the work itself improved, he devised a way to get his attention. One student who worked with both of us came to me in a fury one day, horrified to see that she'd received a C+ on what she was sure was an A paper. Did she read through the comments? I asked. She shrugged off the question without hesitation—saying she didn't have time to figure out the teacher's handwriting.

I suggested that we go over the paper page by page. On the fourth or fifth page, in the margins along with his suggestions and questions, was the professor's signature comment: ''This is an A paper, and that will be the grade recorded. I encourage you, however, to understand that even though you're an excellent student there is room for improvement. I will help you do better work, but only if you pay attention to what I have to say about the work you produce.'' It was his little game, and perhaps a slightly cruel one, but one that taught the student a lesson she needed to learn.

As novelist Jessymyn West observes, "A rattlesnake that doesn't bite teaches you nothing."

Counterplots

Margaret Atwood, a writer who has never underestimated the power of revenge, quotes West at the beginning of her brilliant novel, *The Robber Bride*. In *The Robber Bride*, and in her short story "Hairball," Atwood presents two portraits—one full scale, one a miniature—of the motives for and effects of revenge. *The Robber Bride*'s main focus is the charismatically evil character Zenia, considered by the three women whom she has betrayed over the years as an "aphid of the soul." One erstwhile friend describes her as "pure freewheeling malevolence; she wants wreckage, she wants scorched earth, she wants broken glass."

Beautiful and supremely manipulative, Zenia inspires her friends with affection and loyalty, only to later rouse their envy and destroy their self-esteem. Roz, Charis, and Tony, an unlikely trio of women in their forties, have all had their lives touched and altered in some way by Zenia. They are jealous of her, which is an emotion Zenia cultivates like some kind of unwholesome crop. Roz wonders whether what she feels is rage or a hot flash, realizing finally that what she feels is pure jealousy. "*She's just jealous*, people say, as if jealousy is something minor. But it's not, it's the worst, worst feeling there is—incoherent and confused and shameful, and at the same time self-righteous and focused and hard as glass, like the view through a telescope. A feeling of total concentration, but total powerlessness." This sense of chaos, as Atwood is quick to point out, leads to feelings clearly linked to revenge; jealousy "inspires . . . murder: killing is the ultimate control."

In Atwood's novel, the three central characters must face and accept the knowledge that Zenia is, in part, their own creation. Like Frankenstein's monster, she exists as their nemesis; and so they cannot rid themselves of a connection to her. She has captured their imagination by making herself the embodiment of their most deeply buried selves, part of their minds and souls they want to deny but cannot. In order for them to get on with their own lives, they must revenge themselves on Zenia for the irreparable harms she has committed. And they must do this without becoming as evil or malicious as their enemy herself, always a problem for the revenger. ("I learned long ago never to wrestle with a pig. You get dirty, and besides, the pig likes it" observed Cyrus Ching, summing up the danger of getting too entangled with a rival.)

Atwood's book ends with laughter: The three friends are laughing together in the kitchen, with the "dishes clattering." One is setting out food, the other is telling a story. The third listens, because "that's what they will do, increasingly in their lives: tell stories. Tonight their stories will be about Zenia." "Was she in any way like us?" asks one of the women. "Or, to put it the other way around: Are we in any way like her?" The recognition that the revengers are bound to mirror the very elements they seek to obliterate by removing the focus of their revenge is important to Atwood. But revenge is not in itself censured; if anything, their revenge is the only thing that permits these women to end the novel with their laughter, and with the telling of their stories.

In "Hairball," Atwood takes another revenge scenario and gives it a brief, but fully realized, life. Kat, the central character, has spent the last several years in an increasingly unsatisfactory relationship with her employer. When he decides to rededicate himself to his conventional wife and dully domestic marriage—abandoning Kat after she had an operation to remove an ovarian tumor and firing her in the process—Kat decides to act out her rage as the discarded mistress. Invited to a big party thrown by the happy couple, Kat sends her regrets. As a present, she also sends a large package from the most elegant chocolatier in the city, knowing full well that her ex-employer and his wife will make a ceremony of opening such an ostentatious gift in front of all of their friends. Carefully wrapped under the sumptuous papers, rolled in chocolate, is the tumor removed from her womb.

This is a revenge that is the very antithesis of sweet. The story suggests that for Kat, leaving her "hairball" on someone else's rug is the best revenge. In ridding herself of the part of her that was diseased, Kat can do better for herself, the reader hopes. It is to Atwood's credit that Kat's action is both horrifying and comical, viciously appropriate and wildly anarchic. Having exorcised the worst, she can, perhaps, begin anew.

In contrast to Zenia, Kat is not a character fundamentally driven by a need to revenge herself on the world. But, as any number of writers have suggested, even characters who themselves seem to be consumed by the need to impress the world with their power and wreak a little havoc along the way would be better men and women had they been allowed greater access to happiness.

If You're Happy, It's Easy to Be Good...

To be generous, forgiving, and good go hand in hand with being happy. This is not to say that if you are good, you will be happy, but instead to say that if you are happy it is easy to be good and bear no grudge against the world. Victorian novelist William Thackeray's brilliantly conniving heroine in *Vanity Fair* considers this very point. Becky Sharp has, since her poverty-stricken childhood, been determined to win at life's game of chance. She is driven by a need to revenge herself on all those who have treated her badly because of her lack of status.

When she leaves school, after being patronized and abused by the school's headmistress, Becky shouts, "I hate the whole house. . . . I hope I may never set eyes on it again. I wish it were in the bottom of the Thames, I do; and if Miss Pinkerton were there, I wouldn't pick her out, that I wouldn't. Oh, how I should like to see her floating in the water yonder, turban and all, with her train streaming after her, and her nose like the beak of a wherry." Instead of chastising his heroine for her distinctly unfeminine response, Thackeray has Becky answer her friend's question: "How can you—How dare you have such wicked, revengeful thoughts?" with "Revenge may be wicked, but it's natural. . . . I'm no angel." Thackeray's narrator only reaffirms this when he comments, wryly, "And, to say the truth, she certainly was not." But who needs an angel when Becky's devilishness is what keeps us reading? Not only is she smart and funny, she's the only one to see through society's veils. She then proceeds, like a striptease, to remove (or hide behind) every one of those veils herself. Like Mae West, Becky may be no angel, but she nevertheless remains our heroine.

When she is an adult, with some social success behind her, Becky wonders whether she could be driven by positive rather than negative forces if only her life had been easier. "I think I could be a good woman if I had five thousand a year," Becky muses. "I could dawdle about in the nursery, and count the apricots on the wall. I could water plants in the greenhouse, and pick off dead leaves from the geraniums. I could ask old women about their rheumatisms, and order half a crown's worth of soup for the poor. I shouldn't miss it much, out of five thousand a year.'' Goodness is the heir of leisure and comfort; revenge is born of want and misery, and flourishes in the dark, unkempt gardens of the heart. ''And who knows but Rebecca was right in her speculations—and that it was only a question of money and fortune which made the difference between her and an honest woman?'' speculates the narrator. ''If you take temptations into account, who is to say that he is better than his neighbor? A comfortable career of prosperity, if it does not make people honest, at least keeps them so.'' It is easy to forgive, Thackeray suggests, when life has given you compensations for the losses to which you are subjected. Forced by circumstance to regard other people as either rivals or fools, Becky was never permitted the luxury of doing anything apart from fiercely guarding her own small place in the world.

Vanity Fair is a vast canvas of ambition, lust, and revenge. Thackeray doesn't condemn any of these appetites outright, but he does draw our attention to the ultimately self-destructive nature of holding too fast onto any one of them. Too great a need for revenge, for example, can control the imagination so fully that there is no room for the delights of the world—and Thackeray stresses that even a corrupt world offers an array of pleasures. A triumphant life, one in which an individual can afford to leave alone those things that make her unhappy, is available only if there is enough energy left over from resentment and frustration to make it accessible. If, like Becky, we spend a lot of time attempting to exact satisfaction for old wounds, we deny ourselves the pleasures of generosity and calm self-esteem. If revenge encourages us to spend all our time looking at what we can do to somebody else instead of focusing on what we can do to help ourselves out of the trap of anger and frustration—or even to help others avoid similar pitfalls—then we pay too great a price for it. (Fanny Hill, Becky's eighteenth-century bawdy predecessor, once revenges herself on an unfaithful lover by herself making love on the very couch where she witnessed the infidelity. Although Fanny hugs herself ''for being thus revenged to my heart's content, and that in a manner so precisely alike, and on the identical spot in which I had received the supposed injury,'' she also realizes that her own delight in the lovemaking she just experienced ''plentifully drowned all thoughts of revenge in the sense of actual pleasure.'' Eclipsing the *motive* by enjoying the actual pleasure of the *moment* allows Fanny to forget why she acted and merely enjoy the action.)

Turning Revenge into an Art Form

I knew a young artist who was thwarted by a rival and thereby denied access to a gallery. She vowed to get even. But instead of spending her time thinking of ways to undermine her competitor, she spent her time discovering ways to make herself a more powerful artist. Her work is now well known and her former rival has been virtually forgotten—by everyone but the artist herself. She uses her old rivalry to keep herself moving, keeping her work vibrant and exciting. Her desire to be better than her old enemy remains a small spur to urge her on to better ways of achieving her goals. She has made, quite literally, revenge into an art form. ''The great pleasure in life is doing what people say you cannot do," according to Walter Bagehot. It's certainly a pleasure not to be overlooked.

Looking for a way to rectify a wrong and shift justice back to its proper place is a healthy way of looking at the idea of revenge; thinking only about ways to offend the offender can be, too often, a dead end. Thinking about the whys and hows of revenge can, surprisingly, lead to perspectives and behaviors that encourage constructive resolutions in the long run—but only if the matter is kept in perspective. And perspective depends, finally, on believing that no one is perfect—and no one is immune from the misfortunes inevitable in any life.

Compulsive thoughts of revenge, circling like buzzards in your brain, are inexpedient: they paralyze action, not prompt it. They are birds of prey, not creatures soaring above the landscape in order to get a better picture of it. In such cases, the idea of revenge blocks useful action, and masks the need to accept and work with personal responsibility. For those who become obsessed with repetitive plans for revenge, often relief will come from someone—usually a therapist—who intervenes from the outside to help them understand their perpetually destructive emotions. A little revenge, we should remember, goes a long way—and, like anything too powerful to be taken habitually—it needs to be kept under control.

Revenge as a Lightning Rod

If it seems that at times the very essence of revenge eludes categorization, what remains clear is that revenge serves as a lightning rod for larger emotional and intellectual issues in our lives and in our society. It can act as a catalyst, requiring us to call into question our conventional definitions of fairness, justice, and equality.

Examining the desire for revenge can unhinge the routine belief that we all have the same access to impartial justice; it can help underscore personal—and political—needs for reform. The loss of fear about revenge can be the beginning of the process of working through a need for it. Perhaps instead of seeking a way to restore balance, we should be thinking about the creation of an entirely new balance, one that wouldn't reproduce the same injustice that sparked a craving for revenge in the first place. The desire for revenge can force our deeply hidden beliefs and ideas into the open so that they can be confronted and perhaps even transformed into less threatening and more useful energies. Revenge, as a concept, can oblige us to explain—to others, but more importantly, to ourselves—what we need and want from the world.

The desire for revenge can be transformed into forgiveness—but only if there is a belief that justice will prevail. Swords can be turned into plowshares only if there is a belief in closure coupled with an assurance that the balance of power is guaranteed. Balance, however, can only be achieved if everyone has equal access to power; the powerless are fearless because they have nothing to lose. If the world were anything like what it should be, revenge would be as difficult for the ordinary person to understand as nuclear fission.

The world being what it is, revenge flickers on our screen, fills up our pages, and lights bonfires in our imagination.

notes

Chapter One

Page 7 "Mary Fisher, I hope such . . .": Fay Weldon, *The Life and Loves of a She-Devil* (New York: Ballantine Books, 1985).

Page 19 "this replacement of power . . .": Sigmund Freud, *Civilization and Its Discontents* (New York: W. W. Norton, 1961).

Page 21 "While [social systems] . . ."; "Openly aggressive vindictiveness . . ."; "Self-effacing vindictiveness . . ."; and "detached vindictiveness . . .": Karen Horney, "The Value of Vindictiveness." *The American Journal of Psychoanalysis*, vol. 8 (1948).

Chapter Two

Page 40 "Life as a child . . .": Colette, *Chéri* (Paris: Fayard, 1920).

Page 40 "If women aren't permitted . . ." and "If we lived . . .": Natalie Becker (interview with Regina Barreca).

Page 42 "The threadbare vocabulary . . .": Simone de Beauvoir, *The Second Sex* (New York: Random House, 1949).

Page 44, "a woman's weak and timid . . .": Euripides, *Medea* (New York: Penguin, 1963).

Page 47 "It's time for what . . .": Olivia Goldsmith, *The First Wives Club* (New York: Pocket Books, 1992).

Page 49 "There was some . . ."; "The murders were . . ."; and "One of the most enigmatic . . .": Ferenc Gyorgyey, "Arsenic and No Lace."

Page 54 "She has a wish . . .": Scott Turow, *Presumed Innocent* (New York: Warner Books, 1987).

Page 55 "Get a job . . .": Cynthia Heimel, *If You Can't Live Without Me, Why Aren't You Dead Yet?* (New York: HarperCollins, 1991).

Page 58 "Who am I . . .": Charles Dickens, *Great Expectations* (New York: Penguin, 1985).

Page 59 "The fear of ridicule . . .": Virginia Woolf, *Three Guineas* (New York: Harcourt, Brace and Co., 1938).

Page 60 "few people who saw . . .": Fannie Flagg, *Fried Green Tomatoes at the Whistle Stop Cafe* (New York: McGraw-Hill, 1987).

Page 63 "Revenge. We've got . . .": Maxine Hong Kingston, *The Woman Warrior* (New York: Vintage, 1977).

Page 66 "Let no one think . . .": Euripides, *Medea* (New York: Penguin, 1963), 42.

Chapter Three

Page 79 "The despair was going away . . .": John O'Hara, *Butterfield* 8 (New York: Bantam, 1935).

Page 80 "The lust of hate . . .": D. H. Lawrence, *Lady Chatterley's Lover* (New York: New American Library, 1962).

Page 83 "Only serious diseases . . .": Dan Greenburg and Suzanne O'Malley, *How to Avoid Love and Marriage* (New York: 1983).

Page 83 "Well, if I cannot . . ." and "With frightful vehemence . . .": Emily Brontë, *Wuthering Heights* (New York: Penguin, 1965).

Page 89 "There was too much order . . .": Terry McMillan, *Waiting to Exhale* (New York: Viking, 1992).

Page 89 "If she wants to serve . . .": Marge Piercy, "What's That Smell in the Kitchen?" *Circles on the Water* (New York: Random House, 1987).

Page 94 "It is a curious subject . . .": Nathaniel Hawthorne, *The Scarlet Letter* (Boston: Bedford/St. Martin's Press, 1991).

Page 95 "Oh, it was revenge . . ." and " 'revenge is part . . . ' ": Merry McInerney, "Knife-like Fiction." *New York Newsday* (October 18, 1994).

Page 97 "And if I married him right away . . .": Margaret Mitchell, *Gone With the Wind* (New York: Avon, 1979).

Page 98 "to wreak revenge . . .": Charles Dickens, *Great Expectations* (New York: Penguin, 1985).

Chapter Four

Page 111 " 'Don't get mad . . . ' ": Ernest Brod, "In the Layoff Era, the 'Get Even' Ethic." *New York Times* (January 26, 1992): F13.

Page 116 "alongside giants . . .": Larry Green, "At 96, Feuding Matriarch Opens New Business." *Los Angeles Times* (December 18, 1989): A1.

Page 118 "those who have . . .": Erich Fromm, *The Anatomy of Human Destructiveness* (New York: Henry Holt & Co., 1973).

Page 118 "Oftentimes, their life . . .": Thomas D. Harpley, "Disgruntled Workers Intent on Revenge Increasingly Hurt Their Bosses." *Wall Street Journal* (September 15, 1992): B1.

Page 120 "the urge for honor . . .": Jon Elster, "Norms of Revenge." *Ethics* (July 1990).

Page 122 "to expose to ridicule . . .": Karen Horney, "The Value of Vindictiveness."

Page 125 "given up trying . . .": George Orwell, *Down and Out in Paris and London* (Middlesex: Penguin, 1933).

Page 126 "the mass of workers . . ." and "Let the cooks . . .": Walter Minn, *Sabotage: History, Philosophy, and Function* (Chicago: IWW Publishing, n.d.).

Page 127 "Sabotage as a labor relations . . .": Robert Giacalone and Stephen Knouse. "Justifying Wrongful Employee Behavior: The Role of Personality in Organizational Sabotage" in *Excuses: Masquerades in Search of Grace* (New York: John Wiley & Sons, 1985).

Page 129 "without even talking . . ." and "who, apparently still angry . . .": I. A. Winoker, "Sweet Revenge Is Souring the Office." *Wall Street Journal* (September 19, 1990): B1+.

Page 130 "I have vowed . . ." and "Over the years . . .": John Emshwiller, "Desire for Revenge Fuels an Entrepreneur's Ambition." *Wall Street Journal* (April 19, 1991): B2.

Page 131 "polar disease . . .": Konrad Lorenz, *On Aggression* (New York: Harcourt, Brace, and World, 1966).

Chapter Five

Page 143 "it is illegal . . .": Molly Ivins, *Nothin' But Good Times Ahead* (New York: Random House, 1993).

Page 144 "the universe is made . . .": Mariel Rukeyser in *The Last Word: Treasury of Women's Quotes*, edited by Carolyn Warner (Newark: Prentice Hall, 1992).

Page 149 "a combination of early . . .": Carol Burnett, *One More Time* (New York: Random House, 1986).

Page 153 "We must give . . .": Alan Sherman, *The Rape of the Ape* (Chicago: Playboy Press, 1973).

Page 155 "So I told her . . .": Nora Ephron, *Heartburn* (New York: Pocket Books, n.d.).

Page 156 "When actions are . . .": Charlotte Lennox, *The Female Quixote* (London: Pandora Press, 1986).

Page 161 "a group effort . . .": Linda Anderson, *A Kind of Wild Justice* (Newark: University of Delaware Press, 1987).

Chapter Six

Page 171 "For a man there's something . . .": Henrick Ibsen, *A Doll's House* in *The Bedford Introduction to Literature* (Boston: Bedford Books, 1993): 1517–1567.

Page 174 "Recklessness is almost . . .": D. H. Lawrence, *Sons and Lovers* (New York: Penguin, 1976).

Page 175 "It is generally established . . .": *Mrs. Beeton's Book of Household Management* (London: 1892).

Page 175 "If you are rude . . .": Judith Martin, *Miss Manners' Guide to Excruciatingly Correct Behavior* (New York: Warner Books, 1982).

Page 180 "the aggression is always . . .": Willard Gaylin, *The Rage Within: Anger in Modern Life* (New York: Simon & Schuster, 1984).

Page 183 "But it is a sad fate . . .": Dorothy Sayers, *Gaudy Night* (New York: Perennial Library, 1986).

Page 184 "were not allowed . . .": Alexandra Symonds, "Neurotic Dependency in Successful Women." *Journal of the American Academy of Psychoanalysis*, vol. 4, no. 1 (January 1976).

Page 185 "sacrificers . . . are not the ones . . .": Elizabeth Bowen, *The Death of the Heart* (New York: Random House, 1938).

Page 186 "Suffering is used . . .": Karen Horney, "The Value of Vindictiveness."

Page 187 "When a man wants . . .": Alfred Gingold, *Fire in the John: The Manly Man in the Age of Sissification* (New York: St. Martin's Press, 1991).

Chapter Seven

Page 199 "I'd got in touch . . .": Judith Stone, "Anger: Your Best Power Tool." *Glamour* (July 1993).

Page 202 "anger is a signal . . .": Harriet Lerner, *The Dance of Anger* (New York: Harper & Row, 1985).

Page 203 "Anger stirs and wakes . . .": Toni Morrison, *The Bluest Eye* (New York: Alfred A. Knopf, 1970).

Page 212 "I was benevolent . . ." and "I will revenge . . .": Mary Shelley, *Frankenstein* (New York: Penguin, 1985).

Page 217 "Anger as soon . . .": Emily Dickinson in *The Complete Poems of Emily Dickinson*, edited by Thomas Johnson (Boston: Little, Brown, and Co., 1960).

Page 218 "at all costs he . . ." and " 'Never get angry . . . ' ": Mario Puzo, *The Godfather* (New York: New American Library, 1983).

Page 221 "when revenge . . .": Andrew Oldenquist, "An Explanation for Retribution." *The Journal of Philosophy*, vol. 8 (September 1988).

Page 222 "as capable of serving . . .": Herbert Packer, "Justifications for Criminal Punishment." *Perspectives on Correction* (New York: Thomas Y. Crowell, 1971).

Page 222 "personal revenge we . . .": Karl Menninger, *Love Against Hate* (New York: Harcourt, Brace, and Co., 1942).

Page 222 "emboldened by 'three beers' . . .": Michael Tackett, "She May Be Toothsome, but Biter Has to Pay." *Chicago Tribune* (April 21, 1990): 4.

Page 223 "He told Brodie . . .": *St. Louis Post Dispatch*.

Page 224 "She looked the part . . ."; "Carrie glared . . ."; and "Carrie's whirling mind . . .": Stephen King, *Carrie* (New York: Penguin, 1974/1991).

Page 226 "better to reign . . .": John Milton, *Paradise Lost* (New York: Odyssey Press, 1963).

Page 235 "I came here to hunt . . ." and "Moby Dick had reaped . . .": Herman Melville, *Moby Dick* (Toronto/New York: Bantam, 1981).

Chapter Eight

Page 242 "The other day I murdered . . .": Frank Ronan, *The Observer* (November 13, 1994).

Page 243 "To the happy ...": Fay Weldon, *The Hearts and Lives of Men* (New York: Bantam, 1987).

Page 244 "It is valuable ..." and "Many have thought ...": Howard McGary, "Forgiveness." *American Philosophical Quarterly*, vol. 26, no. 4 (October, 1989).

Page 255 "aphid of the soul ..."; *"She's just jealous ...";* and "that's what they will do ...": Margaret Atwood, *The Robber Bride* (New York: Doubleday, 1993).

Page 258 "I hate the whole house ..." and "I think I could be ...": William Thackeray, *Vanity Fair* (New York: Penguin, 1968).

Page 260 "for being thus revenged ..." and "plentifully drowned all thoughts ...": John Cleland, *Memoirs of Fanny Hill* (New York: Signet, 1965).

bibliography

Altman, Lawrence K., M.D. "Artful Surgery: Reattaching a Penis." *New York Times* (July 13, 1993): C3.

Anderson, Linda. *A Kind of Wild Justice: Revenge in Shakespeare's Comedies*. Newark: University of Delaware Press, 1987.

Atwood, Margaret. "Hairball." *Wilderness Tips*. New York: Doubleday, 1991.

————. *The Robber Bride*. New York: Doubleday, 1993.

Bacon, Francis. "On Revenge." In *The Oxford Book of Essays*, edited by John Gross. New York: Oxford University Press, 1991.

Barreca, Regina. *They Used to Call Me Snow White, But I Drifted*. New York: Penguin, 1991.

Beaber, Rex Julian. "The Social Contract Hangs by a Thread." *Los Angeles Times* (May 1, 1992): B7.

Becker, Natalie. Interview with Regina Barreca, December 1993.

Bowen, Elizabeth. *The Death of the Heart*. New York: Random House, 1938.

Brod, Ernest. "In the Layoff Era, the 'Get Even' Ethic." *New York Times* (January 26, 1992): F13.

Brontë, Charlotte. *Jane Eyre*. London: Oxford University Press, 1973.

Brontë, Emily. *Wuthering Heights*. New York: Penguin, 1965.

Burnett, Carol. *One More Time*. New York: Random House, 1986.

Butterfield, Fox. "Fatal Feud Divides a Village in Maine." *New York Times* (December 27, 1991): A14.

Cheever, Joan M. "The Year of Litigating Dangerously."

The National Law Journal, vol. 12 (October 1992).

Cheever, Joan M., and Joanne Naiman. "The Deadly Practice of Divorce." *The National Law Journal*, vol. 12 (October 1992).

Cleland, John. *Memoirs of Fanny Hill*. New York: Signet, 1965.

Colette. *Chéri*. Paris: Fayard, 1920.

de Beauvoir, Simone. *The Second Sex*. New York: Random House, 1949.

Dickens, Charles. *Great Expectations*. New York: Penguin, 1985.

Dickinson, Emily. *Complete Poems of Emily Dickinson*. Edited by Thomas Johnson. Boston: Little, Brown, and Co., 1960.

Dionne, E. J. Jr. "Capital Punishment Gaining Favor as Public Seeks Retribution." *Washington Post* (May 17, 1990): A12.

Elster, Jon. "Norms of Revenge." *Ethics* (July 1990): 862–85.

Emshwiller, John. "Desire for Revenge Fuels an Entrepreneur's Ambition." *Wall Street Journal* (April 19, 1991): B2.

Ephron, Nora. *Heartburn*. New York: Pocket Books, n.d.

Euripides. *Medea*. New York: Penguin, 1963.

Flagg, Fannie. *Fried Green Tomatoes at the Whistle Stop Cafe*. New York: McGraw-Hill, 1987.

Foley, Helene P. "Medea's Divided Self." *Classical Antiquity*, vol. 8 (April 1989): 61–85.

Foster, George. "The Anatomy of Envy: A Study in Symbolic Behavior." *Current Anthropology*, vol. 13, no. 2 (April 1972).

Freud, Sigmund. *Civilization and Its Discontents*. Translated by James Strachey. New York: W. W. Norton, 1961.

Fromm, Erich. *The Anatomy of Human Destructiveness*. New York: Henry Holt & Co., 1973.

Gaylin, Willard. *The Rage Within: Anger in Modern Life*.

New York: Simon & Schuster, 1984.

Giacalone, Robert A., and Stephen B. Knouse. "Justifying Wrongful Employee Behavior: The Role of Personality in Organizational Sabotage." In *Excuses: Masquerades in Search of Grace*. Edited by C. R. Snyder, R. L. Higgins, and R. J. Stucky. New York: John Wiley & Sons, 1985.

Gingold, Alfred. *Fire in the John: The Manly Man in the Age of Sissification*. New York: St. Martin's Press, 1991.

Goldsmith, Olivia. *The First Wives Club*. New York: Pocket Books, 1992.

Green, Larry. "At 96, Feuding Matriarch Opens New Business." *New York Times* (December 18, 1989): A1+.

Greenburg, Dan, and Suzanne O'Malley. *How to Avoid Love and Marriage*. New York: Freundlich, 1983.

Grimm, Jacob, and Wilhelm Grimm. *Selected Tales*. Translated by David Luke. New York: Viking Penguin, 1983.

Guisewite, Cathy. "Cathy" cartoons.

Gyorgyey, Ferenc. "Arsenic and No Lace."

Hawthorne, Nathaniel. *The Scarlet Letter*. New York: Penguin, 1991.

Heimel, Cynthia. *If You Can't Live Without Me, Why Aren't You Dead Yet?* New York: HarperCollins, 1991.

Horney, Karen. "The Value of Vindictiveness." *The American Journal of Psychoanalysis*, vol. 8 (1948): 3–12.

Ibsen, Henri. *A Doll's House*. In *The Bedford Introduction to Literature*. Edited by Michael Meyer. Boston: Bedford, 1993: 1517–1567.

Ivins, Molly. *Nothin' But Good Times Ahead*. New York: Random House, 1993.

Jacoby, Susan. *Wild Justice: The Evolutions of Revenge*. New York: Harper & Row, 1983.

Johnson, Diane. "Review of Wild Justice." *New York*

Review of Books (February 16, 1984): 31+.

King, Stephen. *Carrie*. New York: Penguin, 1974.

Kingston, Maxine Hong. *The Woman Warrior*. New York: Vintage, 1975.

Lawrence, D. H. *Lady Chatterley's Lover*. New York: New American Library, 1962.

————. *Sons and Lovers*. New York: Penguin, 1974/ 1991.

Lennox, Charlotte. *The Female Quixote*. London: Pandora Press, 1986.

Lerner, Harriet. *The Dance of Anger*. New York: Harper & Row, 1985.

Lorenz, Konrad. *On Aggression*. New York: Harcourt, Brace, and World, 1966.

McGary, Howard. "Forgiveness." *American Philosophical Quarterly*, vol. 26, no. 4 (October, 1989).

McMillan, Terry. *Waiting to Exhale*. New York: Viking, 1992.

Martin, Judith. *Miss Manners' Guide to Excruciatingly Correct Behavior*. New York: Warner Books, 1982.

Melville, Herman. *Moby Dick*. New York/Toronto: Viking, 1992.

Menninger, Karl. *Love Against Hate* (New York: Harcourt, Brace, and Co., 1942).

Milton, John. *Paradise Lost*. Edited by Merritt Y. Hughes. New York: Odyssey Press, 1963.

Minn, Walter. *Sabotage: History, Philosophy, and Function*. Chicago: IWW Publishing, n.d.

Mitchell, Margaret. *Gone With the Wind*. New York: Avon, 1992.

"More than He Could Chew." *The National Law Journal* (May 7, 1990).

Morrison, Toni. *The Bluest Eye*. New York: Alfred A. Knopf, 1970.

O'Boyle, Thomas. "Disgruntled Workers Intent on Revenge Increasingly Harm Colleagues and Bosses." *Wall Street Journal* (September 15, 1992): B1+.

O'Hara, John. *Butterfield 8*. New York: Bantam, 1935.

Oldenquist, Andrew. "An Explanation for Retribution." *The Journal of Philosophy*, vol. 8 (September 1988): 464–78.

Orwell, George. *Down and Out in Paris and London*. Middlesex: Penguin, 1933.

Osborne, John. *Look Back in Anger*. New York: Penguin, 1957.

Packer, Herbert. "Justifications for Criminal Punishment." *Perspectives on Correction*. Edited by Donald MacNamara and Edward Sagarin. New York: Thomas Y. Crowell, 1971.

Piercy, Marge. "What's That Smell in the Kitchen?" In *Circles on the Water*. New York: Random House, 1987.

Puzo, Mario. *The Godfather*. New York: New American Library, 1983.

Rhys, Jean. *The Wide Sargasso Sea*. New York: W. W. Norton, 1982.

Roiphe, Anne. *Torch Song*. New York: Farrar, Straus & Giroux, 1977.

Ross, Alf. *On Guilt, Responsibility and Punishment*. Berkeley/Los Angeles: University of California Press, 1975.

Sayers, Dorothy. *Gaudy Night*. New York: Perennial Library, 1986.

Shakespeare, William. *Hamlet*. In *The Bedford Introduction to Drama*. Edited by Lee A. Jacobus. Boston: Bedford Books, 1993: 233–93.

————: *Twelfth Night*. *The Riverside Shakespeare*. Boston: Houghton-Mifflin, 1974.

Shelley, Mary. *Frankenstein*. New York: Penguin, 1985.

Sherman, Alan. *The Rape of the Ape*. Chicago: Playboy Press, 1973.

Stone, Judith. "Anger: Your Best Power Tool." *Glamour* (July 1993): 174ff.

Symonds, Alexandra. "Neurotic Dependency in Successful Women." *Journal of the American Academy of Psy-*

choanalysis, vol. 4, no. 1 (January 1976).

Tackett, Michael. "She May Be Toothsome, But Biter Has to Pay." *Chicago Tribune* (April 21, 1990): 4.

Thackeray, William. *Vanity Fair*. New York: Penguin, 1968.

Toulmin, Stephen. "Review of *Wild Justice*." *The New Times Book Review* (February 3, 1983): 14.

Tousignant, Marylou, and Carlos Sanchez. "Va. Woman Says She Cut Husband in Self-Defense." *Washington Post* (June 25, 1993): D1.

Turow, Scott. *Presumed Innocent*. New York: Warner Books, 1987.

Warner, Carolyn, ed. *The Last Word: A Treasury of Women's Quotes*. Englewood Cliffs, N.J.: Prentice Hall, 1992.

Weldon, Fay. *The Hearts and Lives of Men*. New York: Bantam, 1987.

———. *The Life and Loves of a She-Devil*. New York, Ballantine Books, 1985.

Winokur, I. A. "Sweet Revenge Is Souring the Office." *Wall Street Journal* (September 19, 1990): B1+.

Wolff, Tom. *The Bonfires of the Vanities*. New York: Bantam, 1988.

Woolf, Virginia. *Three Guineas*. New York: Harcourt, Brace and Co., 1938.

Zipes, Jack. *Breaking the Magic Spell: Radical Theories of Folk and Fairy Tales*. Austin: University of Texas Press, 1979.

about the author

Regina Barreca, a professor of English and Feminist Theory at the University of Connecticut, is author of *Untamed and Unabashed: Essays on Women and Humor in Literature, Perfect Husbands (& Other Fairy Tales), They Used to Call Me Snow White . . . But I Drifted* and editor of seven other books on topics ranging from sex in Victorian literature to the erotics of instruction. She has degrees from Dartmouth College, Cambridge University, and the City University of New York. Recently appointed by the Library of Congress to act as an advisor for a project on Humor and the American Character, Barreca is also a popular talk show guest and media resource for issues on humor, gender, and contemporary culture. She is a regular contributor to the *Chicago Tribune* and her work has appeared in the *New York Times, Ms.*, and *Cosmopolitan*. She lives with her husband in Storrs, Connecticut.